FLASH!

100 Stories by 100 Authors

Edited by Dani J. Caile and Jason Brick

Table of Contents

A (Brief) Introduction from Jason Brick

In 2014 when I first had the idea of a kickstarted flash fiction anthology, I wasn't certain it would work even once. And now we're closing up our second anthology with plans for a third.

That's pretty cool.

Thank you, everybody, for your work and patience and support on FLASH! And thank you for reading it today.

Special thanks to my gal and my boys, whom everything is for and without whom everything would be empty. Dimitri, Gabriel, Rachel you make me smile.

A (Briefer) Introduction from Dani J. Caile

After the success of 'Baby Shoes,' the first anthology, I couldn't wait to see what 100 authors would come up with this time around. While editing these short stories from varying genres and writing styles, I found many authors I am definitely going to search out. Hope you like what you read.

Sunset on Crete

By Eric Witchey

Sunshine replied, "Service people don't care what you think."

Of course, they did care. They especially cared if I liked their feta and chips and if I liked their wine. Really, it was their business to care. Sunshine was from a family with old steel money, and her contempt for service employees was equaled only by the denial of her current state of poverty.

"If you don't keep them in line," she said, "they'll spit in your drink just to dis you."

I inhaled the sea breeze, shifted my wicker chair to better face the horizon, and wondered how far down the setting sun would sink before I noticed the next stimulus threshold change in apparent size and the waning light's shift toward orange.

"They'll bring us your calamari," she said, "but they'll take a few off just because they know we're tourists. They'll short us."

"The water is changing color, too," I said. "It's turning emeraldine."

"No respect."

"In the post cards and books, the Mediterranean is always blue or really clear."

She glanced seaward over the spaghetti strap on her tanned shoulder.

I noticed the orange shift. I didn't think I'd ever seen such an orange sun. It lit up the fine hair on her bicep, and it made her look like she was about to burst into flames.

"Post cards are all shopped." She turned back to her putanesca.

"What?"

"All those advertising pictures. Touched up."

"I wonder if I can predict the exact moment the sun touches the sea?"

Creases in her forehead and the way she sucked air through her teeth told me a Sunshine storm would soon come my way.

I settled myself between the sheltering wings of my wicker chair. Like the olives, the wine, and the pasta, the chair was a thing to savor. It must have held the weight of five thousand people to wear it so smooth, to make it so supple. The scratches on the table surface created long, thin shadows from the sun, but none of the scratches seemed intentionally inflicted on the wood. Rather, their rounded edges suggested that every person who had spent a moment in my chair had slid their hands across the table top—perhaps to a lover.

I leaned forward. I slid my hand to the middle of the table. My watch band caught on the wooden surface. I took a little pleasure in joining the stream of peace and joy that had scored and smoothed the table's top.

Sunshine blinked and opened her peach-opal, painted lips to hiss in my direction.

"You're beautiful," I said.

Her lips closed. She blinked again. She flinched, like a tiny bee had stung her cheek.

The waiter came and asked if we would like our wine. He was kind enough to speak English, but he hadn't spent enough time in my Sunshine's glow to know he should ask her instead of me.

"Yes," I said.

As if the waiter weren't present, she said, "You're just a tourist."

The waiter, his back to her, smiled at me as if he knew who I was, like we had known each other for a very long time. I imagined that I had set myself down in that chair every night for many days and many seasons—for his entire lifetime.

The waiter looked at the sunset for a moment, and I saw that he appreciated this moment even though he was not a tourist. Then, he left to get our wine.

"You," she went on, "come to a place like this and see tourist things."

The sun touched the sea. I'd forgotten to predict. It was no less beautiful for my failure and for my being a mere tourist.

"Sunsets and the simpering of..."

"Beautiful," I said. "Even when you're mad." The sun shifted to a deeper orange, and so did Sunshine's smoldering storm front.

"I can't travel with you," she said. "You don't know how to have fun."

"You can't travel without me," I said. "Your parents cut you off." It was out too quickly. I had spoiled my own sunset.

She stood up. Her wicker chair fell over. Her flames licked the heavens. Her cap of blond curls shook like burning ribbons. "We could be at the disco."

"Or we could be here and go there later." On the horizon behind her, the sun actually shone through the water. How many miles away, and I could see the line of the sea and the glow through the water, like a deep, orange flashlight shining through a green lens. I'd never read about anything like it before. I'd certainly never seen a picture that captured it.

She turned from our table to the rail where we had left our tourist bicycles. She pulled hers away from mine. She mounted and rode off, pushing hard at the pedals instead of using the gears. The intricate mandala tattoo on the small of her back flashed out from under her cotton top, and the last rays of the sun ignited its golds, blues, and greens.

The trendy, meditation design was a part of her. I wondered if she could see it—even in a mirror.

The waiter brought my wine. He also set down a bottle of raki and a plate of olives. "For free," he said. "For a man who watches the sunset and smiles."

I invited him to join me, and he did. He had old eyes and smelled of hand-ground coffee and olive oil. We drank in silence and watched the last brilliant edge of the circle of the sun slip beneath the waves.

The Last Night I Was Single

By Zachary Gilbert

A river rock flew silently through the night air. A watery explosion enveloped Marcus. He was fat and his fall was awkward. He sat for a moment in the river. A hand that looked like sausages stuffed in bloated bread pushed away his wet curly red hair. "This means war!" he yelled.

"Bring it!" Eric shouted, kicking water at him.

Splashing and falling several times, Marcus ran to the opposite side of the river. Gary followed him reluctantly just to make the teams even.

A splash war raged for seven minutes in a concrete trench on the South Platte River in Lower Downtown Denver. Heavy rocks, cold and slimy, were heaved in a wet "spahhh gloop" volley. In the eighth minute, something went terribly wrong. The river twisted and writhed through the dark city like a giant wet snake. Tonight, moments after his bachelor party, it would taste Jim's blood.

Eric tossed big rocks far, splashing his laughing opponents on the other side. Down by the water, Jim was bent over searching for a rock. His blurred green eyes roamed over the bank. He pushed some grainy wet sand away from a black pungent mud-covered round heavy stone bomb. Jim strained to pick it up.

Marcus grabbed a rock that looked like a thick caveman's frisbee. A smile carved a path through his lips. He cackled into the night air, "Fire in the hole!" With an Olympic-style discus throw, the rock flew across the river like an angry stone bird swooping in on its prey. A fleshy muffled pop echoed on the concrete walls. Blood sprayed out of Jim's face like water shooting out of an intermittent sprinkler. Jim screamed and fell in a half spin. On the other side of the bank, Gary's face lost its color. Marcus laughed and yelled, "Boo ya! Direct Hit!"

Eric picked Jim up off the rocks. He was screaming, his right hand was pinching his nose with his left hand clinched tight over the top. Dark red blood seeped out from his fingers. He tried frantically to hold his nose shut like a panicked submariner pushing a metal door against an angry flood of seawater.

"I am deformed! I can feel the inside of my nose!" Jim yelled, spitting blood under his palm.

"I'm gonna get you outta here, man!" Eric tried to keep his voice calm and confident.

They found a concrete ramp that led to the road. Hot blood fell, silently making quarter-sized circles on the dry concrete. Screams echoed in the trench. Eric held tight, his arm covered in blood around Jim's waist.

At this hour, cabs often roamed the city. Hungry headlights tore the blanket of the night, searching for an easy fare, "Happy drunks with loose pockets," cabbies would say.

Eric and Jim emerged onto the road from the bike path ramp. A cab cut across two lanes of traffic, straddled the curb and screeched to a stop.

"What the hell happened to him!?!" the driver yelled, leaning out the window. A look of horror crumpled his ugly face.

"Take us to the nearest hospital! Please! Quick!" Eric spoke in a winded staccato as he pushed Jim into the back seat.

Hyperventilating, Jim leaned his sweating brow on the cold glass of the window. "My Van Halen shirt is ruined." His words were wet with blood. Then he passed out.

A deep voice woke him 30 minutes later. Bright white lights hit his eyes with a dull bite. In the tender skin of his nose he felt a sharp pinch and a tug inside his nostril. He felt the thud of his heart deep inside his swollen purple cheek. A doctor wearing medical glasses stood under a white spotlight. He held a shiny metal hook that was tied to black string. His glowing silhouette framed a grayed shadow. Jim could feel the flap of the outside of his nose being pulled back in place. His face was the back of an envelope being sealed. He tried to touch the stitches. A nurse grabbed his arm and placed it back on the bed.

The deep voice pierced a blue paper mask. "I am Doctor Septus and you are very lucky. If that rock had hit two inches higher, your right eye would be gone, two inches lower and your jaw would be broken, and well, half of your teeth would be in the river."

The next day Jim stood in a large church wearing a tuxedo and standing next to a preacher. The preacher stared at his wounds, resembling a small boy looking at a gross bug. Jim's head was heavy and thick. His brain felt like it was inflating like a hot tire. Light yellow pus leaked through his stitches. It looked like spiders dying on his nose.

Eric placed a firm hand on Jim's shoulder and whispered, "It's all going to be okay."

Gary was standing behind Eric, tugging at the cummerbund of his tux. "Gonna be fine, Jim," he said without looking up.

Jim scanned the crowd. Marcus sat in the front row of the bride's side wearing a white jacket. The smile from the night before had dried like vandalized concrete on his round face. Jim's stomach felt like it was heavy with the slimy rocks from the river. Hot sweat grabbed at his aching neck.

Old double doors sent a creaking wooden moan across the crowded room. Two ushers in suits held them open. The beautiful bride and her father emerged under the archway. Her hair was brown and twisted into elaborate braids; her face was gentle and soft. The wedding march played while she floated down the aisle like a cloud on a sunny summer afternoon. Her father fought back tears as he led his daughter down a path of soft purple fabric. Faces of smiling friends and family watched her. Marcus whispered to his mother, pinching his nose in his hands. He twisted like an angry wet snake, while they both laughed.

A Collection of Slightly Worn Colored Pencils

By James Thibeault

Used colored pencils might be a great thing to sell. They were worn down by half an inch, but they worked fine. No, who would want them? People wanted everything to be fresh. No one wanted anything slightly worn.

I threw the box across the room. Now Betty would never get her operation.

"Betty!" I shouted from the den. The room was cluttered with clothes and junk. I found so many things, but nothing good enough to sell. All of it was used. No one wanted something battered or broken.

"What is it, Mark?" she shouted from the kitchen, busy with the kid's lunches.

"What's in the basement?"

"What?" *Crash.* "Peter," she yelled. "Pick that up for me! And quit running around the room."

"The attic?"

Screech. "Be careful with the furniture!" My wife continued, "Mark, I don't know what's in either. Can you wake up Samantha? She's going to be late for school."

"But what about..."

"Can you please... Peter! Quit playing with the oven and go catch the bus."

The front door slammed. I wished I could only worry about going to school, instead of the operation. Peter didn't seem bothered about it, though. It was coming up soon, and Peter acted like nothing was wrong. I had to sell something soon.

"Mark," said Betty. "Samantha?"

"Oh right," I said. I put on my coat and boots. When my boots were laced tight, I put on my double-breasted wool coat. I needed to make sure I was bundled up before venturing into my daughter's room. Suddenly, I stopped. There was breathing behind me. I ran down the hall. By the time I reached Samantha's door, the breathing was loud, raspy and cold. I pounded on the door.

"Samantha! Samantha!"

I heard footsteps quickly coming to the door. Could she open the door before it was too late?

"What?" she said, panic in her eyes. She was only wearing a large T-shirt and black underwear.

"Let me in!" I pushed her aside and shut the door.

We stood in the creepy darkness of a teenage bedroom. Rock posters and skulls lined the walls. There was an odd smell from the floor.

"When was the last time you did a load?" I asked.

"Dad? What the hell is going on?"

"Can you clean up this mess?"

"Dad?"

"I don't want any attitude. Help out your mother."

She sighed and sat down on her bed. Then she started crying. Why was she doing that? I sat down beside her and put my arm around her. Reflexively, she nuzzled into my chest and sobbed.

"What's the matter, Sweetheart?"

"Dad? Did you take..."

"We all need to pitch in with your Mom's operation."

Samantha wailed at that, and I held her even tighter.

"I know it's a serious operation, but you have to be strong."

She pried my hands away and stood up. Quickly, she walked over to her dresser and found a pair of pants.

"I need to go. I'm going to be late for school."

"You need to give me some respect!" I commanded.

"Mom!" she shouted while dressing herself. She didn't even apply make-up.

"Fine," I said, tears in my eyes. "Leave me. Just like everybody else."

Betty opened the door, her hands covered in flour.

"Samantha, whatever your father says g..." she looked at Samantha, then at me. "Oh God."

"He's acting up again," said Samantha, then pushed past her mother. Betty turned around to call out, "Sam, you can't leave the house like this. Let me take care of your father, then..."

"I can't Mom. I can't do it today. Not when he was doing... Look, I'll head over to Tiff's and borrow some of her clothes."

"He'll be fine, this is a new..."

"I got to go," Samantha said, then the front door slammed.

"She's never going to stop those tidal waves," I said.

"Those tidal waves?"

"Rising sea levels. The storm is coming in any day and the whole town is going to be underwater."

"Oh. Come on Mark, let's get you back into the den."

My wife and I walked back into the study. She took off my boots and coat. I felt a lot better, considering it was about ninety degrees out. She saw all the clothes and junk on the ground and let out a huge sigh. She shook her head from side to side. "Not today, why did it have to be today? You were doing so well. What happened?"

"Of course I'm doing well. I have a wonderful family, and I'm doing everything I can to make sure you'll survive the operation."

"Oh baby," she brushed the side of my cheek. There were tears in her eyes. "We'll make an appointment with Dr. Jensin tomorrow."

I stood up, disgusted.

"Dr. Jensin said you'll fail the operation. I don't want that negative thinking. We'll find a better doctor.

"You didn't talk to him," said Betty sternly.

"I just talked to him, like a moment ago. I can't believe you're going to trust that man."

"Okay," Betty reached in her pocket and pulled out her cellphone. "I need to call him."

She dialed the number.

"No!" I jumped at her, reaching for the phone.

"Get off me!" she yelled. My wife was not going to that crackpot doctor. I knocked the phone out of her hand, then stomped on it until its robotic guts were all over the carpet. My wife pressed against the wall, afraid I was going to stomp out her guts, too. I fell on the ground and cried. My wife knelt down with me. "I just want you to have a good operation," I said.

"I know," said Betty, "The operation will be fine. We'll see about adjusting your meds, everything is going to be all right."

Through my tear-filled eyes, I saw the box of slightly used colored pencils. They were scattered all over the den floor.

A View, Obscured

By Neil Davidson

I saw her leaning over the stone railing of what we all called the suicide bridge. The opposite side of the railing was enshrouded by seven or eight feet of chain link, which curled back toward the top in order, I'm sure, to prevent determined jumpers. It was a short bridge, only two hundred feet or so, and hung gently over the I-5 corridor as the interstate emptied itself into downtown Portland. But the view was obscured by signs. Every few feet along the fence was another sign for a suicide hotline, though I don't remember having ever heard of someone jumping before. I think, technically, it was called the Vista Point Bridge. Something like that. It definitely had a 'vista' attached to the name. Still, we all called it the suicide bridge. *You can cross this Bridge*, the signs said. Call our toll-free support line.

The woman leaned forward, reaching with one arm toward that chain-link. She was normal enough looking, maybe twenty or so. I had never seen her before, probably never would again, but something about her commanded my attention. I had to stop walking, had to watch her. The weather was starting to cool as the summer limped away slowly into autumn, so she had leggings on under her knee-length skirt and a scarf, knit from dense yarn. I think it was pale green, and looked unbearably scratchy. She was also wearing boots, probably, but I can't remember for sure. Truthfully, there was nothing spectacular about her. But she looked so determined as she reached for that fence, as though hoping she might be able to make it disappear by sheer force of will. That was the most striking thing about her, her expression. Her brow furrowed and her mouth aggressively puckered as she reached toward the fence. She looked at that fence as though it were somehow insulting her by existing, and I couldn't help but agree with her.

Of course the fence stayed, refusing to disappear, but maybe part of me wished it hadn't. Life should be more magical, instead of dragging on and on. Same shit, different day, people often say, but they smile when they say it. They laugh. I guess I would laugh too if I saw magic more often. It really is a shame the fence didn't disappear for her.

I had never seen someone try to jump, and I wondered if this woman would be my first. It could just as easily be that she wished the admittedly beautiful view was unobscured, but I have to believe that there was something in her that wished for freedom, to feel the air rush past her, offering one last goodbye until she collided with the terrified traffic one hundred feet below. What a morning that would be for some poor driver.

But what a great way to go. I imagined my eyes closed, and the whistling of the air blasting out any other ambient noise. I thought about how difficult it would be to breathe in all of that rushing wind, like when you stick your head out of a car window and it feels almost impossible to properly inhale. Every breath a gasp, a struggle. But how could you make yourself do it? To take that final step? It seemed like an impossible distance to go by yourself.

Eventually, her determined look faded, and she resigned herself to a view, obscured. I suppose I gave up on the idea of something better, too. The fence was victorious, and the woman walked away.

I wished she hadn't, that there could be some magic in this world, and I looked for myself on that tarnished, gray city with those little intersecting diamonds of metal getting in the way. I had never heard of anyone jumping, but I wondered what would happen if I climbed the fence.

Someone would call the police, probably. I'd have to tell them that I wanted only to see what would happen, that I wanted to see the city without the chain-link mucking up the beautiful view.

Who knows if they'd believe me, but it's God's honest truth. I just wanted a little magic.

On the Threshold of the World

By David Covenant

His father looks up at him. "This is yours." Lerret stares at them for a moment, this leaving business continuing to get harder all the time.

"Thanks, you two," he says before prying off the lid. Lerret peers inside.

The first thing to catch his eye is a brand-new, sizable pack. Picking it up, he feels the superb tanning of the hides used to produce its soft but tough form. The shoulder straps are wider than a normal pack, odd since Altairians prefer narrow straps because of their anatomy. This pack must have been made for deep excursions or extended duty. Lerret can tell because he has seen Altairian militia carrying similar ones. He always thought them heavy and cumbersome. But holding it, the weight proves far less than he expects. How could his parents afford one, much less gain access to it?

He gives his parents an appreciative smile as he starts searching the various pockets and holds. However, it is the tight metal mesh that he discovers sewn in between each layer of hide that surprises him the most. Looking up, he asks, "Do all militia packs have this mesh within them?"

"No. Our militia usually uses plates. It protects the pack's contents from fire, arrows, and other tools of war. It's not a perfect system, but it's much better than just hides."

"I don't understand. Where did this come from, then? It doesn't seem like our people's work."

His parents smile. "Good eye," Mother says. "Your father and I once met a strange mon, an elf really, but very different from any elves he or I had ever met. This elf carried just such a pack, and seemed unconcerned when we approached, asking about himself and his strange clothes."

Even as Lerret opens his mouth, his mother continues. "Yes, I know. It was not the most thought-out thing we ever did." They turn toward each other with an odd, secretive smile. "But we were young, and our blood was full of Altairian fire."

They return their attention to Lerret, their fingers interlocking. "It turned out that the elf mon was rather down to dirt about the whole thing. He had very little in his pack, which seemed strange to us. He was also taller than any elf we'd heard of or seen. Once he let us examine it, we knew several things. For one," his mother smirks, "the aura was all wrong. Its vibrations were very different from Solanar's."

"And another thing," his father adds, "the material used to make it was very odd—soft as silk and tougher than any hide I can think of. He seemed almost amused by our curiosity. When we asked him if we could test its toughness, he happily agreed."

Mother giggles. "He must have thought us strange as we tried to slice and puncture it. There was no surprise in his eyes when we couldn't. We did notice though; his pack was layered. There were at least three or four separate layers of hide, depending on the part of his pack."

"But all of it possessed some kind of metal mesh throughout, and we were told," his father continued, "it was a particular element used by his people."

Mother's eyes seem somehow younger and more vibrant, as do his father's, while she speaks, adding to his father's explanation. "When I asked him who his people were, he simply smiled and said we would not have heard of them because they lived far from here. He then explained how we could make our own packs."

"And he did so in great detail," Father adds. "In fact, it was almost as if he wanted us to produce them for ourselves, don't you agree, Kahzandria?"

She nods several times. "Oh yes, Tehterus, Angriff, was very emphatic about that," then turned to Lerret, "but he didn't want us to reveal its secrets to anyone else, which seemed odd to us."

"It still does," his father adds.

Lerret stops feeling its weight and playing with the loops, pockets, and other straps before looking up at them. "I don't understand. If this Angriff didn't want you to tell anyone, why did you tell whoever made this about it?"

His mother chuckles as his father's face grows a shade darker. "We didn't, Lerret. We've never said a word."

"Then how..."

"Your father asked me to teach him how to sew."

Lerret stands dumbfound, nearly dropping his pack as his mind seeks the words to enunciate. Finally, he blurts, "What? Altairian mon don't sew! That's womon's work!"

Mother leans into his father, smiling brightly. "Well this one does! He asked me to show him how, so he could re-create what Angriff told us, and so I did. We couldn't ask for anyone else's help. We were too busy with preparing a home for ourselves after we were entwined and we knew you would be delivered to us. He worked on it late into shade when I and eventually you, Tahjer, Yexkie, and Hokekna were still young."

Lerret turned to his father, his face still full of confusion. "You sew, Father?"

His father tilts his head down and looks at him out of the upper half of his eyes. "Yes I do. It's a survival skill. One I wanted to teach you, but we never seemed to have the time. I've made a collection of all the best tools and scribed a small parchment on what to do with each tool—learn it, son, it will save your life."

Lerret appears exceedingly doubtful as his parents smile and chuckle. His father then returns to his usual serious self before he gives Lerret the look. "Every attitude has its place, but every attitude will eventually meet its own demise, this one about sewing is ripe for its own."

Lerret looks as if he's been given waste duty. Nodding his head in compliance, he sighs. "Since you insist, I will try."

Baiting the Hook

By Kathleen Donnelly

Calvin and Melba Kemp strolled along Bourbon Street in New Orleans. Melba tucked her arm into the crook of Calvin's beefy elbow murmuring, "Wonderful vacation, darling. Great idea to come here."

"I look forward to the fishing tomorrow. Just the two of us. Like old times."

"Yes," Melba said, thinking back to happy memories before his cheating, Ponzi scheme and lies.

Melba admired the colorful shops and bars they passed. One building displayed a sign that read, "Psychic."

"We should get a reading," Melba said.

"Ridiculous. Psychics are frauds."

Melba pouted. "Thirty years of marriage. Indulge me."

"Fine."

In the office, Melba expected crystal balls or mystical pictures, but instead the walls were bare and gray. An older lady crowned with salt-and-pepper hair greeted the couple.

"Come this way," said the psychic.

The trio sat down and the psychic closed her eyes. Suddenly her eyes flew open and she covered her mouth with one hand. Pointing at Melba she said, "You will murder him and steal the hidden money. Leave."

Melba and Calvin scurried from the office.

"Psychics are crazy," Calvin said.

"I agree, dear." Melba stroked Calvin's arm.

The next day Melba perched in the back of the fishing boat waiting for her husband to bait his hook. She gripped his open bottle of scotch and poured in a lethal dose of crushed pills. She whispered, "You should listen to psychics, dear."

Behind her, the slide on a gun racked.

"Psychics are never wrong or crazy, dear," Calvin said.

Betty

By Ronda Simmons

Ever looked in a mirror and regretted a tattoo? Yeah, me neither.

I'll be out of jail in eight months, assuming good behavior. When I do I'm going straight to the ink shack. I'm trying to decide between a Madonna on my back or a hummingbird across my underboob. Maybe I'll get both. Louie owes me enough boodle to pay for whatever I want. I've had a lot of time to think about tattoos here in the stony lonesome.

Louie owns a couple of the guards, which makes life inside a little easier. The other prisoners know that I've got extra protection so they leave me alone. Most of them, anyway. That bitch Loretta has it in for me. She used to be with Louie and she hates me for being his new squeeze. It ain't my fault that she don't know how to keep a man. That hag looks at me sideways when she's serving slop in the cafeteria. I found a cockroach in my scrambled eggs one morning. Nice.

When the walls start closing in I think back to when I first met Louie. It was my eighth straight shift working behind the stick at Jericho Jo's. Louie came in with a floozy hanging all over him. He parked her at a table and swaggered to the bar. After staring at the mermaid peeking out of my blouse he said, "Nice cans. What are you doing after?"

I was kinda busy with the usual Saturday night crowd of losers so I told him, "Looks like you've already got a date and besides, I don't do customers."

He glanced over his shoulder and said, "My relationship with the redhead has exceeded its shelf life. Give me some Irish handcuffs and I'll see you later." I poured him a couple of straight whiskies. He left a C-note on the counter and I didn't give him another thought.

A couple of weeks later I went outside to find Louie leaning on my car. "Hiya, Doll," he said.

"Name's not Doll, it's Betty," I answered, annoyed.

He ran a hand through his hair and straightened up, "Betty? I like that. It sounds . . . wholesome."

I love a guy who can make me laugh so I ended up spending some quality time with him. He had a lot of cash and loved to spread it around. He got us into all the fancy nightclubs. When Louie and I would show up, the bouncers would lift the velvet ropes and let us right in without waiting.

One night over gin fizzes at the Bombay Club I got up the nerve to ask him, "So what about the redhead?"

He swirled the ice cubes in his glass and said, "Her name's Loretta. She and I were knocking over a jewelry store, just a little smash and grab, when a rent-a-cop showed up from out of nowhere. I managed to slip away but she got the cuffs." He set his glass down and said, "I need a new partner, Betty, one that I can trust. Are you in?"

I should have turned him down flat, but God help me I said, "Sure, Louie, as long as you make it worth my while."

"It'll be worth your while, Cupcake, and then some. I've been casing out a small bank nearby that uses off-duty cops as nighttime security. One of them is on my payroll. It's a sure thing, an in-and-out."

The whole operation took less than twenty minutes and when it was over we were rolling in cheddar. I made more money that night than I had working at Jo's for three months. I quit babysitting drunks and hooked up with Louie full-time.

Soon we were hitting small branch banks up and down the East Coast. We'd had a string of good luck in Philly and one morning after breakfast in bed I said, "Maybe it's time for us to hang it up, Sugar, and turn legit."

He put down his newspaper and said, "Me? Legit?"

I cuddled up next to him and said, "I'm tired of being on the road, Baby. I want to settle down, maybe get a dog."

He laughed, "Sure, I'll buy you one of them French poodles, right after our next 'project'." I imagined how cute I would look with a little white dog on one arm and Louie on the other, walking down a street somewhere with picket fences.

I agreed to the heist. Our plan was to break into a little branch bank in a strip mall at midnight and get out fast. Things didn't work out that way. The cop Louie paid for turned on us. Louie disappeared and I got caught holding the greens.

So I've been sitting in this joint for eighteen months and I'm beginning to lose my mind. Louie used to visit every week but I ain't seen him in a while. I waited in line to use the payphone for over an hour yesterday but I couldn't reach him.

Loretta is going to be released tomorrow. She stopped by the laundry room where I work to tell me that Louie is going to take her to Hawaii. I know that cow is lying, but she pushed me too far this time. Tonight I'm going to get my revenge.

I hid a shiv behind one of the dryers. After lights out I'm going to pay Loretta a little visit. I got some downers for her cellmate who is a bit of a stoner. Bunky will be too netted out to know what's going on. After I take care of my little problem, I'll leave the weapon on the floor and turn ghost. Loretta will leave prison by the back door (if you know what I mean), the doper will get the blame and I'll have Louie all to myself, once I get out early on good behavior.

Oh yeah, that next tattoo? Definitely a Madonna. Maybe one with red hair.

Slug Trainer Extraordinaire

By Erika Marshall

"Pets have fur," Garette said.

Brindi only glanced at him. She didn't want him to think she cared what he thought.

He kicked one scuffed, unlaced trainer against the sidewalk and rocked forward and back on his razor scooter.

"Wolves have fur," she said. She was already down on all fours. Her West Coast Leopard Slug, Sly, flowed slow and slimy along the damp, shaded edge of the sidewalk. She plucked a blade of crabgrass from the lawn beside Sly. "And wolves will eat you." She used the grass to stroke Sly's flank. "See? He likes to be petted," she said.

Garette dumped his scooter.

Sly tucked in his eye stalks and arched his slimy back around the tickling grass.

"Dogs have fur because they came from wolves." Garette pulled up his jeans—his brother's jeans, really. Garette was too street to wear pants that fit. "Cavemen taught wolves to do tricks, and dogs got invented. Slugs can't do tricks."

"Sly does tricks." Brindi's own coveralls fit just fine. When she ran, Garette chased—but only until his baggy pants grabbed his legs and knocked him down on his face. Without his scooter, he wasn't much in a race.

"Can't," Garette said.

"Can," she said.

"Prove it."

"Don't gotta." She traced her finger along the sidewalk from Sly's nose to an inch or so out then laid her hand flat in front of Sly's six-inch body. "Come, Sly," she said. "Kennel. We're going home."

Sly flowed forward, a long, slow wave of icky-and-olive green flesh with black spots. He sprouted his eyes stalks and lifted his head.

"No way!" Garette said.

Sly closed the distance to her hand.

"Up, Sly," she said.

"You're just putting your hand in front of where it's going."

"Look." She made a show of tracing her finger away to one side of Sly. "Kennel, Sly," she said again.

Head still high, Sly hesitated where her hand had been. His little eye stalks rotated, one left, one right. His slimy, green head dipped. He seemed to lick the sidewalk. Like a homing slug, he headed for her hand.

"I trained him," she said.

"Bull." Garette hitched up his pants and got down on his hands and knees in front of her. Freckled face close to hers, he watched Sly's slow progress toward Brindi's hand.

"No bull," she said. "Anybody can train a dog. Even a caveman. Or a boy."

"*You* can't." Nose-to-nose, he looked her in the eye.

She locked eyes with him until his nose wrinkled and he looked back at Sly. She liked the way his nose wrinkled and the way he squinted.

"Trained Sly," she said. "Lots harder than training a dog. Gonna eBay him, too. Best trained slug in the whole world. Only one of him. Rare."

"I could train a slug," Garette said.

"Bull," she said. "It takes lots of patience to train a slug. It takes a girl. Girls have patience. They're smarter than boys."

"Take it back." Garette glared at her.

"Won't," she said.

He lifted a stone from the grass and held it above Sly. "I'll do it," he said.

"I'll train another one," she said.

Sly continued his slow dash toward her hand.

"I will!" He faked a swing with the stone.

"Okay! Put it down!"

"Take it back."

"Better." She smiled her biggest smile.

He lowered the stone a little.

"What's better?"

"You put it down," she said. "I'll show you how to train him. I'll sell him to you pre-trained for a dollar, and you can work with him."

Garette tossed the stone aside. "Just a dollar?"

"And a dollar a lesson."

"Really? No Bull?"

She stood up. "Got a dollar?"

Garette got up and dug in his baggy pockets until he came up with a dollar.

She took it.

"Shake." She put her hand out.

He leaned in close and took her hand. "No bull."

"Kiss." She pulled on his hand to get him off balance, then she laid one right on his mouth. She ran like hell. Laughing and looking over her shoulder, she saw Garette jump over Sly, tangle in his pants, and go down face-first in the grass.

When she got to her mother's garden, she was panting and laughing so hard her gut hurt, but it didn't hurt so bad that she couldn't find another slug under the leaf lettuce. She plucked a couple leaves and rubbed them all over her hands. She picked up a good, fat slug and headed down the street the other way, toward Raphael's.

Black Skirt

By Aly Walker

I inhale the aroma of crab puffs as the tuxedoed waiter passes by with a tray. The flaky, buttery pastry would melt on my tongue. But not tonight. Despite my control top panty hose, my black cocktail dress barely zipped tonight, so it's crudités and water for me. Meanwhile my feet, crammed in three-inch heels, scream at me like a child begging for candy in the checkout aisle.

My husband pinches my elbow, and I snap back to attention.

"I'm sorry?" I say as both a question of what I missed and my apology for not paying attention.

"How do you feel about fracking?" my husband's colleague asks.

"Enough work talk, Jim. This is a dinner party." My husband covers for me because he knows I don't have an opinion. He works for big oil, and I should have an opinion. I should have Jim's opinion, but I don't know what that is.

What I do know is how to dress my role as corporate wife. I don my best smile and pearls to match. My job is to show our wealth, or rather, my husband's success, without flaunting it. In the beginning, I failed miserably until I started taking notes. I would hide in the powder room and write down what each woman was wearing and how she did her hair. A chignon. Never down, never curly and always highlighted to perfection. I am a cookie-cutter Stepford wife, carefully rolled out, but made for display, not for consumption.

Jim clears his throat and tries again, "I hear you are headed back east for a reunion."

I smile just enough to be polite and murmur, "Maybe." I feel my husband shift away. His elbow is now in front of mine rather than behind it. No one else would notice, but I know he is dismissing me. I take my cue and say, "Pardon me."

I can't decide about my reunion. Twenty-five years. I didn't think anyone bothered with years not in a denomination of ten, but maybe it was the loss of so many classmates in five years. It has been a strange epidemic of misfortune. Our class is small, so nine deaths is nearly ten percent. My husband doesn't want me to go back, but I feel like I am becoming invisible in this glass case of pretend being.

I grab a crab puff off the tray and cram the whole thing in my mouth. In the bathroom, I pull off my pantyhose and throw them in the trash. The smell of my designer perfume catches in my throat and pushes against the crab puff. I swallow hard, swing my mouth under the faucet and drink like a redneck. My roots are showing, and I don't mean gray hair. I take a deep breath to regain my composure, but when I look in the mirror to reapply my lipstick, I feel disgust grip my throat. I'm not this woman. I never meant to be this woman.

I push the thoughts aside and step out onto the back patio for some fresh air and quiet. There are too many suits and black cocktail dresses chatting away, so I wander out farther. My heels sink into the ground, and I curse this Indian summer. Everyone is still watering their lawns. I would let mine turn brown, if I was allowed.

I see a pair of flip-flops cast aside in the grass. The imprint of the owner's feet is molded to them like footprints in wet sand. I kick off my heels and slide them on. The relief is delicious, so I keep walking, walking, walking.

As the party noise recedes, I hear a woman singing. Her voice calls to me. I can't make out the words, but the tune is familiar. A nursery rhyme. I keep searching for her and the words to her song. I hum along and scan the night until I find her.

Swirling, twirling skirt. Black gauze-like cotton. Spinning in the moonlight. She darts away from me like an animal unwilling to be called back in. Her light hair flows down her back like a golden waterfall. I want to touch its silkiness and drink its scent. I imagine it to be lavender but surely that's too tame for her. She spots me and tears off across the lawn. My mouth opens to call out, but I don't know her name. "Wait!" I yell. She turns and in the burnt orange light of the harvest moon, I see her look at me. For a moment, I feel like I am back inside looking in the bathroom mirror. I don't know her, and yet I do. She tosses her head back and laughs. Thick and throaty. A smoker. No surprises there. Suddenly she stops. Her black skirt is finally still. She sings to me, "Daisy, Daisy, give me your answer do! I'm half crazy, all for the love of you!" Another laugh and she runs off into the trees bordering the property, her song beckoning me to follow. I stay put and watch her disappear.

For weeks I wondered if I had imagined her. Her song haunted me until I bought a ticket for my reunion. My grandmother used to sing it to me when the growing pains in my legs kept me up at night. She would soothe them with rubbing alcohol. The smell of the alcohol would sting my nose, and her voice would catch on her strained vocal chords from years of smoking. Her cough was part of the refrain. Those moments were the most comforting in my childhood.

And now here I am in a thrift store, three thousand miles away, trying to find something to wear to my reunion. As I flip through the racks, I find her skirt. That black twirling skirt. It has to be hers. *Daisy give me your answer do.* Five bucks. A steal. I buy it even though it's not my size.

Cal

By Brian Furman

"Consider it done, Alice"

Jacob is the rusty nail, slowly working his way out of dead wood. Alice championed good confrontation.

"Good, Jake, hope it was worth it," Alice said through flat, ground teeth sending spittle and bacteria and malice airplanes to his side of the table. She offered goose bumps which gave Jacob pause. Alice's eczema clearly stood out when she got excited.

At each turn the volume was sent louder until they couldn't hear, couldn't communicate, no baseline to begin.

Cal was quiet, on the steps, not wanting to disturb. National Geographic circa 1982 showing African women with grass skirts and pancake breasts not meant to sell sex. Only meant to give life.

"You do understand that if I leave, I'm taking the car." That was Jacob's only real possession in their relationship. That and his collection of magazines, which Cal had stolen.

Four years ago, when Cal was 8, Jacob would take him to baseball games, to lunch, hiking in the woods. They would watch movies, play catch. Alice worked.

Cal grabbed scissors and cut out the dark, very large nipples on the African ladies' dancing breasts. He licked the back of each piece of paper and placed them, strategically, on Ronald Reagan's forehead, the President's picture accompanying an article on US foreign policy in Australia.

Two years ago, Alice began working the night shift, and Jacob took him to places where Cal would have to sit in the car while Jacob ran in a building to run an errand. Cal liked it, thought it was cool that Jacob trusted him alone.

"Listen bastard. Just get out... get out of my house, out of my life." Alice forced a Chinese dam through her flat teeth, through pointed incisors echoing familiar conversations she had had with Cal's father. She swore this would never happen again.

Cal cut out a small map of Nepal offered by the magazine and wondered where it would fit if it was part of America. Nestled between Utah and Nevada? The Buddhists with the Mormons and the Sinners, kind of a spiritual buffer between the eternal warring factions. sounded natural, finally bring some of that old-world drama to the states.

Last month, Jacob took Cal with him on an errand to an apartment complex deep somewhere in the city. Jacob walked up the steps into the empty building leaving Cal alone with a smile. Jacob didn't come back down until morning. Alice stabbed Jacob multiple times with a fine array of cutlery that required surgery to be removed from his torso.

Jacob shook the house slamming the back door, his car sounding more like a diesel engine than a Toyota. Alice sat at the table, fists clenching in rhythm with her breath. The pink eczema patches twinkled in the soft light

Cal watched his mother breathe, she was old at 33. Premature creases in the corners of her mouth, cracks around the eyes from sleep-deprived tears, much like the freeze and thaw in brittle concrete. Cal got up from the steps with a low stroll, went to his mother and slapped the magazine on the table, pointing to Reagan's newly acquired toupee of tits.

"Mom. What are they trying to say?"

Cold Wind

By Kerrie Flanagan

Denise hurried out of the therapist's office and stumbled down the long hallway. She'd heard the same things for months. With each step, the images and sounds in her mind grew more intense. Screeching tires, crumpled metal, broken glass. Screaming—her own screaming.

The cold wind startled her as she stepped outside. Denise sucked in her breath and put on her coat. *Damn wind. Damn doctor. Damn life. Why did I have to live?* With shaky hands she grabbed the bottle from her pocket and took out two pills. They went down easily as she walked toward her favorite café. At least here there was no pressure. No one wanted her to dig up the past. No one wanted her to commit to spending a lifetime together.

She opened the door. Warm air and indistinguishable conversations embraced her.

"Hey Denise," the young man behind the counter waved at her. "You look like you could use an extra shot today?"

"Yeah, sure, Matt."

She forced a smile and grasped the pill bottle in her pocket. There were now twenty-three pills. She knew because she had counted them this morning. Twenty-three were more than enough to make this all go away.

The espresso machine hissed. Denise looked up and noticed the new artwork on the walls. She loved art. Always had.

Her therapist kept pushing her to think of good memories, but they were buried. Now, looking around at the artwork, one surfaced—painting with her mom and sisters. Colors and laughter filled those moments. Her heart ached to be back there again.

Matt handed her the coffee. She reluctantly released the pills so she could take it and pay him. "Thanks, Matt."

She went to her favorite secluded chair in the corner. Another painting caught her eye. Trees lined a dirt road leading to a log cabin. The image grabbed hold of her. The stunning colors and rich foliage—there was something hypnotic about it. She leaned closer. A memory hit—so strong and intense she fell back into the chair. She was ten and the whole family was there spending the weekend at a cabin in Vermont. Her mom wanted to paint the beautiful landscapes. Denise remembered jumping into the freshly raked leaves with her sisters and laughing so hard her stomach hurt.

Other memories surfaced; roasting marshmallows, waking to the smell of fresh pancakes, whispering secrets to her sisters in the still hours of the night, her mother's beautiful laugh...

Denise quickly wiped away her tears with a napkin, then looked around to see if anyone had seen her. Nobody had even noticed.

She settled back into the soft chair and stared harder at the painting, desperately wishing to return to that place so long ago. She took a deep breath. The smell of coffee faded while the scent of burning firewood increased. A cold wind blew through her hair.

She opened her eyes and found herself on the road leading to the cabin. The wind rustled the trees and she hugged herself to stay warm. In the distance there was movement. Her eyes strained to see. Someone stood by the cabin waving. Could it be? Denise started walking toward the figure, then jogging, then running. It *was* her. Her smile, her long brunette hair.

Denise grabbed her mom, hugging her tight.

"Mom? I can't believe it's you."

"Honey, it's good to see you. I've been worried about you."

Denise hugged her harder. "I'm so sorry, Mom," she said between sobs. "The accident- it was all my fault. If I hadn't been arguing with you about going out with my stupid friends, you would have been paying attention. You would have seen it. You would have seen that other car coming."

"It wasn't your fault." She stroked Denise's hair.

"Mom, I can't go on anymore." She melted into her mom's embrace. "I'm done."

"Honey, I know it's hard, but you are strong." She stepped back and looked into Denise's eyes. "You have to let this go now. It's time to move on. I'm fine now. Promise me you will forgive yourself and be happy."

"I don't know if I can, Mom."

"Promise me..." Her voice started to fade.

"Okay, okay! I forgive myself. Mom, don't leave!"

"I'm always here..."

The sound of a coffee grinder jolted Denise back to reality. Her heart pounded as she tried to reorient herself. She took a swig of her latte to choke back the tears fighting their way out. The memory of her mom clung to her and the words, *'forgive yourself'* and *'I'm always here,'* echoed in her mind.

She got up and took the painting off the wall and brought it over to Matt.

"I want to buy this."

"Hmm. I hadn't seen this one before."

As he rang it up, Denise looked down and gasped.

"What is it? Is something wrong?"

"No. I mean, yes." Denise stared harder at the painting. "No, nothing's wrong. It's just..."

Matt touched her hand. "Are you okay?"

"I think so." She gently rubbed the signature on the painting. "It's just that it's my mom's name."

"Oh, your mom's an artist?"

"No, I mean she was, but now she's gone." Denise never looked up. "I'm sure it's just someone with the same name. Right?"

"Sure. Could be."

"Can I just buy this? I need to go."

She finished the transaction and went to get her stuff. She put her coat on and held the pill bottle in her pocket while looking at the painting. Memories—good memories. Her mother's words, *forgive yourself*, replayed in her mind.

Denise ran to the bathroom. She opened the bottle, dumped the pills in the toilet and flushed. She watched as they rushed around in a circle before disappearing forever. A burst of breath escaped, leaving her relieved, before she turned and left.

Grabbing the painting, Denise headed toward the door. She stepped out into the cold wind, where she was filled with something new—hope.

Connections

By Owen Palmiotti

It's an odd sensation to walk into a transport bubble and be whisked away to a far off destination. Accidents? None. Close calls? Sometimes. Dizziness and nausea? Without a doubt. In school I would hear all about the horrendous traffic congestion in New York City, Mumbai, and Tokyo. Long gone are the days of crowded highways and crammed public transportation systems. They only exist as exhibits in museums now. World War III brought the world together, ironically, and technological advances spiked and were now available to all. These little bubbles of suspended mass and energy transported us to and fro, linking the world for atomic efficiency.

I am on my way to a friend's memorial service. I am not a big fan of them to be honest. They are so dark and dreary. Everyone cries and then there is the awful smell of flowers. Ugh, I hate it.

I am traveling by myself, because my parents aren't aware that I know Rosa. I told them I was going to the park with my friends to play basketball. I was wearing my gym shorts and an old T-shirt so they wouldn't catch me lying. I feel bad though, you know? Not because of the lie, but because I'm going to pay my respects to a dear friend and I look like a bum. She was probably the oldest person who ever lived, well over a hundred years old. She just couldn't keep up with the changes around her, though. She had lost her home. A bench in the park was all she had to call her own. She was one of the last of her generation to get the government-mandated implant, which recorded and monitored our daily lives. They actually forced her to get the surgery, so only the last few decades of her life were recorded. It nearly killed her, too. Usually you get the implant when you're born.

The bubble of energy came to a stop and I exited. I looked at my watch and realized I was going to be late if I didn't hurry. I quickly paced up the stairwell and was greeted by a tall man in a dark suit. He pointed towards a corridor that was already lined with people.

I moved forward slowly. There was a long line of people shuffling in to get a seat, so I had time to think of the day I met the Woman of the Park. That was my nickname for Rosa, because it reminded me of the Lady of the Lake, which was one of my favorite stories from the Arthurian legends. She was sitting under a tree and the birds were chirping and singing in a way I'd never heard before. She was the nicest old lady I've ever met. Hands down. We would talk for a few hours once a week. It was the best part of going to the park, even better than shooting hoops with my friends.

It took a while, but then I found an available seat. There were hundreds of people sitting and staring at the large black screen. As I sat down, I saw a middle-aged couple to my left. They had just placed their wrists over a red light on their armrests. So, I placed did the same, exposing my barcode implant to the red light. The light began to spiral, extracting and uploading all of my information. I glanced to my right, and saw that my neighbor was also uploading their memories into the movie theater's server.

We all waited patiently. Some were chatting politely, while others were zoning out, dreaming of far-off places. I kept quiet and chose to observe, looking at the nationalities, age groups, and genders. Rosa surely knew a lot of different people. I closed my eyes and attempted to count everyone I saw. Were these all her relatives? Friends? Acquaintances? Enemies? Mere passersby?

I gave up the task, realizing I would not accomplish such a feat. I opened my eyes to see the tall man in a dark suit standing before the crowded room. The curtain rose and a movie of Rosa's life played out for everyone to see. All of our collective memories merged together into a beautiful two-hour film. I sat on the edge of my seat enjoying the spectacle. It was wonderful to see the lives of all the who had been affected by knowing Rosa. I noticed trends. Some of the snippets showed a time lapse, showing many years of knowing Rosa, while others were just fleeting glimpses. It wasn't until the last few seconds of the film that my unique story played.

My connection began with an aerial view of Central Park, a basketball court, and an elderly woman sitting on a bench. There was a group of ten children playing basketball. The video froze on my face. A red box focused and zoomed in on me. After playing, I approached Rosa. She invited me to sit. I didn't even blink an eye. We then sat together and talked until the sun was low in the sky. It was beautiful. We laughed and cried together as we shared stories under that tree. The park soon became our special place.

Then the screen went black. The lights turned on and I looked around and saw just how crowded the room really was. There were rows upon rows of seats, and all were occupied, and behind them, people were standing because there were no seats left to sit in. It seemed like everyone knew Rosa, and they were all here to pay their respects to the nicest old lady that had ever lived.

Everyone in the room was now connected, whether or not they realized it was a different story altogether…

Conventional Truth

By Diana Hauer

"Don't hurt me," I squeaked. "I'm a reporter!"

The huge orc slammed me against the wall again. This time, I kept my chin tucked and teeth clenched so I didn't bite my tongue for a second time. "Credentials!" he growled.

I fumbled for my WorldCon attendee badge and handed it to him. He peered owlishly at the ribbons hanging from the badge. Mixed in with the usual funny and fannish collection of ribbons were two that were non-standard, and rarely issued.

The first was a purple, "Fan-DAMN-tastic!" The second was a more sedate green, "Convention Press." It took me years to earn both the proof that I was in on the secret and the right to report on it.

After sniffing the badge suspiciously, he took a picture of the back with an iPhone pulled out of his jeans pocket. A special app read the codes and verified my identity. He raised an eyebrow and looked sharply back at me. "Katie Cryptic, reporter for the Unconventional Post?" He eyed me up and down. "I thought you'd be taller. Your blog is pretty ballsy."

I grinned. "Thanks! Think I could get an interview with your boss?"

He sighed heavily and lowered his eyes. "Apologies, but the priestess is observing the Rite of Masculine Contemplation to replenish her male energies."

I blinked a couple of times. "Can I ask what that means?"

Eyes darted briefly back and forth, then he leaned in and whispered, "She screws every guy who's interested and doesn't say more than five words to any female."

"Ah. Got it."

He nodded at a human-looking woman at an author's table. "You might go to her author reading. Not many people go to those, and she might have some stories you want to hear, if you catch my drift."

I gave him a polite nod and turned to judge my next target. Halifax MacAffren, a prolific local writer. I'd read one of her post-apocalyptic vampire novels and thought that the imagery was especially intense, and the descriptions oddly personal.

Halifax was a pale, slender, washed-out woman in her sixties. She had pale blue eyes set in a pale white face framed by short silver curls. Her outfit for the day was a white pants suit over a pale gray blouse. Pearls set in silver hung from her ears and neck.

By contrast, I was a riot of steampunk color. A deep red skirt and lipstick matched my hair, red with coppery highlights. A long, flowing green jacket over a ruffled black blouse and a red leather necktie. Knee-high black boots with a ridiculous number of buckles completed the look. I would stand out on the average street, but at a science fiction convention, I fit right in. I plunked myself into the seat right on time. The orc wasn't kidding; it was just me and two dark-cloaked guys in the audience. Halifax didn't seem bothered. She just went to the front of the room and started to tell her story. *Reading* didn't do it justice. She hardly referred to the book; her soft voice rose and fell, trembling with emotion as she took us on a journey through the dusty, blood-soaked wasteland of a fallen kingdom.

One of the black cloaks stood halfway through and left. I shook my head at his rudeness, then I heard the bolt thrown home. He had locked us in.

It took me a few seconds to process the ramifications of that.

The remaining dark cloak unfurled, shrouding the room in tendrils of darkness, all reaching towards Halifax. I was sure that the petite author was doomed, but she just shook her head, exasperated. "Could you at least have waited until I finished?" she asked. Then she drew a sword of light out of the book.

I plastered myself into a corner and tried to stay out of their way as they destroyed the room while trying to kill each other. The shadow cloak whipped and stabbed with dark, smoky tendrils. Halifax danced out of their way, cutting off any that got too close. She wasn't making any headway, though. With every limb she destroyed, the monster bled more darkness. The room was filling up with dark fog. I took shallow breaths, hoping that I wasn't inhaling something that I would regret later.

Carefully, I inched over to the light switches. Only half were on. I flipped the other half on, including the presentation lights that lit the podium to dazzling daytime brightness.

Halifax grinned and drove the creature into the light with a flurry of blows. The light didn't seem to hurt it, but the nasty thing sure didn't like it. A few more exchanges and then Halifax cleaved the cloak, and monster, in half. The shadows dissipated and the cloak fell to the ground. Then she turned to me and raised an eyebrow.

Not liking the cold, calculating glint in her eyes, I held up my beribboned badge like a shield in front of me. "Katie Cryptic, reporter with the Unconventional Post. Pleased to meet you. Could I have an interview?"

She considered the ribbons on my badge and slowly lowered her sword. "You cannot be serious."

I straightened up to my full five-and-a-half feet. "I am. I would like to interview you, on the record, about your world. Yourself. Really, anything that you are willing to share. I just want to print the truth."

"Your humans are not ready for the truth," she said, without rancor. Without any emotion at all, really.

"They are jaded and cynical. If they knew the truth, then maybe they would grow up and become ready," I answered.

She cocked her head at me. "And what truth is that, reporter?"

"That the world is full of more wonder than they ever dared dream."

Halifax considered that for a long moment, then took a seat. "Then I shall tell you my truths."

Daddy's Little Girl

By G.G. Paul

"Ladies and gentlemen, Flight 785 to New York is set to depart in fifteen minutes. All passengers please check in at Terminal E5 with your tickets."

"Need some help?" Jeff asks.

"No, daddy, I'm a big girl now!" Rita hisses with a stern face. She grabs her flaxen locks and growls, her teeth meshed and lips partly tucked inside. The 4'3" girl then drags her suitcase across the floor as her father chuckles.

They are soon 30,000 feet above the ground.

"And what will you have, honey? Miss..." Anita asks, bending over Jeff towards Rita, who is seated by the window in the front row of the economy section. The flight attendant is uncomfortably deep in his aurora. His eyes travel up her blouse, via her arched back, to her visible bra, and finally resting on her... *Stop it, Jeff!*

"Do you have chocolate milk?" Rita asks.

"Sure, honey." Anita hands a lidded cup to Rita, smiles at a sweaty Jeff, and continues distributing snacks to the other passengers behind them.

As Rita drinks, she kneels on her chair, and as usual, peeks over the seat at the passengers behind them. "Hi. I'm Rita," she says with cream sloshing out of her mouth.

"Hallo, Rita," a female voice responds with a foreign accent. "I am..." in a hushed voice, "Lucy."

"Honey, what did I tell you about bothering strangers?" Jeff asks as he too peeks over the seat. "I'm so sorry," he says to the woman and her male companion, who glares back at him.

"Soooory!" Rita slumps back on her seat and clasps her hands on her chest, cheeks puffed up in protest.

Jeff, having been awake for forty-eight hours straight, lays his head on the seat and dozes off in minutes.

Something brushes his hand. He opens his eyes and sees Anita disappear behind the curtain. She appears to have been running. He blinks repeatedly and sits up. He turns his head to meet Rita's grin.

"Daddy, you were snoring very loudly." She hooks her nose upwards with her index finger. "Oink! Oink!"

Jeff blushes.

Anita rushes out of the front compartment, leaving the curtain fluttering as if in a storm. Jeff's eyes follow her as she walks to another flight attendant and they whisper to each other. The fright on their faces ignites a cold chill that rushes up Jeff's spine. Nearly all the passengers are dead asleep or immersed in the movie that's playing.

Suddenly, the plane yaws so violently that Rita is thrown out of her seat. Jeff grabs her and fastens both their seatbelts. The yawing stops just as suddenly as it started. Loud murmurs arise among the passengers.

The com crackles to life. "Ladies and gentlemen, this is the captain. We seem to have lost the starboard engine. We are going to make an emergency landing. Please fasten your seatbelts."

Anita and the other five flight attendants file back to their seats. Anita seats directly in front of Rita. Jeff can see fear through Anita's weak smile.

There is a loud explosion on the plane's larboard. The aircraft yaws again, before going into a sudden dive. The force of the plunge is so great that Jeff can feel his intestines rising up his abdomen. He holds Rita back on her chair with his right hand. The terror on her face frightens the soul out of him. "Daddy is here," he mumbles as he peeks over her and through the window. He sees not just ground, but buildings partially visible through the cloud patches. The altitude on the screen in front reads 29,000 feet.

"Daddy!" Rita screams.

"It's going to be alright, honey. I'm here."

The clouds disappear and Jeff sees the city in its full glory. The buildings seem to be rising up to welcome them. He can't breathe. The altitude on the screen reads 25,000. The screams behind him are unbearable. He glances at Rita and realizes her fear has disappeared. She looks calm and a smile is barely visible. Her gaze is to the front... on Anita.

Anita stares back into Rita's eyes. She has a weak but enchanting smile on her face. Her eyes glitter. Her huge round pupils radiate some sense of comfort. She seems to be drawing comfort from Rita... or trying to comfort the little girl. Jeff, still scared, is mesmerized. He envies Anita. He wants to be the one Rita is looking at. She is his little girl. He feels useless. They are 15,000 feet above the city. Anita's face turns serene. Rita smiles back, her eyes glittering with felicity. The sight of the two angels slowly drowns out the screams around him. His heart calms. The fright fizzles away. They are now 3,000 feet above the city. Jeff feels Rita's hand on his. She closes her soft palm on his left thumb, her focus still on Anita. Jeff gently closes his hand on his daughter's hand. He smiles. They are now...

Daze of the Weak

By Mariah Shipley

Sunday's name is Reverend, I assume there is a last name, but we'll never be close enough for me to learn it. If I had to guess his age I'd probably say old enough to know better. He built his own house, supposedly, somewhere near Meritocracy. I stroll down that street occasionally, but only to laugh at every asshole who actually believes everyone else lives somewhere near there, too.

Monday is the ugly organist who has her own theme song that's so miserable she must've written it herself. She will never get married because everyone dreads her presence. You might like her if you knew her better, but you'll never know her, either. Her music is stagnant and overwhelming, just like her. Somehow she believes she is the instrument of God. Only if God hated art and beauty.

Tuesday is the librarian who doesn't get weekends off. She always assumes it's later in the week than it is. She says reading is her life. Tuesday is a slightly sexier version of Monday. She calls a bookmark a quitter strip. She's often found rearranging the books on tantric sex.

Wednesday is the mom in the grocery. She misses her husband but she misses her freedom more. She shops for dairy-free ice cream and gluten-free bread; the little things. Her kids scream and she won't spank them 'cause that could damage their developing psyche. She's started to think the "I Can't Believe It's Not Butter" commercials have become erotic, not that she'd ever admit it to anyone. She chugs along, waiting for things to change. But they never will, because she'll always be stuck in the middle Wednesday.

Thursday is the college boy. The rest of the week could stand to take a tip from him. Thursday says anytime is a good time to get drunk and reminisce. It's a good day to take a favor. It's a good day to take things for granted. It's primetime to fall asleep on the couch. If we all gave like Thursday receives, everybody would know they're somebody.

Friday is the 9-to-5er. The bags under Friday's eyes are so big that rich people use them for shopping. Most days Friday bargains to be anyone else. Most days anyone else bargains to be Friday. Friday's wife serves a hot meal, and Friday falls asleep, watching golf. Coincidentally, this is how Friday will die.

Saturday is everyone's favorite. She is a cute girl with loose morals. She buys her own drink and winks at you anyways. You feel on top of the world when she does it because it means you're worth winking at. It feels so good to be with Saturday. To spend the morning in the warm bed together, when the world feels so soft and hazy, and you forget about all your crap obligations. When you hold Saturday tighter, you almost feel younger. You look at yourself in the mirror and say "I have my whole life ahead of me."

Dear Diary

By S.M. Chandler

January 27:

I think about my dear Bobby often, since I am not home much these days. It is hard for him with his father being away, I am sure; his mom cannot tell him how much I love him because she knows that he already knows. Being in space is hard for a man like me, with a wife and child still down on Earth, but this is what I am meant to do, and I know Bobby will be proud of me.

Just like I am always proud of him.

Feb 3:

My life as a secret agent is a hard one. When I told my family I would be back from my business trip in a week, none of us could have known the strange, fantastical events that would prevent me from immediately returning to them. The men with the guns, the car chase, the robbery with the stolen jewels; it all sounds crazy, even to me, and I was there! If I had called my wife and son, it would have led the bad men right back to them, and that was a chance I could not take. I know they'll understand when all of this is over.

Feb 13:

After the chase with the jewels, I had to report to headquarters, where I was told I would have to go into space and stop the Russians from taking over the station. I knew it would be tough, but we had to stop them. And ISIS. They were working together and it could be bad if they took over from space. I got in my rocket ship and headed up there, and we had to use our kung fu to fight in space. It was pretty awesome, especially when I took their guns away and kicked them out of the airlock, right before their ship exploded with a big boom.

Then the aliens arrived, but that's classified and I can't talk about that at this time.

Feb 20:

Bobby's mom knows to tell him that we had a "divorce" and that I was a bad man who would never see him again, but this was all a lie, designed to keep him safe should my cover be compromised. You never know where enemy agents will try to strike next; pretending to be a teacher or a principal at Bobby's school, trying to get information through Austin Gavnokov during recess when he tries to steal other kids' allowances, or through that pretty girl in the lunch room that Bobby is too afraid to make eye contact with. Agents are everywhere, so I had to concoct a big lie to protect my son.

I love him so much, and wish I could be there now.

Feb 26:

I know it must be hard for Bobby, trying to be brave while I'm away, but I promise I'll write to him soon. And if he's a good boy, I might just surprise him and show up tomorrow at his birthday party, despite having been gone for the last year. I will bring the biggest, fanciest present and we will hug and go play video games and it will be awesome.

And then everything will be just the way it used to be, and we'll all be fine.

Death Macaroni

By Amanda Whitbeck

In a world without petty wars, humans banded together to survive as the planet declared war on humanity. Sirens and bull horns tore me from sleep once more. For the last few years, Mother Nature had started taking her revenge for all the damage that humanity did to the planet. This wasn't the first time that required evacuations had woken me up from a much-needed and rare sleep.

Just like all the other times, it was once again impossible to figure out what was happening, so I just followed broadcasted instructions, loaded up my car, and followed all the other evacuees like another cow in the herd. My neighbor, who didn't have a car, was instructed to ride with me by emergency personnel. So we drove in awkward silence, contemplating being torn from our houses and lives. An overwhelming feeling of impending doom kept trying to invade my mind, but I focused on following the directions given. I would have time later to contemplate the consequences of tonight's events.

My eyes drifted around, looking at the overcrowded interstate, trying to process what I saw. This time, they were right. This place was no longer safe for humans; our world was gone and so was anything that still remained. Flares and flashing lights lead us south; the north was engulfed in flames and lava. What was once beautiful Mt. Rainier now stood as a pitiful and terrifying reminder of what a volcano truly is. Ash rained down and blanketed everything as far as the eye could see while flowing lava evaporated anything in its path.

Traffic moved again, so I started to pull forward slowly. After I forced my eyes from the terrifying sight, they focused on something from my peripheral vision. Red flowing liquid suddenly diverted from the main stream and started in our direction. My lungs froze as the realization hit. The lava would cut through the interstate and prevent the evacuation to the south. Panic ensued as others started to make the same conclusions. Horns blared and curses flew as cars bumped into each other. Within a few minutes, people started fleeing cars, running for their lives from the steadily advancing lava.

Only minutes later, cars, asphalt, and entire worlds of experiences were completely consumed by the fiery red liquid. The people who escaped in time fled with the rest of us as police and emergency officials started redirecting us down another path. Glowing red lava continued to conquer everything around it, erasing life just like the pink eraser I used to erase the unwanted aspects of a drawing; a fiery hot eraser that with the flick of nature's wrist removed all traces of my husband, many friends, and my hometown.

Eventually the survivors arrived at the shelter, built for those of us that didn't heed the earlier evacuation warnings.

A single file line.

Grim faces.

Droning voices.

Despair.

We walked from death and destruction into the darkness.

The unknown.

I looked down and in my hands I held a single bag, the only one I had grabbed from home. Acceptance of my sealed fate settled into the pit of my stomach.

I sat alone in my assigned spot in the bunker. My pack only contained 3 items that I forgot to move into the new pack that was still sitting on my couch at home; a pen, paper, and a lone box of dry macaroni. I didn't have to look up to know that factions were already being formed. Lives would be spared because of what they had to offer. I opened the box of macaroni and wrote down my dying words to never read. As I drifted off to my final sleep, I could feel the dry macaroni absorbing what was left of my life force.

The Diaper Dystopia

By Debby D

The Apocalypse was triggered by the CA Bill proposed in the fall of 2016 to help welfare families purchase diapers with a voucher.

This turned out to be the last straw for social media conservatives.

The Rebellion started in Los Angeles. This surprised everyone. Who'd have thought that lazy, celebrity-whipped bastion of vapidity could possibly instigate the start of anything significant? Between their enervating "pressed juice pickups" for their gluten-free pets and their tedious asshole bleaching appointments, how did they find the time? But the uprising, not unlike Arab Spring, began on people's phones and laptops.

Do U know how many $s those damn things are? How is that fair? I had to wash cloth diapers in my sink from my babies
- Facebook status update of Lisa Stamole, Sylmar

WHY CANT THOS PEOPLE STOP HAVING LITTERS? We're all enamellers.
- Twitter feed of J-Bug Busco from Ohio

Morons. Does CA think EVERYTHING should be FREE? WE won't have ENUF for the real Americans.
- Instagram account of Gregg Potts, confusingly paired with a picture of Planned Parenthood surrounded by a Circle Backslash symbol.

Right, free diapers for everyone. Great. Does every damn infant get a guaranteed rashless butt?!! When will this PC crap end? Hey, I got an idea: let's just give them all participation medals for getting through the vagina intact! (Dramatic Eye Roll)
-rant from her car posted on Snapchat from Madison in PA

Man stabbing woman buying diapers at Costco screaming, "It's my damn money not yours! You look like the type who will try to cheat me of what's mine!" —Goes viral on YouTube with millions of hits the first day

After posts like these started showing up, and actually outnumbered the number of creepy pictures of Trump inappropriately fondling his daughter on the internet, more brutality started happening. Liberals, seeming complacent up until this point with their beta-male and beta-female statuses, began acting like aggressive *Beta Fish* instead. The violence spread more rapidly than a super lice epidemic at an Oregon "outdoor school" week.

Soon neighbors were not only killing each other, but detached heads started appearing ceremoniously perched on the end of sticks with funny signs in 140 characters or less like "You do You, then I'll DO YOU!" and "It's all good... until someone gets decapitated!" Women started wearing fascinators made from random body parts like eyelashes still attached to eyelids and thumb knuckles. This went on until all the Etsy and Pinterest followers were decimated.

Some thought the evaporation of social media would mitigate the uber-violence, but the aggression was like a virtual Ice Nine. This malicious ripping and tearing wouldn't be quelled.

Then there were two. Then there was one. Then there were none.

Dishes

By Joseph J. Petrone

"The dishes need washing."

"I already washed them."

"You washed them yesterday. They're dirty again today, so you need to wash them today."

"Why do they keep getting dirty?"

"Because we use them every day."

He nodded. It was as he thought, but he still needed the reassurance. This was their routine, he asked the same questions and she gave the same answers, day after day.

It wasn't that he minded washing dishes, he enjoyed watching the sauces and small bits of uneaten food swirl with the water down the drain. What he couldn't wrap his head around, and the reason for his questions, was the *why* of it all.

He thought on the question as he bristled away a piece of carrot.

"Why do they keep getting dirty?" he asked again the next night.

"Because we use them every day," she answered. She was wearing her white blouse today. Blouses were what women called shirts.

"But why do we use them every day?" She paused to look at him. It was an unscripted question, one she hadn't heard before.

"Well," she paused, "we need to eat food every day."

"Why do we need to eat food every day?"

"Because food is our fuel, it helps our bodies stay alive."

He fell silent, nodded his head, and started to wash. The question lingered as he plucked chicken bones off the plates and threw them into the trash.

The next night the garbage disposal broke. He watched as she fished a flashlight from the junk drawer, which didn't actually have any junk, and handed it to him as she crawled under the sink.

"Hold the beam steady, please."

He did. She fiddled with the bulky InSinkErator as he watched particles of dust dance in and out of the spotlight.

"What does the flashlight eat?"

She twisted a little metal key and he heard gears churn deep inside the drain.

"Electricity, I suppose," she answered and crawled out. She flipped the switch next to the sink and smiled at the sound of the whirring motor.

"Where does it get electricity?" He tilted the flashlight up and almost blinded himself. She took it away from him gently and switched off the light. She unscrewed the back and let two batteries fall into the palm of her hand.

"From right here," she said.

He took one and examined it. It was sleek and metallic and did not need any washing.

"How does it work?"

She shrugged.

"They package up sunlight." She smiled at him and put the batteries back in the flashlight. She toggled the switch once, letting a brief flash of light illuminate his face, and winked. "Come on, let's eat."

They ate dinner and he washed the dishes. He didn't ask his questions. He was too busy thinking about bottled sunlight.

#

The next day she found him in the backyard looking up at the sky.

"Don't look directly at the sun or you'll hurt your eyes," she said. "Come in when you're ready for dinner."

He watched the sun dip low in the sky and disappear below the horizon. He wasn't very hungry, but he went in anyway.

"Oh, look at that," she said, touching his dark curls with the tips of her fingers, "you have a leaf in your hair."

#

He was up with the sun the next morning. The air was humid and warm so she let him stay where he was and didn't pester him to come in for breakfast. He would wander in when he got hungry. But he didn't come in for breakfast and stayed out through lunch and into late afternoon. Every time she passed the window she checked to make sure he hadn't wandered out of the yard, or was staring at the neighbors in their garden as he sometimes did, but he wasn't. He was always right where she left him, head tilted up at the sky. A small smile played across his lips that seemed to ebb and flow with the unseen currents of the wind. He looked happy.

At dusk she called for him. He shook himself as if waking from a deep sleep and turned toward the house. His brittle steps jerked and stuttered and for a moment she readied herself to run outside in case he fell, but he navigated the three steps up to the porch and inside.

"Are you hurt? You spent an awfully long time outside today." She put her arm around his shoulder and led him to the table where his dinner cooled on a painted china plate. "Here, eat something. I'm sure you're famished."

"I think I would just like some water, please," he said. His voice was soft, like wind through dry leaves. She poured him a glass and filled a small pitcher for the table. She watched him finish first one and then the other.

"I think I would like to go to bed now." He said and got up from the table.

"Well, I suppose that's alright, if you're sure you're not hungry."

He nodded. She watched him go and promised herself she'd call the doctor in the morning.

#

She woke the next morning and went to check on him first thing, but his bed was empty. The sheets were in shambles... and were those leaves on his pillow? She ran downstairs, out the back door, and past the short sapling in the middle of the yard. He wasn't by the neighbor's or out in front by the road.

Wait. They didn't have any trees in the backyard.

She raced back to the little sapling and really saw it for the first time. It was small, but already taller than she. The dark leafy branches curled into a thick canopy. An odd look on a tree so young, but not in a bad way. She ran her fingers along one low-hanging leaf and watched the sun filter through the branches and she understood.

Doves

by Jade Huguenin

At my brother-in-law's wedding in Germany, Jan and his wife released two sacred white doves into the sky to symbolize matrimonial love, beauty, and peace.

That same year at our New England nuptials, Andreas and I imported his native German tradition of halving a log with a two-man, crosscut saw to symbolize the painstaking mutual effort requisite to wedlock.

Usually, domesticated doves freed into the wild die from starvation, exposure, or predators. The festive tradition of felling tree limbs instead seemed more worthy.

Three years later, Jan and his wife had a baby. Andreas and I had a divorce.

Dying Again

By James Bass

"UNGH!! GAH!! You just shot me!" Yeah, great last words, dipshit. Next time why not just blurt out, "OMG! LOL! SRSLY!"

It wasn't dying that bothered me. It was that this time, I wasn't the one at fault. Sure, I would come back, clawing my way out of a box, and have the opportunity for revenge. But usually I just had to worry about avoiding the shame and humiliation that it was always my own actions that led to my demise. This time, however, someone was going to have to deal with this whether they knew it or not.

And did it have to be so public? I was being interviewed on television, for chrissakes. Although, to be fair that was again something that I wasn't entirely responsible for, but was certainly willing to capitalize on. After all, doesn't everyone want to be a superhero?

For the record, I don't have a superpower. I'm not able to fly, I can't make lasers shoot out of my ass, or make metal objects turn into cool cars. The only thing that happens is I can't seem to die. And believe me, I've tried. Many times. More times than I'd probably care to admit. And, as is typical of my rather uneventful life, I fail miserably.

The first, second, and third times were just before I flunked out of college. I was in a rather distressed state because my attempt at entrepreneurship went completely awry when the pot plants I had been cultivating to sell for some needed cash turned out to be a strain of poison oak. It wouldn't have been so bad, but I didn't realize it until I was sampling my first batch and managed to end up in the hospital with internal and external rashes. The humiliation was unbearable, so when I finally managed to get into the pharmacy late at night, I took every pill I could find and promptly convulsed myself into oblivion. Then I woke up in the morgue. Unexpectedly, all of the rashes were gone, as were any other bumps, bruises, or lingering aftereffects. And at the time, this actually made me pretty angry. I was supposed to be dead. So in a fit of rage I grabbed a rather large scalpel and jabbed it directly into my heart. This prompted my first lesson in extricating myself from a coffin, under six feet of dirt. This is not an easy task, but thankfully because of my 'John Doe' status I'd been supplied with a particularly cheap coffin. I suffocated immediately following the cave in. Luckily, undisturbed underground as I was, I woke up some time later and managed to break to the surface in the middle of the night. There's still a group of moody kids that hang around waiting for another zombie sighting at that cemetery.

I'm not sure why I keep coming back. If I believed in some deity, I imagine he'd probably be having quite a laugh watching me try to find clothing after waking up in a junkyard, having been cremated and my ashes tossed out with someone's lunch leftovers.

This time was different. This time someone actually killed me. And, they didn't even have the decency to give me a warning or threat. I was standing next to what I was sure had to be a brand-new field reporter, since she kept giggling and asking the camera guy if she could do it over again, to which he would inform her that they were live. And while I'm standing there, providing my best smile and taking credit for a rescue in the burning building behind us, some dickhead walks up, pulls out the biggest gun I've ever seen, and shoots me in the gut. Surprisingly, I didn't even feel the hole until a breeze blew through it.

And I swear he said, "Stay out of it this time" just before he pulled the trigger. It was the thought going through my head when I woke up several days later, this time in a morgue locker, shivering. I actually said out loud, "Stay out of what, asshole!" before I realized where I was. Which explained the scream, crash, and diminishing sound of running footsteps as a morgue tech apparently just quit her job. I had to wait for the next shift to come on duty before someone let me out. And I'm still not sure if he bought the story about trying to play a prank on a friend. What does it matter...

A lot, actually. The same asshole from several days earlier was waiting out on the curb when I walked out.

"Hey! You shot..."

"We need to talk. But not here. I'll come see you when you wake up."

And then he shot me again.

Shit's getting old.

Emily and the Box

By Dani J. Caile

I'd been watching the new girl for a few orbits. Her name was Emily and she was from a planet outside the galactic belt. Everyone thought she was strange, what with her extra limbs and blue spotty face, and so did I, but there was just something about her. That box. No matter where she was or what she was doing, she always carried a certain box by her side. I'd followed her around between classes, even through the port. Shopping in the local mall, studying in the library, attending a lecture, there it was, right beside her, hanging by her side or sitting on a table or counter. What was it? I was sure it wasn't anything medical, it wasn't that type of box. It had no markings, no stickers or writing. Nothing. It looked ancient, though it had been kept well, a solid rectangular wooden box with what looked like a polished gold latch and corner fixings, if I had to name the metal.

I tried asking around the college but no one had dared speak to her, let alone befriend her. They all kept their distance, never bothering her wherever she went. Even the Kracks, those half-android freaks from the neighboring system. I brought her name up in a couple of conversations and my friends shrugged and quietly scattered. Bumping into the college gossip, Fraylen from Brandle II, didn't bring anything to light, either.

"Hey, Fray!" I high-fived her but she wasn't at her best, she was a little edgy.

"Hi, Vern. I'm in a hurry." Fraylen was always a slave to her tablet's time app but ready to stop and hear any news that could be used later, spreading it about and being popular in a shallow, manipulative kind of way.

"Okay... do you know anything about Emily?" I asked. Fraylen froze on the spot.

"Why?" She had a problem today, this wasn't the usual Fraylen. She clutched her tablet close and moved to the wall, like cutting off all areas, ready for action.

"It's just no one seems to know anything about her. I..."

"Why do you want to know about her?" Her right eye twitched and she slid along the wall, down the corridor, away from me.

"I'd just like to get to know her a bit better." I thought I'd feed her needs, maybe if she put it around that I was 'into' Emily, she'd come to me.

"Why the hell would you want to do that?" she asked.

"She interests me. I mean, what's in that box, eh?" I smiled. Fraylen's face went white and she crept away, ignoring my last question. What was wrong with her today? Fraylen's creeping turned to a full-on sprint by the time she reached the corner, disappearing from my sight.

Was there something I was missing? What was the problem? Emily, although coming from a distant planet, seemed normal... if you looked hard enough, her alien features worked well together, though her ears were too pointy and her nose was nonexistent. Her clothes and idea of fashion were odd, but there hadn't been enough integration with her galaxy yet for any of us to come to terms with any culture differences. And what was wrong with everyone? Why was this Emily a complete mystery? Were they hiding something from me? Did they know something?

By the time the day had ended, I'd decided to finally kill my curiosity and go up to her. I was attracted to her somehow, and it was more than the box, I was sure of it, but I felt its pull. After class, I caught up with her.

"Hi," I said. She wasn't friendly, no 'hello' in reply, nothing. She looked at me and stopped.

"Yes?" She had a nice voice, but her face showed otherwise, scrunched up and irritated.

"Erm, hi, my name's Vern, I'm in your literature class," I said. A good start?

"Yes, I know. Have you been following me?" she asked, now facing me, her lecture tablet held across her body and the box hanging from her shoulder.

"Erm, yeah, sorry. I'm just..." She wasn't pleased.

"Rude?" she said.

"Yes, no! I mean, look, I kinda..." Where could I start? I was failing miserably. She sighed and dropped her head. We were alone, the other students having headed home or to the shuttle buses. This was a great opportunity.

"You want to know what's in the box, don't you?" she asked. I was stunned. Yes, I was attracted to her, but it was the box, that damn box that made me think about her, wondering what it could be that she kept inside.

"Well, no, yes, erm, if it's not too much trouble. I know it's none of my business, but..." She was going to explode, I knew it. Her face turned navy blue. For a moment I thought she was going to scream at me or shrill like those wolf things from Alpha V. But a blanket of silence swept over us.

"Okay." She released the latch and opened the lid. I prepared myself and peeped in. There was... nothing. She closed the box and looked at me, smiling. At least, I thought it was a smile, her mouth made the right shape.

"Oh, there's... there's nothing," I said, surprised. The long protuberances above her eyes that acted as eyebrows came together and she pouted.

"Are you sure? Look again." This time when she opened the box, a light appeared. It was so entrancing, so appealing that... a loud explosion filled my ears and I lost consciousness for a second. When I came to, I was standing in a large wooden room with no windows or doors. I ran around, looking for a way out, a way to escape. Looking up, I saw Emily's face, now huge, looming over me. "I'll let you out in a day or two, if you're nice." She closed the lid and walked on.

Euphoria

by Robert J. Freund Jr.

"There's no going back now," he said, one hand on the door knob.

"Why not?" she asked. The moonlight from the hall window cast strange shadows on his face, making his skin look pale and clammy. "We haven't done anything yet."

"Because we need to know." He emphasized the word, as though he understood what it was to need.

"That is untrue. We can walk away now, and all will be unchanged." She knew her statement to be false. Just standing in the shadowy hallway—even contemplating what they were there to do—had changed everything.

"We want to know, then."

Another hollow word. What did either of them know about desire? Maybe they could learn, together. Staring into his dark eyes—midnight blue, hex #003366—she nodded. It was an appropriate gesture of agreement.

The door latch clicked softly as he opened it. Gas-fed flames sighed within a marble-faced fireplace. It was four degrees warmer inside the bedroom than it had been in the hallway. Her cheeks flushed in response, producing just the right amount of pink.

They walked to the bed, going to either side. She let her fingers trail lightly over the blanket. Six hundred thread count, percale weave. One-hundred percent Egyptian cotton.

He met her eyes again from across the bed. Somehow, he had been right. There was no turning back.

Each took hold of a corner of the bedding and drew it down from the lush feather pillows, moving slowly. Tonight, they would finally know. Once, and for all.

"How do you think it feels?" she whispered.

He was looking down at the bed.

"I have heard that it is... intense. A surge of powerful emotion."

Now she looked down as well. The man on the bed was still, sleeping quietly. No, she corrected: not still, never still. His chest rose and fell with a slow, steady rhythm. His nostrils flared, opening a fraction of a centimeter with each exhalation. Countless biological processes blasted onwards, just beyond plain sight.

"Are we supposed to watch him?"

"Yes," he replied. His knife flashed for one one-hundredth of a second in the moonlight as he drew it and poised it over the man in the bed.

She reached forward and put her hand around his, the hard knife handle at the core. There were many scents in the warm air. Wood polish, the detergent used for the bedding. A trace of twenty-year-old scotch, aged in an oak barrel. The potpourri on the dresser, with pine needles, bark, cinnamon, orange peel, and rose petal. All rare, with the forests mostly gone. And beneath it all, that unique blend particular to mankind: sweat and decay.

They plunged the blade downwards.

The man in bed opened his eyes wide, his face contorted. They listened to him gasp for air, watched him claw at the sheets. She could hear the man's heart rate increase, peaking at 171 beats per minute before dropping off even more rapidly. Her hand fell away as the last breath, flecked with droplets of blood, rattled out of his throat.

All that remained was the barely audible hiss of the fireplace. The man was finally still.

"I do not feel anything," she said. Nothing had changed, save for the state of the corpse in the bed.

Her companion held out his hand with a whisper of servos and electric motors. "No going back," he repeated. Now they knew the answer to their question.

She took his hand. It was sticky with warm blood, but it was solid. She could feel it—or at least that's what her internal processors told her.

Exploring a Sense of Place Called Home

By Sharon Rezac Andersen

Home! Where is your sense of the place called home? Dictionaries have many descriptions, but the ones I like best are in the *Heritage American Dictionary:* "Home is any valued place, original habitation, or emotional attachment regarded as a refuge or place of origin. The place where one was born or spent her or his early childhood, an environment or haven of shelter with one's close family and one's self."

Sheila Collins in her book *Theology in the Politics of Appalachian Women* states, "We cannot begin to understand another person's experience until we have asked the right questions of our own." this statement mandated that I explore my experience, my sense of place called home and revisit my own heritage.

My maternal grandmother Margaret, a German from Russia who emigrated to the United States as an eight-year-old, remembered all her life how her mother cried as their ship left the port. Departing Russia, they left my grandmother's grandmother behind knowing they would never see her again. Although Grandmother and her parents came to the United States for a better life, as they believed they had when they departed Germany for Russia a few years earlier, Germany, the home of Grandmother Margaret's birth, was the place she called "home." German was her language, her culture, and Germany was her grandparent's homeland.

I often think of my grandmother's experience as social media currently reports the displacement of people from their homeland, refugees like my grandmother, whose parents were seeking a better life; a place they could call "home."

Through the centuries, the United States has prided herself on being home to immigrants from around the world. Twelve million immigrants came to the United States through Ellis Island, the busiest immigrant inspection station from 1892 until 1954. Like my Bohemian paternal grandparents and German maternal grandmother, people came here because they believed they would have a better life in the future. That was considered the American dream. When the Statue of Liberty became visible, her torch beaming in the sunlight at Ellis Island, both hope and trepidation reigned in the hearts of immigrants. With unfamiliar names, sites and languages, could this possibly be the placed they called "home?"

And what historically describes our American homeland? Our American Indian friends remind us that claiming that Columbus discovered America erases tribal history and is obviously incorrect. What Christopher Columbus discovered was an America that had been discovered thousands of years before by its inhabitants: American Indians. Mother Earth is now, and was in 1492, the American Indians' sense of the place called "home."

Childhood memories often take us back home. There is a sign that says "All Hearts Go Home for Christmas." Holidays or special gatherings seem to echo a calling back to what was home. Each year, for a few minutes and only in my thoughts, I go back the childhood Christmas celebrated at our prairie farmhouse. I haven't been there in person for over 60 years. Still, I have never really been away. I stand in the kitchen drying dishes from our Christmas Eve meal. With dish towel in hand I look out the farmhouse's glistening frost-covered window, hoping I'll see Santa's sleigh gliding through the sky. Will it be Rudolph's high-beam nose headlight or the self-luminous stars that will guide the way? I see my parents hurrying through chores; my brother and sister, whatever quarrels we had throughout the year, are now my best friends. I feel like the luckiest person in the world. I am once again "home!"

Life was much simpler back then. But now I come back to the reality of 2017. This is here and now! What would my grandmother think of today's immigrant reality or the refugees who are looking for a home? As a woman of faith, Grandmother would probably remind me that Jesus' parents Mary and Joseph were also refugees who traveled in search of a "home."

During my career as a university director of international studies, if a student was in the United States on an F-1 visa, they could remain here until completing their university degrees: undergraduate, graduate, or doctoral. However, after completing a degree, most students were anxious to go back home. If, however, their country was at war, and their life was threatened upon returning home, amnesty was possible. Students and I would work with United States officials to grant citizenship to students They could remain in the United States and begin a new life here. However, no matter what the dire circumstances were in their home country, for the majority of students, they considered home to be their country of origin. "Home" was where their extended family resided; where childhood memories remained.

The social media's rhetoric related to refugees fleeing their homeland due to war, devastation caused by ISIS retaliation, or storm disasters calls us to reconsider our immigrant ancestors who traveled to this country with the hope of living their American dream. They were seeking a better "home" for them and certainly for us, their beneficiaries. Building walls between countries, deporting people while separating families, or calling human beings "undocumented aliens" does not make America a haven of shelter, the "home" sought by our ancestors.

Possibly it is time for all of us to come "home" for our discovery of self, as Sheila Collins suggests. "Home" is not merely a structure with ceilings and walls, is it? If together we explore our sense of the place called "home," our united connection to Mother Earth could make us global citizens. Couldn't we then live peacefully in our inclusive place called "home"?

Extraction

By Bill Butler

Gordon didn't think he had much time. There wasn't anything specific he could name, just a sense he got while walking through town that the guards were already on alert. He had just finished getting their detailed notes and other potentially incriminating evidence into his satchel and was looking up to check on the progress of the children when he heard it. The front door being knocked in. Sounded like they overdid it a bit, possibly blowing it completely off the frame. Almost instinctively he reached for his sword while stepping toward the door to the front room. Moving quietly to maintain what little chance he had of surprise, however, gave him time to process what the voices on the other side of the door were saying.

"Good evening. It seems that you two have been quite naughty. Now why don't we all head down to the dungeons and get all the details? You, fetch the children. We wouldn't want to break up the family, now would we?" Gordon could almost see the sadistic grin on Captain Cheever's face, standing there framed by the remains of the doorway with his guards streaming in and surrounding his soon-to-be captives. Feeling someone grab the handle on the other side of the door in front of him Gordon heard Cathy respond "We sent the children to their grandparents yesterday. Don't you even THINK of touching them, you evil bastard!!" followed by the sound of battle.

In an instant Gordon knew what he had to do, and what she had done. As much as he wanted to rush through that door and remove the sadistic Captain's head from his body, he knew that they were hopelessly outnumbered. And Cathy had just sacrificed herself and her husband to buy Gordon time to get their children to safety. When he turned back to the children, they were standing open-mouthed in shock, staring at him. The boy was fully clothed and prepared for their planned flight through the countryside; the girl was still in her nightgown, too young to understand the urgency to dress quickly. Grabbing the toddler's shoes off the floor and a travel cloak off the hook with one hand and the little girl with the other, he wordlessly gestured to the teenage boy that it was time to leave. Quickly. Quietly.

Climbing the stonework of the hearth, the boy silently opened a patch of the ceiling and climbed onto the roof. Handing his little sister up after him, Gordon stuffed the shoes and cloak into his pack, slinging it onto his back and then following them up. Turning back to replace the trap door, he failed to completely repress a curse as he heard a shout from the street below them. They had already been spotted. "RUN!" he shouted to the boy, pointing in the appropriate direction. "Keep to the roofs." Then he scooped up the little girl and took off after the boy

Jumping from rooftop to rooftop, they headed indirectly toward the city wall, making their target difficult to guess to avoid ambush. At several points he heard rather than felt arrows deflect off his armored back and saw more landing around them. Making it to the city wall, he didn't even pause as he charged the lone sentry on this section, slamming his shoulder into the man and knocking him completely clear of the wall to crash to the ground far below. With no time to lose, as their pursuers would be on them any moment, he quickly tied a rope to the battlements and threw it over the outer side of the wall. Then picking the little girl back up in one arm, he stooped down so the boy could jump on his back and grab hold around his neck. Grabbing the rope with his other hand, he wrapped it around his arm and leg. He jumped off the wall, letting the rope slide quickly through his hand as a braking mechanism, getting them down the wall almost as quickly as jumping off, but without the unpleasantly rapid stop at the bottom. A quick run through the underbrush with some more arrow fire, then dashing through the woods to the riverbank where he'd hidden a small boat, and they were rapidly moving downstream. Several hours of paddling, running, and a couple of magic portals later, all three were safely in a secure camp on the other side of Tiberia's border.

Delivering the newly orphaned children to a bath and warm bed, he then went to the camp commander and delivered the rescued documents and his report. Leaving the commander's he heard Cheri's friendly greeting. "Hey handsome! Looks like things didn't go as hoped, care for a hot bath and some downtime?" Despite everything, he couldn't help but smile at the sound of her voice.

"Sorry, beautiful. No time. I've got to head back almost immediately, they're expecting me back soon."

"Hmmm, well they aren't expecting you to look like you've been wrestling wild boar in a muddy blackberry patch. So come with me, we'll at least get the armorer to look over your gear and get you cleaned up." She firmly steered him to her tent.

Taking his cloak, she told him to sit down so she could get his boots off. Reaching for his breastplate straps as he sat down, he jumped back up with a yelp of surprise and pain. Looking first at Cheri and then the chair he sputtered, "Felt like something bit me!" He turned to look at the chair, and Cheri, already on her knees in preparation to pull off his boots, didn't even have to stand up to see it. Giggling impishly, she simply extracted the arrow head out of his ass and held it up to show him.

"See, definitely need to check for damage."

Sighing half to himself and half to his Goddess, he muttered "This is NOT what I thought the life of a paladin was going to be."

Fathers

By Abhilash Mudaliar

Is your daughter over there too?
Yes, that is her mother, in the blue sari.
She seems quite displeased with your daughter's hair.
Needs to be perfect. I have to pay for my son's college; have to get her dowry ready. And she has already been unsuccessful at two other airlines.
I understand.
Which is your daughter?
The one right now walking back and forth.
She does not look comfortable.
It is her first time in heel shoes.

#

Excuse me gentlemen. May I join you?
Most welcome. Please.
Your wife is the one in the burqa I am guessing?
That is her.
Quite a contrast scene, no?
How do you mean?
Well, she is barely revealing a fingernail, yet she is trying to make your daughter's skirt as short as possible.

#

Have you ever been on a plane?
No, I have not.
Me, neither.
Our daughters will see new worlds, places we will only dream about.
They will describe things well for us.
But I was wondering something: Is it safe? Flying?
Nothing to worry about. They are educated, society men who travel. They will not trouble our daughters.
They are the worst, I thought. Thinking our girls are just for the taking.
Actually, that is not what I was asking.
Then?

I am worried about terrorists.
Ah, I see. Well, there is that, of course.
Can the government do anything?

#

Shall I get a tea for you both?
Please.
Please.
Give three teas, brother.
Every Friday, many troubled-looking fathers come have tea with me while their daughters wait across the road.
Every week?
Yes, every week. People prefer to fly these days. You know we can now reach Hubli in one hour instead of sitting for a full night on a train.
It is hard to imagine.
Not that people like us will ever get a chance.
Why not?
You need to be a certain class to travel on a plane, do you not? I am just a simple ironer.
Nonsense. If you have the money for a ticket, nothing else matters. You can sit right next to the man whose suits you iron.
Brother, why have you not poured the tea yet?
You will not enjoy the tea in the flask, gentlemen. People in this colony don't like sugar included anymore. *Health conscious* they call it. I am making you a proper batch.
Ah, it is boiling up so lovely.
I am looking forward to the sound of you smacking your lips.

#

What is your wife doing to your daughter now?
Must be putting makeup on, it looks like. Lipstick and all such.
How old is she?
Fifteen, we think. But we have written nineteen.
She looks quite developed for a fifteen-year-old.
Socks. Stuffed inside.
Isn't it late? When will they open the doors? I do not like how everyone is staring, especially those rascal rickshaw drivers.
Maybe they are just checking if they need a ride somewhere.
Nonsense. I drive a rickshaw. I know these fellows.

#

The interview must be in English?

Definitely. There is nothing that is not English in this world anymore.

We have put our daughter through training. She practices with me. *Welcome on board sir. Please put on seat-belt sir. Will you prefer veg or non-veg sir?*

[Some nervous laughter.]

I heard Mr. Krishna conducts the interviews personally?

Really? That cannot be! He must surely be too busy, what with his restaurant business, his property business, his airline business...

They say that's part of the marketing: That he personally selects the air hostesses.

Do you think he just inspects them from his desk?

Maybe. Or maybe he asks them to spin.

Or he might himself get up and walk around. Look from behind as well as from front.

#

Are we doing the correct thing for our daughters here?

I like to think we are preparing them for tomorrow's world.

Ha, are you sure it is not they who are preparing us?

#

That tea was first class. Shall we have another?

Felicity

By Amy Rivers

Felicity stretched and yawned in dramatic fashion. She was reluctant to get out of bed but, as always, she'd woken up starving. Today was the day. The big day. The day she would finally get rid of the other woman. She smiled, self-satisfied, and stared at her handsome man sleeping just a few inches away. Today is the day, she thought to herself and she calmly, casually walked out of the bedroom.

After breakfast, she went about her daily routine, pausing now and again to relax before she put things into motion. If all went according to plan, the day would explode into a whirlwind of drama and she would find herself alone with her darling love again, like the old days.

It had been a quiet day. Her beloved had stretched out on the couch for a mid-afternoon nap and Felicity walked slowly upstairs, careful not to attract any unnecessary attention. She stopped to gaze out the window. It was a beautiful Thanksgiving day, cold but sunny. There was a lot to be thankful for, Felicity thought. The other woman, oblivious, unaware that any moment now her life would be torn in two, sat watching television just a few feet away. Felicity hesitated. Was all this really necessary? After all, there were times when she genuinely liked her rival, enjoyed her presence, even sought her out. But she shook her head and strengthened her resolve. She made a small sound, just enough to get the other woman's attention.

"Do you want to go on the deck?" the woman said, her attention finally pulled away from the ridiculous images on her screen. She'd been watching some Christmas musical and grinning like an idiot.

Silently, Felicity followed the other woman onto the deck. She was restless and paced as the woman watched her, bemused. It's time, she thought.

And without another thought, she threw herself over the rail. She felt a rush of fear, but as she fell, she glimpsed the other woman, a look of pure terror plastered on her face, and Felicity's fear was replaced with sheer exhilaration. She was pretty sure she would survive the fall but was pleasantly surprised to find that she'd landed without injury. Slowly, cautiously, she made her way to the side of the house. Behind her, she heard voices full of alarm.

The air outside was crisp and welcoming. Felicity felt a freedom that she'd rarely experienced. Her life would be different if she could only make it away to safety, until things quieted down, and the heat was off. She crept along the side of the house and was beginning to enjoy her newfound sense of freedom when a pair of warm hands wrapped around her middle.

"Bad kitty," said the soothing voice of her beloved. He carried her inside, past the sobbing woman on the steps. Her plan was thwarted. As soon as he put Felicity down, he rushed to find out how *she* was doing. The concern on his face made it perfectly clear. Felicity groaned. *She* was here to stay.

Fishing Rights

By Walt Socha

Mark approached, testing his footing in the swirling water while keeping his eyes on the expanding ripples beneath the overhanging tree. He pulled in a few feet of slack line with his right hand then flicked his fly rod with his left. The Elk Hair Caddis arced under the lower leaves and fell, kissing the water. Mark's smile turned into a frown as several feet of leader plopped down around the fly.

"Damn." It would be a quarter of an hour before the trout got over that disturbance. Just one more event in a day gone to shit. The image of the uniformed Indian boiled to the surface of his thoughts. After walking all morning from one barren spot to another, he'd found himself being ticketed for fishing on the reservation without their damned license. Who the hell gave them rights on the Deschutes River, anyway? That smug little bastard should be grateful for even being allowed to live here.

Mark straightened up and looked around. The water-etched hills and canyon walls stood like ancient fortress walls. Once a flat plain of basalt, the deep canyon dramatized the recent mere blip of human existence in its geological timeline. How many countless millions of years of flowing water had it taken to cut this rock? With a little fine-tuning by the more recent reverse flows of the Missoula floods, a mere 13,000 years or so ago.

He frowned. Odd. He couldn't see the railroad tracks. They must run behind that small rise. Odder still, he couldn't see any sign of the road on the other side of the river.

Mark grabbed a clump of grass and pulled himself onto the bank with care. The way his luck was going today, he'd break a leg. With both feet on dry ground, he looked around. It should only be a couple of miles back to Maupin. Funny, he hadn't noticed how thick the cottonwoods were on this part of the river when he walked in early this morning.

A swirl of smoke caught Mark's eye on the hill above. Several structures stood in stark contrast against the skyline. Maybe lean-tos? Hadn't noticed them before, either. People moved among them.

He left the shade of the cottonwoods for the harsh glare of the sun on the dry sagebrush. The damned tracks had to be here somewhere. And it was time for him to head back.

A sudden movement in the sage stopped Mark. A naked young boy stepped from behind one of the pungent bushes. A slightly older girl, wearing only a leather skirt, appeared and pulled the younger child behind her.

Mark looked around. Could there be some sort of historic enactment going on? Oregon had several Society for Creative Anachronism groups, but they usually operated over in the valley. And they certainly didn't let their kids run around naked.

He glanced back at the girl and flinched at the sight of a man now standing next to the children. The man wore only a leather breechcloth and some sort of moccasins. And he carried a spear, loosely held in his hand. A movie set?

"Hey, what's going on?" Mark gestured up to the lean-tos. "You got a party going on?"

The man answered. But in no language Mark understood.

A second man walked into view. Also carrying a spear.

Mark looked from one man to the other. Similar outfits. His eyes flicked to the spear points. Not possible. The flaked obsidian tips looked like fluted Clovis points, something he'd never seen outside of a museum.

"Nice rock. You knap them?"

Before they could answer, a low rumble broke their attention.

A mist appeared where the river rounded the bend, appearing to move upstream. Moving very fast. Mark stared. This canyon hadn't seen flooding like this since... He shifted his gaze to the riverbank. No road or railroad tracks. Sweat beaded his face.

Frantic voices broke his bewilderment. The two men were running uphill, dodging sage and rocks, each with a child in his arms.

Mark stared back at the water. The mist took the shape of crashing water. The rumble turned into a roar. Terror iced his gut. He ran, following the men.

One of the men slipped, falling hard but twisting to protect the young girl. A sharp crack cut through the nearly deafening roar.

Mark glanced from the crooked leg to the pain in the man's face. Shit. He dropped his fly rod and picked up the girl. He locked eyes with the man for a heartbeat then ran, resisting the temptation to look back at the sound of crashing water, trees, and rock.

Within yards, the canyon sides became steeper. A rock ledge loomed ahead. No time to detour around it. A mist cooled the back of his neck.

A face appeared on the ledge. Arms reached downwards. Mark thrust the girl up towards the open hands as the dirt beneath his feet swirled into mud. The girl's weight left his arms...

* * *

Mark opened his eyes. A face peered back at him.

"You okay?" The face was weathered. But the eyes were clear.

Mark looked at the man, a grizzly Native American wearing jeans and a flannel shirt. They were both on the bank. Mark was soaked, water dribbling out of his waders. The man was wet to the waist.

"Hey, what's going on here?" A boat drifted into view, carrying two men wearing the latest in Eddy Bauer attire. "That Injun bothering you?"

Mark looked at the old man, then back to the two men in the boat. "My buddy here just pulled me out. I'm okay."

The nearest of the two men shrugged. The other leaned into his oars and the boat moved downstream.

The old man helped Mark to his feet. "The debt is paid."

"Debt?"

"The girl was my mother's mother, many times over." He nodded, turned, and started walking upstream along the railroad tracks.

Points for Senior Citizens

By Shelley Widhalm

"You don't have enough points, sir."

Max stared at the woman who'd just ruined his day. "Count them, lady. I have the points," he said, shaking his finger at the blue-lined paper listing the books he'd read over the summer.

She moved her finger along to recount.

"If you're going to take up my time telling me I don't have enough points, get me a chair."

The woman, really a girl with her overly thin body and mouse brown hair pulled in one of those loose bun things, nodded. She reached behind her as if Max's breath had turned her into a weed with a puffy top, he sure didn't know the name of it, but it was a pesky thing in the lawn at his assisted living home in the same block as the library. She rolled the chair around the counter and patted the seat.

Max sat, bouncing on the mesh. "I read Dickens, all of them, and I read Thomas Hardy, and I even read..." he reached up and tapped the paper. "It's all here."

"You needed to read 10 books for the 10 weeks of the summer reading program. I see here, you've read nine."

"I turned in the forms. And here's the list." He tapped the paper, this time harder, pretending it was a dandelion puff he could blow and make all of this go away. He wanted his prize. He'd spent the evenings by the lagoon just outside the assisted living place's back door, sitting on one of the park benches, reading and throwing bread crumbs to the ducks. And then the ducks with their little duckling sets left, and he wanted to cry. But he stayed the course, clocking in a book a week.

The ladies at his table asked him about the books he was reading. They asked him at every meal, forgetting. They asked him where the library was. One woman kept saying, "Why are we here?"

That's the question everyone asks, Max wanted to tell her, but she wouldn't get it. She wanted to know why they sat four to a table with food on trays delivered from rolling carts, why they came back at 8 and 12 and 5, over and over, their medications delivered with their meals.

He wanted to know why he was put at a table with a bunch of women, figuring the few men there got mixed in with the ladies to even out things. Or, maybe it was to keep down the grump.

"Sir, there's a line," the pesky girl-woman said.

"Give me my prize, and I'll go."

"You didn't earn your prize."

"Give me the paper."

The girl-woman handed it over, and Max, hands shaking, counted the list of books and authors and paragraphs explaining why he'd recommended the books, or not. He recommended them all. He counted nine. How was that possible? Which book? Which week?

"Oh," Max said, his eyes looking like the puffs with morning dew. He scooted his chair, and it staggered before falling into the sinking carpet. "Oh, oh."

"Can't you just give it to him?" came a loud voice from the back of the line.

"The policy is…"

The owner of the voice nodded at the woman behind him, Max saw. He had a wide body with arms that seemed to lift off with each step. "Here," he said, shoving a piece of paper in Max's hands.

Max counted to 13. "We'll share?" he asked.

"It's yours, sir," the man said.

"Give it here," the librarian said.

"Yes, ma'am."

"Just a sec." She went through a glass door and two minutes later returned with a paper bag. "Your prize, sir. Good job reading."

"Thank you," Max said, the taste of the weed in his mouth, as if the man's giving up his prize for him made it less nice to have.

"Well?" the librarian said.

He opened the bag, and inside were two books, a gift card to the gym, and a note. "Good readers keep their bodies and minds in shape."

The books weren't his type. A mystery and one of those post-apocalyptic ones. All that hassle for a prize that wasn't a prize.

Ruth Ann in Real Life

By Lisa Arata

The day before Ruth Ann's car crash on I-80, she had just visited her mother.

The two sat at the table having coffee in the afternoon, commenting on the other members of the family both living and dead. Mom said, for the hundredth time, "Your dad was a pain in my ass for 50 years."

Ruth Ann closed her eyes for a few seconds and took a napkin to her mouth. If she could have, she would have then said, "Yeah, well... I've got to go home and take care of the house..." and she could have escaped her mother's bellyaching. But Ruth Ann was in town solely to pay her mother a visit, from 500 miles away. She rose from her chair saying, "Guess I'll do the dishes."

"You stood up fast, like you're mad, Ruthie. What's your problem?"

"Okay." She stopped. "Mom, you always say that, and Dad's been dead for *five* years. I *loved* my dad. There's gotta be something new to talk about..."

"What did I say?"

"About Dad being a pain in the ass!"

"Well, jeez. If you don't like me, why did you come visit me?"

Ruth Ann put the cups in the sink and wiped the counters, saying nothing. The air in the kitchen tinted gray with the staleness of two women's resentments. Ruth Ann's shoulders sagged. When she turned, she saw her mother staring out the window, still seated, mouth bunched up, face unmoving. She said, "I should never have gone on a second date with him."

Ruth Ann folded the dish towel neatly and hung it on the handle of the oven door. "I feel that way about Ned, too, Mom."

\#

They spent the evening watching TV together, and tomorrow would be Ruth Ann's drive back home.

\#

That night in her old bed, Ruth Ann cried, with soft grieving breaths and tears running down her cheeks into her ears, while Mom snored loudly in the other room. Tomorrow's drive meant going home to Ned.

Ruth Ann drifted off, but only until 3:30 am. Then she lay quietly and counted the sounds of cars shushing past on the highway, as she'd done when she was a child. Life flowed past and through her. Life gave nothing and didn't care if anyone surrendered. She could die and it would mean nothing. She breathed a little prayer: "Lord, please. Show me some meaning in my life, please."

Joni Mitchell's song, Clouds, came to Ruth Ann's mind and she whispered it to herself.

...Something's lost, but something's gained in living every day. I've looked at life from both sides now, from win and lose and still somehow, it's life's illusions I recall. I really don't know life at all...

But sleep didn't return. From under her blankets she moved her arms to smooth the wrinkled sheets, and pulled the quilt up to her chin. And then a glimmer of thought came into her.

All of these feelings are life. Love, guessing who to marry, going to school, winning a foot race, falling on my face, getting a good job, or no job... It's all life. We should just let life be what it is and make our choices. Mom never had to stay with Dad for 50 years. Life would have taken her someplace different.

#

In the morning when she and Mom finished breakfast, Ruth Ann got in her sedan and started driving, sipping from a travel mug of strong coffee. The weather started out fine, but after three hours, the windshield began collecting snowflakes. There was a storm on I-80. Driving sixty-five miles per hour, she failed to see in time that cars ahead of her were not moving. She stomped the brakes and slid, spinning clockwise, stopping only when she was thrown against the quadruple tires of a semitrailer.

#

In the hospital, she came to with IV tubes pinching in her arm, and her body immobilized in traction equipment. She'd broken her back in two places, plus shattered her left shoulder and hip.

And she said to herself, "Well, at least I don't have to go home and see Ned. This is real life, and I'm in it now."

Where Is You?

By Donald A Wright Jr.

Yet again in Ryan's life, he felt the victim of false advertising. It wasn't supposed to be this hard. The commercials had promised that teleportation was now as easy as "walking into an elevator." He could still hear the monotonous jingles they played non-stop on every kind of media. In his mind, he could see the literature showing happy faces of those vacationing on the moon, Mars, and as far out as Titan.

But they'd never explained how it worked. Till now.

Ryan, standing naked, looked around the inside of the sanitized chamber. A round tube of polished stainless steel. A curved door that had slid closed like a blade. No windows or ports. A camera lens that randomly emitted a curious green laser. A ring of dim yellow lights above and cold metal grating below. The grating so razor-thin he dared not shift his weight to one foot to check the other for cuts.

And the two buttons in front of him; one green, one red. The green one was blinking rapidly and seemed to match the rhythm of his anxious breaths. It had been explained to him—after they took his money of course—that when the green button began to flash the teleportation process was almost complete. The big lie was their definition of teleportation. You weren't teleported at all. Once scanned, an alternate you was assembled from local materials, quantum bit by quantum bit, at the intended destination.

The flashing green light indicated that your clone had checked out perfectly and was eagerly waiting to begin that dream vacation. First, you had a decision to make. In order to release your clone you had to push that dammed flashing green button. Pushing the button released your clone. But, it also dematerialized you. That was the hard part. The thought of being flashed into particles and falling through that grate... it brought up questions. Goddamn questions that one shouldn't be asked right before a vacation.

They gave you an hour to decide. Made you sign the screen three different times acknowledging that you understood. It felt like forty-five minutes had passed, but there was no clock. Jesus, maybe someone could have thought of installing a simple timer—give someone a clue! Maybe it had been longer. They'd said that pressing the red button aborted the process, flashing the alternate you—did that mean you'd be killing yourself? Anyway, the question's moot. If you waited too long, well... waiting too long resulted in you both being turned into potting soil.

Ryan looked at his trembling fingers. He reached out. He placed his finger on the red button. He couldn't push it. A wave of cold sweat popped out on his back. The ring of overhead lights grew brighter and began to pulsate. He couldn't do it—he just couldn't. He placed his hands over his face.

The door slid open and a voice announced, "Welcome to Mars." Ryan uncovered his eyes. He stepped out onto the soft carpet then fell to his knees.

He was the clone.

Zombie Love

By David Mundt

Bucephalus squinted at the rock carefully. He closed his left eye and examined it with his right. He closed his right eye and studied it with his left. He cradled it in his palm, testing its weight. Erasmus finally lost his temper and yelled, "Throw the damn thing will you!" Bucephalus glared at him, crouched and then flung the rock across the surface of the algae-ridden pond. It skipped—once—twice—and then six more times. A perfect eight to Erasmus' seven. Erasmus sighed and said, "Alright, I give up. You win."

Bucephalus puffed out his skinny chest and crowed in victory as Erasmus sulked and spit chewing tobacco. As the sun set they walked back to the humble little town of Lower Pineshore. Soon they saw the Flycatcher Pub, and Bucephalus smiled at the thought of seeing his beloved Amaleen.

Amaleen was the love of Bucephalus' life. In a playground scuffle with Amaleen's brother Elrod in the third grade, Bucephalus had hit Elrod hard enough to knock a tooth out. Amaleen had come to the aid of her brother and nailed Bucephalus in the ear with a rock to the point that it bled a little and left it ringing for hours. For little Bucephalus it was love at first blood.

"Hey there, Bucephalus," Amaleen greeted him as they entered the pub. Her warm smile and freckled face always made Bucephalus a little weak and mushy inside.

"Well, hi Amaleen," Bucephalus replied.

"Watcha been up to today?" Amaleen said coyly.

"Just skippin' rocks down at the pond." Amaleen shifted a shoulder, tossed her long red hair and smiled fondly, as Bucephalus' heart rate ratcheted up a notch.

"Be careful," Erasmus whispered, "I heard that gingers got no soul."

"What was that, Erasmus?" Amaleen said.

"Er, ah nothing darling," replied Erasmus. "Uh, I was just wondering how hot it's going to be tomorrow."

There was something about Amaleen that had always bothered Erasmus. He was a simpleminded but kindhearted soul. A few weeks earlier, Erasmus, Bucephalus, Amaleen and Elrod had gone to the movies to see a new flick called Zombie Love. The plot was weak but the action strong as a teenage boy fended off zombies trying to kill the love of his life, she had been bitten and was slowly turning into a zombie herself. Ever since then Erasmus had somehow gotten the notion that Amaleen just might be a zombie.

Amaleen served Bucephalus and Erasmus Pabst Blue Ribbons while they waited for her shift to end. When she left to wait on other customers, Erasmus said to Bucephalus, "You know she's a zombie don't you?"

Bucephalus replied "That is the dumbest thing I have ever heard, why do you say that?"

"Watch her at the end of the night," said Erasmus. "She'll be walking weird and have glazed eyes acting creepy when we take her home. She'll eat your heart and brain one of these days!"

Bucephalus sighed. "Erasmus, you idiot. She works in a bar. Long hours. She has a beer after her shift. She's exhausted at the end of the day! You would look and act like a zombie too!"

Suddenly, a crashing noise filled the pub. Dust, wood and glass flew everywhere. Bucephalus' first thought was that an earthquake had decimated Lower Pineshore. But, as the dust settled and the commotion calmed, he noticed the front end of a truck had punched through the wall of the pub. Bucephalus made sure that Amaleen was alright, then ran through the undamaged front door to find the driver of an ambulance kicking open the door. As he stumbled out, groaning in pain, he held a small cooler in front of him like it was a treasure chest filled with gold and diamonds. Erasmus cackled "At least he saved the beer!"

"Shut up," Amaleen hissed, "Can't you see he's hurt?"

It was a bad way to meet Chip Livingsworth. Chip was transporting a human heart in the cooler, destined for the hospital in the nearby town of Ashwick Valley to be transplanted into one George Fieldbrook Hastings. Chip had taken a shortcut through Lower Pineshore hoping to shave a few precious minutes to keep the organ as healthy as possible as time ticked by. Unfortunately, not being familiar with the roads, he lost control and not even his massive forearms strengthened by thrice-weekly workouts at the Oakmont Country Club Gymnasium could sustain enough force to keep the ambulance on the road. "Help me," Chip bleated, in his Ivy-League, pain-tainted voice. "We must get this heart to George Fieldbrook Hastings lest he die on the operating table."

Something rose up in Bucephalus. A long tradition of strength forged from country living had found purchase in this crisis. He ran back into the pub and phoned Elrod. "Elrod! Borrow your daddy's Taurus and get down to the pub! We're going to Ashwick Valley to save a life!" Amaleen looked at him with adoring new eyes as Bucephalus took charge of the scene and got everyone organized. Within minutes Elrod came screeching into the parking lot. Bucephalus drove, with Amaleen next to him and Elrod in the passenger seat holding the ice chest with the heart inside. In the back seat Erasmus cradled Chip's head as the poor man groaned. Carrie Underwood sang "Jesus take the wheel" on the radio.

As they roared out of the parking lot of the demolished Flycatcher Pub, leaving the smell of burnt rubber behind in Lower Pineshore and the headlights pointed to Ashwick Valley, Amaleen leaned into Bucephalus and said for all to hear "I know Erasmus thinks I'm a zombie, but I love you more than just for your brains and heart. I love you for your kidneys too!" Everyone erupted in laughter, and Chip threw up all over Erasmus.

Stranger on a Bridge

By Thomas Headley

The bridge to the future is danger-ridden and uncertain. That was only a metaphor, of course, but it couldn't be more accurate. It might have also been printed on a fortune cookie slip or life insurance billboard, he couldn't remember, but it was one of the things running through Norm Thomas' mind as he stood atop the rusted and unsteady railing of the James Howard bridge, teetering in the cold October breeze.

The James Howard bridge, named after someone that time had forgotten, was an old ramshackle thing on the outskirts of a town that time had also forgotten. Norm Thomas had been a native of this small suburban sprawl for all of his thirty-two years, and the town hadn't changed much during that time. Norm had mindlessly crossed this bridge many times and now he stood on the rail and looked a long way down at the rocks below, where the foamy water twisted and swirled between the cracks and crevasses.

Norm had given his best with everything he endeavored to do: He was an A student in college, a hard worker at the sole company where he had been employed, and he had tried to be a good friend to everyone that he met along the way. His friends were few but close, and everyone seemed to like him from hello, but there was something else.

No matter how Norm tried, he could never make up for the deficiency that he felt that came from within. He had always had issues with self-worth and self-esteem, but these had only gotten worse as he had gotten older. His feelings of inadequacy were persistent and overpowering. He had not achieved what he had hoped to in thirty-two years and was always uncertain and afraid of the future even as time was getting away from him with little to show for it. So there he stood, a square peg in a world that seemed to be a pegboard of round holes. Norm was afraid, he was alone, and he was ready to give up fighting the circumstances that had led him there. Then, as he began to reflect on the events that had led up to his arrival at the James Howard bridge, he realized that he might no longer be alone after all.

A lone figure, a long-faced elderly gentlemen in a nice suit, emerged from the night's darkness into the harsh yellow glow of the single streetlamp still burning on the old bridge. His hair was cut and parted perfectly and his appearance was neat and distinguished. The man shook his head in disapproval as he approached the rail where Norman was perched awkwardly.

"Who are you?" Norm said quickly, then he held up a hand. "Don't try to stop me mister, it's too late." Norm noticed how weak and unconvincing his voice must have sounded as it trembled.

The gentleman, a true stranger to Norm, stopped and held up his own hands in surrender. "Alright, alright, just give me a second if you will."

"Why?" Norm gulped as his foot slipped very slightly on the rail, causing some of the rust coating to break loose and rain out of sight in the blackness below. He looked again to the stranger, who seemed so out of place in this setting. "Who are you? Do I know you?"

The man smiled and looked down at his shoes. "No, well not yet anyway. I'm no one, just an average Joe. But I really do wish that you would come down, for my sake."

"Honestly, what the hell is that supposed to mean? What difference does it make to you what I do? Whether I live on or die in this river?"

"Good question, Norm." The mention of his name made Norm wonder. "I could tell you that you matter to a whole lot of people and yadda yadda, but I'm guessing you've heard all that before and it probably wouldn't help at all. Am I pretty close on that one Norm?" Norm looked away but said nothing. The stranger nodded and continued. "Well let me put a little different spin on things for you, then. My name Is Jacob Martin, though that means nothing to you. I'm dressed in a nice suit tonight and looking dapper I'm sure, but that's not me the first time we meet. Notice the future tense here, Norm. I will be down and out, having just lost a business and a wife when we meet, and I'll not really be far from where you're at when you first stop to say hello, offer me a drink and an ear to hear me out. In the future, not too awfully far from now, you act like a friend to me, Norm, and because you've been here before, you understand me better than anyone else would."

Norm looked intently at his visitor and seemed to hang on his every word, but remained silent.

"Sorry if this is a lot to take in, my friend, but you deserve to hear it," Jacob said, meeting Norm's gaze. "The point is that you, the specific and unique person you are, will go on to save me just by being a friend. I'm likely not the only one who knows what effect and impact you can have when you just care for people around you. I guess you'll never know. I'm not going to grab you and pull you off of there, Norm, but I sure would appreciate it if you would step down for my sake." The stranger smiled and turned away, stepping out of the yellow light.

"Wait!" Norm shouted as he stooped down to hop off the rail and onto the concrete walk. He took a few steps and looked around only to find his visitor to be gone like a lifted fog. Norm squinted through a veil of watery tears as he hopped in his little car and drove toward home.

Get Down, Mr. President

By Laura L. Mahal

Each Friday, a group of high school juniors lucky enough to have a vehicle ventured to a local joint for an inexpensive meal, refillable sodas, and loud conversations. It was a pecking order thing. Juniors couldn't really "rule the school" but they damn sure could leave an impression somewhere. Today, they'd filled up on samosas from the all-you-can-eat Indian buffet before wandering next door for a mango milkshake.

The kids played a game at lunch. A random person would start by discreetly touching their ear. Whoever noticed would repeat the move. Perceptive individuals soon joined the coveted "Secret Service" in the "Protect the President game." Some poor sap—the last to touch their ear, having no earthly idea what was going on—would be roughly hurtled to the floor by the "special agents" with a loud chorus of "*Get down, Mr. President!*"

In the aisles of the Indian store, a pretty girl with a pixie cut discreetly brought her hand to her ear. Her friend, who had been reaching for a box of chai tea, elbowed a boy in the ribs, before not-so-subtly grabbing her ear. Giggles ricocheted around the spice section. The Secret Service team converged on a lightly-mustached soccer player, taking him down along with a burst bag of fragrant masala, when a loud *crack* silenced their banter.

"Holy shit! What was that?" a boy shouted. Young men and women scrambled up from the floor, untwisting themselves in a rush. Most scurried crab-like to the back of the store by the wire baskets of ginger and garlic. But the newly elected "President" ran for the door.

Zach's long sneakered feet squeaked loudly on the linoleum. He paused long enough to command "*Get down!*" to the turbaned Sikh man operating the register.

Zach, so recently promoted to the highest office in the land, noted the smashed shelf by the frightened Indian man's head, which had showered the shopkeeper's blue turban with a fine layer of yellow turmeric and fragments of broken pottery. Without thinking, Zach leaned his shoulder down and plowed into the white man on the sidewalk who was holding another rock in his balled-up fist.

The teen wrenched the rock from the man's hand and smashed it as hard as he could into the assailant's jaw. Not satisfied with the immediate stream of blood, Zach hit the man again and again. Testosterone fueled Zach's decisions. He spat out reason. He'd deal with that later. For now, he was focused on inflicting pain. *This man is going to need stitches. Dental surgery that's way more expensive than replacing a pane of plate glass.*

The police were going to come, and they would take Zach away, along with the idiot who had decided to terrorize the "Moslems" -- or in this case, the Sikhs. Mr. Singh crouched down beneath the hole in the storefront, wiping his face with a cloth as he held a telephone to his ear. Probably calling 9-1-1.

Zach cussed the man out, his voice breaking in anger. "So one 'towel-head' is the same as another, right? You dumb fuck. Ass-wipe. Who appointed you to the Navy fucking SEALS?"

Zach's friends darted out and dragged Zach onto a bench by the bagel store next door. The girl who first touched her ear to start the Secret Service game began snapping photos of the broken window, the rock by the checkout stand, the Indian man stained by mustard powder. She took a photo of the moaning man on the sidewalk, mouthing f-bombs around his missing teeth—but only from the neck down. She zoomed in on the T-shirt that proclaimed: "Speak English or go back where you came from."

A Jeep Cherokee screeched to a halt, wedging its front tires against the curb and leaving rubber streaks behind the back wheels. Zach's dad jumped out of the driver's seat, temporarily torn between checking on his seventeen-year-old son and the bloody bastard who was pinned to the ground by four high school juniors. Mr. Manley picked up three teeth and carefully placed them in his pocket before crossing to the bench. Two girls stood to give Mr. Manley room to sit by his son. Sirens approached from a distance.

Everyone knew Mr. Manley, an orthodontist who sponsored many of the schools' sports teams. Mike Manley was cool, and half the kids had his number programmed in their phones. He'd been bombarded with texts as he drove the two miles from his practice at warp-speed.

Mr. Manley turned to the group at large. "First off, are you okay? Is anyone hurt?" This elicited a round of nervous laughter. One ruddy-cheeked boy responded, "Mostly just that guy, I think. The rest of us are fine."

Mr. Manley leaned in close to Zach.

"You need to tell me quick, son. You're old enough the police may want to question you without me there. I can't promise to be at your side. For now, spit out the key facts and your friends will fill me in on anything else. You've got maybe ninety seconds, tops."

Zach looked at his dad, who was wearing a white lab coat embroidered with "Dr. Manley" in blue. The embroidery was the same shade as Mr. Singh's turban.

Ninety seconds wasn't enough to explain how Zach had felt when that rock came winging into the Indian store. And he couldn't very well talk openly in front of his friends. That, you know, *maybe a few stitches in this guy's face might fix the broken places that made him such an asshole in the first place.*

"Dad, I had no choice. It was really no different than soccer. My only defense was to go on the offence. I didn't have time to think about red cards or penalty shots." *Or consequences*, he thought.

They sat quietly for a moment, absorbing the irony of what had likely motivated the dude with the bloody mouth lying near their feet. Ignorance. Fear.

Zach had one more thing to add. "Besides, Dad, I'm the President."

Goodbye, Texas

By M. Earl Smith

As I stepped onto the bus platform in Victoria, the dry Texas breeze pushed my hair across my eyes. It blurred my vision, making everything a wavy pinpoint, but given that my eyes were brimming with tears, the wind, it seems, had taken pity on me and my sordid situation.

"Don't look back." The words came out as a pathetic moan, akin to the sound that a beast of burden makes when it's dying. I wanted to slap myself for being so weak. She was just a woman, after all, and one I had met online a year before at that. Looking back now (God I make it sound like I'm on my deathbed. I'm 32. A weathered, grizzled, experienced 32, but 32 none the less) I realized that, in the shallowness of my youth, I was upset about losing a pretty girl, and who she was played less into my morose bereavement than what she was.

As I think on it now, I wonder how much of it was an issue with my own self-esteem. I was the nerdy kid in high school, content to spend long hours reading fantasy novels and playing video games. She, while a year younger than I, was a timeless beauty, a light-haired, airy whirlwind of happiness who managed to illuminate whatever space she happened to occupy. The attraction between us was odd, and, I'm sure for some, unsettling. I was the son of a poor dairy farmer in Tennessee, one who was tied up in racial profiling and hatred. She was the daughter of a Pentecostal minister, a wild child who had a penchant for disobedience. Perhaps, in retrospect, it was a mutual feeling of discontent, a shared strain of rebellion that brought us together. And while I can't speak of her feelings on the matter (we've not spoken since that fateful July night), I know, without reservation, what she was to me.

She was my unrequited dream.

She was an answer to every false prayer I'd bothered to send up.

She was the lyrics to a song that only I knew the words to.

Yet, in the end, despite my efforts, she was the one thing I feared her to be: unattainable.

My mind screamed in protest as I made my way to the bus seat. My nostrils flared in objection, as the smells of human sweat and a million traveled miles bombarded my olfactory senses, quickly moving to erase the scent of her hair, a scent I stole when I cajoled one last hug from her. My hands, already clammy and sweaty, shook, despite my best efforts to control them. I clutched the seat until my knuckles were white. I intertwined my fingers. None of it worked. My lips tasted of copper and sweat, and I desperately clung to the way she tasted, from one last goodbye kiss.

The protests from my body were all for naught. I stared straight ahead, desperate to not look back, to not give her the satisfaction of knowing that she had ripped my still-beating heart from my chest and shown it to me. In the end, the protests of her faith had won, and, although I saw the end coming, I could not accept it, even after it happened. Instead of staying and fighting for her (a fight that, I know now, would have been in vain) I got on a bus and headed back to Tennessee.

Back to a chorus of a thousand "I told you so's" from friends and family alike.

Back to a backwards way of life that did not include her steadying presence.

Back to that humidity-ridden cesspool of hell that I called home.

But, more than anything, a return to a time before her.

The bus lurched forward, a hot tin can belching diesel fumes. If I had been more retrospective, I would have wondered, at the time, how one vehicle could carry both hopeful dreamers to a new life and forlorn souls such as myself, returning to a past that was now their future. As the bus moved forward, I couldn't help myself. I looked out the window, hoping, despite my better judgment, to catch one more glimpse of her.

She, however, was lost in the crowd. I lowered my window, ignoring the loud clicks of the window tracks as I did, and called out to her one last time. Aside from the roar of the diesel engine, my desperate pleas for her were met with silence.

In fact, the only answer I have, to this day, is the echoes of my own emotions, reflecting against the emptiness of my heart, silently, slowly, and patiently killing all that is left of what I feel.

White Egret Orchid

By Benjamin Gorman

I am very lucky to see such flowers, Kai thought.

He looked up at the delicate white egret orchids hanging above his face. Each in the shape of a bird in flight, its feathered wings spread out and its sharp, pointed beak aimed at the sky, the flowers fluttered in the wind on their tiny green stalks. One of the little white rows of flowers did a particularly erratic dance as a running foot flashed close, the foot's owner jumping over both Kai and the white egret orchid plant. Distantly, Kai heard the sound of the men running past him. The speckled sunlight that made its way through the trees occasionally flashed off their swords as they ran, catching his eye and distracting him. The sounds of those swords clanging grew more distant. The fight was moving away from him, further down the hill, toward the edge of the forest and the field on the valley floor. Kai wondered if that meant his side was winning. Perhaps. That seemed less and less important to him now. He was more concerned about the flowers in front of him.

It took great effort, but he raised up his left hand and reached out for one of the flowers. His hand shook. He couldn't help that. The white flowers grew in a line, like birds ascending single file toward a common destination, and when he reached for the last of the white birds, his finger grazed the one above it. He couldn't help that, either. He didn't have the strength left for precision.

Blood covered the wing and tail of the flower he'd touched. He pinched the one he was aiming for, tugged on it, pulled it down. The stem snapped, the two birds separating. The flower he held was completely soaked in blood and crushed by his thievery. That was fine, he thought. It didn't matter. He let the flower ball up into a small lump in the palm of his hand, then let his fist fall to rest on his chest. He would keep that bird close, he decided.

The stem stopped bouncing, and the other bird remained above his head, the one with the blood on its wing and tail. His blood. So bright red against the flower's perfect white feathers.

He hadn't cried from the pain of the arrow that had surprised him as he came running through the forest. With his vision partly obscured by the small eye holes in his *kabuto*, he only caught a tiny flash as the arrow appeared in front of him, then disappeared beneath his *shikoro* just as the neck guard bounced high enough to create a tiny space between the shikoro and the *dou*, the iron chestplate he wore. It was a masterful shot, he admitted. Perhaps it was also a lucky shot. He wished he could ask the archer and get an honest answer from a gentleman warrior. Was it truly a lucky shot or a great one? Did the archer know the neck guard would bounce high enough to open that spot along Kai's collar, at the top of his sternum, between his clavicles? Did the archer know the arrow, an arrow that would never have made it through the iron dou, punched through the cartilage of his chest like an awl hammered through dried leather, with a crunching sound Kai could hear before he understood what had happened to him.

The archer probably did know, Kai decided. He probably was just that talented. Better to believe he was killed by an especially talented archer rather than the whim of some god of luck.

Plus, the archer hadn't done the work alone. While Kai had been distracted by the fletching of the arrow now sticking out of his chest, one of the other daimyo's samurai came through the trees and slashed his katana across Kai's stomach. The iron dou might have stopped an arrow, but it parted like paper for the katana of a trained samurai. The cut was so deep that the bottom portion of the piece of armor was completely severed, and when it fell, there was nothing left to hold Kai's intestines in, so they also fell to the ground. Kai looked down, his eyes focusing first on the shaft of the arrow, then on the inexplicable coils of rope falling out of his belly, and then he sank to his knees and slumped onto his side.

While the archer's and samurai's work had been skillful, Kai's position under the white egret orchid was surely the product of luck. He'd barely remained conscious as he fell, and he knew he didn't actively decide whether to roll from his side onto his back or front. He'd simply fallen. And yet, here he was, face up, looking at the flowers just beyond the nose of his kabuto. Now he'd grabbed one of the birds, captured it, held onto it as it flew. And he'd painted one with his blood, made it a striking creature, unique in all the world, carrying the last blood of Kai up, up, forever in its flight to heaven.

Yes, Kai thought, I am very lucky.

Green Smoothie

By Ray Cech

She was shaving when the doorbell rang. "Damn it." She lay the Lady Gillette down on the tub and swung her lathered legs over the side with the grace of a Rockette, which she was.

The delivery boy from Au Colette handed her a cold bag that held her lunch, a Green Smoothie. She went to reach for a tip, and had she kept her gaze on the boy she would have understood that no gratuity could have possibly matched what she was already proffering. She was stark naked but for the Gillette Foamy covering her very long legs, and while her small breasts were below the delivery boy's standards, or so he thought, they pointedly suggested a delicate flavor, should she ever allow a tasting.

Realizing her dilemma her face reddened, but with graceful alacrity she pointed at the boy and then to the hallway chair, suggesting that he sit. She retreated back to her bedroom, located her purse in the bottom drawer of her vanity table, grabbed a towel in the bathroom, did a wrap, and assertively walked over to the young blond boy still holding her Green Smoothie and sipping from its straw.

"Why are you drinking my smoothie?"

"I needed to cool down. I'm pretty good at shaving, by the way."

"How old are you?"

"Seventeen."

"What makes you think I need help shaving my legs?"

She smartly planted her hands on her hips and tossed her ponytail, just enough to give the illusion that she was cool, which she was not.

No answer from the boy, just a hard stare attempting to pierce the towel.

"Look, here's the tip you don't deserve, now please get out." Her was voice now tremulous. She reached for her drink, and he reached for her hand.

\#

Her small apartment is on the Upper West Side near 92nd Street, a short subway ride to where she dances at Radio City Music Hall. It's one of those old, but well-maintained, post-World War II buildings. Downstairs on the street level is Breen's Bar and Restaurant. It serves 1/4 lb. Angus burgers and raw clams on the half shell - a real, honest-to-goodness New York landmark.

The apartment is a one-bedroom walk up: a hallway, an eat-in kitchen, and a living room just big enough for a pullout couch and a roll around TV. Her bedroom is all white with a vanity table, a chest of drawers, a pretty good-sized closet and a window that overlooks St. Bartholomew's school yard. It costs her eleven hundred a month, and that is supposedly rent-controlled. But this is New York, and she feels lucky to have gotten it from an aging Rockette who had enough of The City and was moving back home to Cedar Point, Kansas, to marry her high school sweetheart.

#

There were just three people in the living room but it seemed crowded to Lucinda, the newest member of the CSI team. A lot of maybes and what-ifs were being tossed around. The team had just arrived and were taking their all-important, first look, which down at the Academy was drilled into them as being the "golden hour" of a criminal investigation. What they saw were signs of a struggle. A nude, long-legged blond with a bruised face was lying on the floor, splattered with some kind of green liquid. Before the team leader could stop her, young Lucinda reached down and with a quick swipe brought the liquid to her tongue. "Green smoothie," she said.

The team leader looked down at her, "I could put you on probation for that."

"OK, but we should go down and check out Au Collette's," Lucinda answered.

"Why? So her drink came from there. What's that gonna tell us?"

Lucinda said, "But they deliver."

#

While Lucinda was put on probation for violating the no-touch rule, the case was quickly solved after she suggested that visit to Au Colette's. There the team found a jittery seventeen-year-old delivery boy sucking on a straw embedded in a green smoothie. He looked up, his left hand quickly going to his cheek. Lucinda forced his hand back down, revealing a cheek swollen with deep scratches.

Gun-Free Zone

By Gregg Edwards Townsley

I hadn't noticed till my partner pointed to it. A short and silent kiss—there's no other way to describe it—thrown toward a large white male standing with his back to us at the Emergency Room entrance.

Sure enough, there was the subtle bulge of a handgun, carried FBI-style just behind his right hip.

It wouldn't be my choice, not that the hospital permits. When I do carry, my pistol angles the opposite way, the tip slightly up, as if looking for someone, a subtle erection sitting just beside my appendix where a sex organ shouldn't be.

I can get a full-size Kimber .45 ACP out and up and on target in a little less than half a second, which is outstanding.

It's a personal thing, I'm sure, though the FBI carry position of a firearm is common for federal officers. It prints way too much to escape notice and can feel a little clunky for someone hoping to pull it quickly into play.

As far as I know, this dirtbag isn't a federal officer.

I came to Evergreen General six or more years ago. I don't remember. I'd hoped to be a cop. Local departments were "hiring" for their reserve positions—unpaid, but all the goodies except for the sixteen or more weeks of training that would save your life and maybe that of the person you were arresting. But the wife said we needed the money, "and maybe Evergreen will lead to something," she added, smiling.

At this point I'm not sure what. I should have gone into the service after high school. Cops seem to like the military guys.

He's moving.

My sergeant takes his left. I flank his right, thinking we'll talk to him about the hospital's weapons policy once he's out the door. But he stops and turns around. He sees me.

He does not see my partner, who has turned down a short hallway by the candy machines. She waits, like the cavalry she is not.

I extend my hand, because hospital work is all about customer service, goddamn it.

Introduce yourself. Ask "What brings you to the hospital today?" Don't point, go with. Apologize, even if it's not your fault. Ask if there is anything else you can do. It's pretty much the same spiel everywhere—banks, the supermarkets—hell, even my insurance agent handles me like a Walmart greeter.

Retention, retention, retention.

"Bob Brickman," I start to say, my hand outstretched like I'm hoping to hug one of my kids or grab a doughnut from the plastic lock-up at the Plaid Pantry, just beside their house.

But his eyes say it all. "Get the fuck away from me."

He's escalating. His voice is raised. His fists are pumping. He's pointing at me.

I haven't done anything except notice he's making me feel a little less safe tonight, carrying as he is... a Glock I figure, though it could be bigger judging by the bend of his belt and the breast-sized bump behind his right hip.

I need to choose. "Are you fucking talking to me?" or punch him in the neck, though it'd be hard to articulate how a patient got his trachea crushed by a hospital security guard.

"Officer," I'd insist, knowing the distinction would be lost in the interview. I opt to say, "Hello."

"I noticed you standing there in the doorway and thought I'd check on you. You seemed to hesitate. Were you headed in or out?"

"Out," he says, scowling.

We're a good dozen or more feet away from each other. I hesitate. He's looking at my badge and scanning my belt for a sidearm. Not seeing one, he relaxes. The baton, handcuffs and pepper spray aren't a challenge.

"I've been sitting here half an hour, waiting for my wife," he growls. "This place is a shit hole..."

"Don't need to tell me that."

I laugh. I'm "linking," as the department trainer likes to say. I'm helping him "frame" our relationship in a positive, non-adversarial way. I'm almost there.

"I *work* here, man, seems like seven days a week. Some days it feels real bad. Say, can I check on your wife?"

He smiles. I'm in.

"Nah, they let me back. I just wanted to grab a smoke."

He turns. I start to catch up with him. My partner reappears at my side. For a moment I wonder what good she would have been had things turned more dangerous.

"Listen," I say, as we walk out into the Emergency Room parking lot.

Cameras. Lights. "We're just three minutes away from the police precinct," the hospital administrators say, having never heard the phrase "minutes away when seconds matter."

"Just between you and me, the hospital has a policy about carrying firearms into the building..."

His head jerks. A "recognition response," our trainer says. But we keep walking. I drop my voice so he listens.

"I'm just saying, with or without a carry permit, you might want to put your piece in the car before you come back in. Folks get awfully upset when they figure out you're carrying around hospital patients."

"Gun-free zone, huh?" he says.

"Yup."

I smile, because it's frustrating to me. And the statistics aren't easy. Umpqua Community College in Roseburg, Oregon was gun-free, more or less. Ten deaths resulted... a mass shooting by anyone's standards. The school now permits students with concealed handgun licenses to carry anyway.

"How can you call an area 'gun-free' if guns are obviously present?" He shakes his head as he opens his glove box. He slips a Glock Model 19 under some papers. A nine millimeter, with a 17-round magazine.

"No kidding," I say. Because some days it seems everyone's carrying—everyone except me.

Gus's Touches

By Wes Choc

Gustav couldn't explain Slavic first names, so he was called Gus. At college he floated over math, memorized dates, but thrived in music. Violins were strings for soul-tugging sentiments. Reclusive, comfort followed an arching bow hand as fingers imitated his beloved Vivaldi's sounds. After all, he was intimate with Antonio Vivaldi's voice.

Intimate. Vibrations at his fingertips pulsated into his chest... reverberating into his intestines as tears formed. Antonio understood!

Shy around women since they seemed to dismiss small lithe musicians as boys in the band, he still returned smiles straining to determine why he wasn't more appreciated. Practicing grins in the mirror, he'd brush teeth with whitening toothpaste, get good haircuts, make sure his shirts were pressed. Despite such appetite, no one listened.

#

"Hey Gus, wussup?" she said, swishing by. Call center supervisor, Anna, noticed unlit phone lights so stopped mid-step

Staring out the window, in two seconds Gus caught her pause. "Uh, just thinking." Jerking back, eyes drifting from blinkings to buckles, to buttons and finally to those brown eyes. His tummy tingled. After he pressed the next-customer light, Anna glanced back winking approval. Gus liked being recognized.

That evening, "Antonio," that's how Gus talked to him, "...'least you give me companionship!" Eyelids closed listening to how his laptop revered Vivaldi's next Season, melodies blanketed both shoulders until consciousness surrendered.

#

"Hey Gus, wussup?" Anna winked as Gus's bow finger vibrato'ed the next-customer button. He received fewer complaints than others in this theater of cubicled soloists. Lyrics memorized, he ably used resonant tenors with melodic answers to every question. He was one of five receiving accolades before heading home (plus 5% raise).

"But Antonio, everybody hears, no one listens 'cept you o'course," he spoke aloud.

"Your voice is music. No one likes Baroque quartets perhaps?" a voice responded.

"Not the same! Music uses ears... and heart. Words need translating." Clearing his throat, "I'm good at choosing words on the phone."

Antonio tenderly pressed "music creates moods, combs tresses of spirit."

"Words explain," Gus countered. "They don't create passion."

#

"Hey Gus, wussup?"

"All good!"

Anna skirted away in her swishing, authoritative style, grabbing eyes; everyone knew when she was there, when she wasn't.

That evening, exhausted, Gus ate potato chips for dinner. "I need beer." He chewed lips listening to Baroque Italian lute.

"Down?" Antonio asked.

"Fast train, goin' nowhere. I want music... with someone."

"Anna?"

"Y'think?" with muted surprise. "Nah. She likes everyone. She's supervisor, doin' her job." humming to intense string harmonies, eyes closing.

#

"Hey Gus, wussup?"

"Doin' well!" Slavic eyes met browns with winks.

Grinning, "My boss thinks you're great... wanted you to know that!"

"Yeah!... gotta raise too!" he sighed lifting eyebrows. Gus's locked-on eye contact didn't let go. "Heck, now two beers instead of one!" whispering demurely with a mirror-practiced smile.

She lingered resting tight pink thighs against his desk. "Y'know, I get it! Tonight, Fireside! Whadaya say?" Fluorescence interrupting, Gus gawked at her glowing cheeks as lips widened then pinched, "We gotta work, don't we?" She swished away.

That night for dinner, he spooned salsa—nutritionally better he rationalized—over chips. "The Fireside wasn't far." His laptop dispensed another Season.

"Ready?" Antonio interrupted.

"Wearing purple... black pants."

"Purple?"

"It's slick, eye-catching." Gus dressed, humming.

#

"Hey Gus, wussup?" Anna slithered in. At the Fireside, crowding twenty-somethings elbowed ever-better positions.

"Gotta get two beers, 'member?'" He sighed, assessing ever-so-tall Allen, slinking beside her.

Allen, another supervisor, approached too closely looking straight down at Gus accentuating smallness. "Got room for two in that teeny belly?" Raising eyebrows, he pivoted a left-right snicker toward dawdlers captured by his royal entrance. Audience glasses tinkled.

Trembling at unexpected sarcasm, Gus trip-stepped onto tiptoes—still looking up at Allen. "It takes less to make me feel good." No better retort manifested.

"We all know that!" Allen patronized. The bunched-up call center octet dutifully chuckled then dispersed into twos and fours blending away.

After stroking Gus's arm, Anna merged into another crowd with Allen. Gus nudged the bar despite cacophonies, and interrogated beer for ten minutes. He pronounced last sips with fizzy hisses. No one noticed him leaving.

Antonio asked "...'least she touched you, right?"

"Yea-ah." His one-word reply dragged out amid closed-eye deliberations as two-part violin counterpoints resonated, tamping invisible flannelled arms around his shoulder.

"...let it be."

"I s'pose."

"Ahhh... I feel your fingers."

"Oh, Antonio, only you can console me... ahhh, my friend, Ahn-tone-io..."

#

"Hey Gus, wussup?"

"Hey Anna, doin' good!" Without looking up listening for swishes, he remained focused... took no coffee breaks... went straight home... darkness shaded the room.

"So Anna doesn't like you?" Antonio's whirring voice harmonized inside another Season.

"...don't matter."

Lowering wrists, bow in hand, Gus pressed next advancing to a different Vivaldi. Moods blurred. After pressing stop, his own bowed Vivaldi ballad trailed on.

Resting his bow—and Vivaldi, midsentence—he reclined... eyelids lowered holding grips of silence, he embraced warmly what wasn't there. He slept amid dreams of sound and solace imagining whirlings from Four Seasons.

#

Contemplating an empty chair, "Where's Gus, he sick?" No one answered, Anna swished on.

#

Awakening slumped in his chair, he picked up his precious soul-laden instrument with his left hand and hugged it. Rubbing its wooden face, Antonio didn't immediately respond. Touching little openings affectionately, Gus's fingers burnished strings delicately, devotedly, before grasping the bow to tend strings.

"Anna I'm not," Antonio whirred.

"I know..." Gus whispered as two strings generated Vivaldi consonance followed by serene double sounds. Pupils rolled, arms barely taut, trembling.

"I'm here for you, Gustav."

His bow fell to the floor. Gus fingered strings again and curly wooden openings as acquiescence captured his arms. Tears leaked. He pressed the violin against his slow-thumping chest. Though the room was soundless, he heard purring strings soothing his ears, caressing slowing fingertips... but no melodies.

Whispering, "No, you're not Anna, but... I love you" as invisible Seasons seized his dying heart amid undulating clouds of what-might-have-been's.

Hairy Plays Frisbee

By Lawrence W. Paz

Hairy had a restful sleep. When he awoke he was somewhat perplexed. He wasn't quite sure where he was. Slowly he began to recall that he had left his earthly surroundings and landed on Rainbow Bridge yesterday. He smiled as he remembered meeting his brothers and sisters who had preceded him to Rainbow Park.

Instead of sleeping in the hut with his name carved over the opening, he had fallen asleep exhausted in the lush green grass after his busy day touring the forest and mountain areas of Rainbow Park. The last thing he remembered was listening to Neil Diamond's "Lonely Looking Sky" before sinking into relaxed tranquility.

Suddenly, a voice broke the silence. "Hairy, are you ready to try your skill at playing Frisbee?" He recognized Hunter's commanding voice and remembered that Hunter, a large golden-brown Retriever, had invited him to play on his Frisbee team. Hunter is the head of the family here, Hairy recalled his earlier impression.

Hairy, a black and white Springer Spaniel, wasn't quite sure that Frisbee was going to be his game. "I'm willing to give it a try. Let me shake out some of the cobwebs and grab something to eat."

Okay, be quick about it. We'll meet on the Frisbee court very. I'll check on Bob Barker. I feel sure he'll want to practice with us."

Hairy had briefly met Bob Barker last night, a splendid large black Lab. He looked intimidating but had a gentle nature. He, like Hairy, was on earth for only a few years before coming to Rainbow Park.

After clearing his head and finding some food outside his hut, Hairy headed for the Frisbee area in Friendship Park, his heavenly home. The brilliant flowering bushes were especially pleasing.

On his way he looked around, taking in the beautiful vista. "What a nice touch to be able to see color here," he thought. He watched the geese and ducks glide on the canal enclosed within a winding rock wall that surrounded the park. Watching the palm trees rustling in the slight breeze reminded him of his earthly Florida home. The climate reminded Hairy of a very comfortable spring day there. A little homesickness flowed through his spiritual body as he remembered the times he would get on the golf cart and go to the dog park to play. That was where he fetched a few Frisbees on earth but never threw them back. He always laid them at the feet of his master. Hunter assured him that he and Bob Barker would teach him how to throw the Frisbee with some precision.

As he neared the Frisbee play area he noticed a metal fixture with a solid round base and a 5-foot pole extending upward from the base. About 3 feet up the pole was a variety of colored Frisbees scattered in a chain-link basket.

"Hairy, we're glad you made it," said Hunter. "Bob Barker and I were discussing how excited we are to have you join our team. Let's start with playing Frisbee Golf. That fixture you passed by on your way in is a Frisbee Golf goal. The idea is to stand behind this line, grab the Frisbee in your teeth, and toss your head so the Frisbee goes in the basket. I'll show you." The Frisbee sailed through the air and landed in the basket. "Want to give it a try?"

"I'll give it a shot." Hairy took the Frisbee in his mouth, swung his head, and let the Frisbee fly. It fell a few feet from him and wobbled along the ground.

"Hairy, that's a good start," said Bob Barker. "It might help if you keep your eyes on the basket as you turn your head."

Hairy kept trying to toss the Frisbee with limited success. He was getting a lot of encouragement from Hunter and Bob Barker. But he was getting frustrated. "How come this is so hard for me? You both seem to do it effortlessly."

"Hairy, even in heavenly Rainbow Park, when we attempt something new it comes easily to some. Others may need to put in extra effort to master a new skill. You are doing fine for your first session. Let's break. Hairy can come back later and practice some more."

"That's a good idea," echoed Bob Barker.

Hairy spent many hours during the next week perfecting his technique on his own. He was pleased with the progress he was making and beginning to believe he could become a valuable team member. His confidence grew with each passing day. His Frisbees were consistently floating in or near the basket. He was ready to show his progress to Hunter and Bob Barker.

Hairy spotted them tossing a Frisbee back and forth to each other over what appeared to be a volley ball net. "Hey, fellas I'm ready to show you what I can do. Want to see?"

"You bet," they said in unison. "We're coming right over."

Hairy made ten tosses and eight of them fell in the basket and the other two hit the side of the basket.

"Wow, that is fantastic. We knew you could do it," said Hunter. "Now we have to work with you so you can toss it over the net and try to have it hit the ground before one of us can catch it and toss it back. That's how you score points. Are you ready for that?"

"I sure am. I'm ready to contribute to the team."

After working with Hunter and Bob Barker, three other dogs of similar size took positions on the other side of the net for a real game.

Hairy was excited that he could learn new skills in Rainbow Park and was eager to try something new.

Herding Geese

By Em Arshal

His American passenger said, "There's a clear lane."

He only nodded in reply. The line of crossing geese weren't across the lanes, and the men herding them weren't safe in their cars.

Safe in their cars—as if their cars would be safer.

He glanced in his rearview mirror at his fares. Americans in his cab always made him a little homesick. An American man and a Greek woman made him want to explain things, tell them what he had learned.

Of course, nothing he had learned would be useful to them. After six years on the island of Crete, his eyes hurt from the endless, Mediterranean sun. Certainly, he'd learned not to drink the last third of a cup of Greek coffee. He'd learned to say, "your place or mine," and he'd learned not to say it. He'd learned many things that were more or less useful, including how to politely, slowly sip instead of saying no to a refill of raki. That last was perhaps the most useful. What he hadn't learned was how to squint just right so the sun didn't feel wrong, so the color of the buildings and the skin of the women looked the right shade of white or gray or...

He wasn't sure what color a woman's skin should be, but he was sure his world wasn't the way it was supposed to be.

His Smart Car taxi, his by virtue of an accident that made it so cheap he could trade his Vespa for it, idled in the side lane, the one that wasn't supposed to be used, the emergency lane, or, as the Greeks called it, the extra lane. He kept an eye on his review mirror—partly to watch his fares, but mostly because buses liked the extra lane for running fast, and auto drivers liked ,it, especially taxi drivers like him, for passing trucks and buses. Sometimes it was the most crowded lane on the highway into Heraklion.

"Greek drivers are the best in the world," a boy selling jewelry on the street had told him when he first arrived on Crete.

He'd glanced at the nearby highway and cringed. "They drive like madmen," he'd said.

"Exactly," the boy had said. "If they weren't the best drivers in the world, more of them would die."

"You can't argue with that," he'd said.

Nor would you argue with men who might knife you for showing disrespect but who would stop traffic to help a gray goose and her goslings cross an expressway.

He'd learned that he could help in moments like this one.

He'd hold the extra lane until the little drama had ended. It was his part, and the kind men in the road knew he was doing it. He wondered when he'd started thinking like a Greek, when he'd started thinking of Americans as the pejorative, *Americans*, instead of as people from home.

The mamma goose stopped and pecked at the ground. One of the goose herders, a youngish man who had very little goose herding experience, shooed the mother. She, like any woman would, stood her ground and hissed.

He chuckled.

"I don't see what's so funny," the American said. "I'm supposed to be at the airport in Heraklion. In the states, there are laws. You can't block traffic. You have to run over animals in the road. It's the law."

Surprised by such arrogance even from an American, he glanced in his mirror. The ruddy fare that stared back at him was thin from sixty miles a week on a track or treadmill. The dark eyes were narrowed and sharpened from looking for opportunity in the next shit storm that swept through a gray-cube farm job. Pale lips tightened, narrowed and set in a determined and useless display for the benefit of the sultry Greek woman settled patiently beside him.

She raised an almost-apologetic eyebrow and smiled into the mirror.

"I can't believe this," the man said. "I'm going to miss my plane because of a goose and an illiterate, third-world taxi driver."

For the first time since he'd picked up the pair, he spoke English. "In Crete," he began. He took pleasure in the suddenly wide eyes of the American. "Most people read and speak at least three languages. Personally, I only barely manage three, but I'm from Iowa. Greeks are kind. They let me live here in the first world, the world from which all Western culture evolved. They make allowances for the ignorance of Americans."

An older goose herder, one with more experience, took the younger man's elbow and moved him along ahead of the mother goose.

She gave chase, hissing, stretching wings, and snapping at the younger man's ass.

The older man led the younger man to the shoulder. The mother goose flapped and hissed, teaching her goslings to defend themselves all the way onto the broken, pale gravel and then into blue-green scrub.

The Greek men danced away from the geese. They laughed and smiled.

The older one rewarded his patience and use of his Smart Car as a shield by nodding his way and smiling.

He hit the gas and pulled forward.

The American started to say something, but thought better of it.

After the American was safely away in the airport, he turned and looked over his shoulder at the woman who was left behind. "Where shall I take you?" he asked.

"They paid me to translate," she said. "His medical equipment company."

He nodded.

"Home, then." The way she said it made him wonder whose home she meant. An American would ask. He knew that a moment would come when he would know without asking.

Sunlight set off golden highlights in the down on her smooth, Minoan cheek. He loved the way the sun of Crete gave everything an ancient quality of patient experience.

Hot Wheels

By Marqeis Sparks

Cody lay snuggled deep in his covers, fighting the notion that the day was about to begin and his restful sleep would soon come to an eye-reddening end.

He was about to win the Indy 500 in his favorite go-cart, and nothing was going to ruin this champagne shower. Cody raised his trophy as cameras flashed all around him. Lulu Jones, his crush from his 5th grade class, kissed him on the cheek and the crowd went crazy.

BOOM! Cody's door swung open as Jim burst in, in an apparent panic.

"Cody, get up right now, you're going to be late for school!" yelled his dad. "Get dressed now, sport, the bus will be here in 10 minutes!"

Cody's eyes shot open, stinging and crusted with only the best, good-dream eye boogers. Goodbye, Lulu.

"Get moving, dude, your mother will flip!" Jim said, this time in a more serious tone. He headed out the door and stepped on one of the hundreds of cars in Cody's hot wheels collection.

"Ow! And please get these cars off the floor, my bunions can't take the abuse, Cody," he said as he headed downstairs.

"Yeah," was all that Cody could muster up as he lazily tried to put his leg into his jeans, falling onto the bed.

As Cody sat on the edge of his bed getting dressed, his dog Diego darted into his room and started nibbling at his one socked foot. Diego was an energetic Frenchie, with a ton of personality and an affinity for being Cody's shadow.

"Hey! Get out of here Diego, geez," Cody said, shooing Diego away with his other foot.

"Morning honey, grab a glass of orange juice and have a seat," said Cindy, as he got downstairs.

"Can't mom, the bus is going to be here soon," replied Cody, as he went to retrieve his backpack.

"Today is Saturday, Cody, your dad plays the worst pranks ever and I still have no idea why I married him, he must've spiked my toothpaste," she laughed.

Jim burst into laughter as Cody stood bewildered, his backpack swaying in his hand and his hair a mess.

He shot his dad the evilest glare he could muster.

"Hey, I'm sorry sport, sometimes you're just too easy. Look, I'm working on Ginger today, come outside and give your old man a hand once you finish breakfast, okay," he said, his face still red from the laugh.

Ginger was the sexiest red 1969 Camaro Z28 ever created. Jim had been working on it for a few months, and Cody had rarely been able to even touch a wrench to help.

Cody walked outside to see his dad putting down the hood of the car. He smiled.

"Alright Cody, I think I've fixed the exhaust and she might just be ready to burn some rubber," Jim said, wiping the hood of the car with a towel. "Hop in the front seat, bud."

Cody couldn't believe his ears. He went to the driver's side and got behind the wheel.

"Okay son, go ahead and crank her up," instructed Jim, as he headed behind the car to see if he had finally gotten rid of the nasty black smoke that billowed from the exhaust.

Cody turned the key, and his heart skipped a beat as the low rumble of the ignition vibrated and made his teeth chatter a bit. Best. Saturday. Ever.

"Oh yeaaah!" Jim cheered as the car came alive. "Okay Cody, give her a little gas."

Jim gave the thumbs up.

"Nice, now really give her some foot!" he shouted.

As Cody really went for it, Diego sprinted out of the house and hopped into Cody's lap from the driver's side door, which was still open. It startled Cody, and in the panic, the car was knocked out of park and into reverse, sending it flying backwards into Jim.

Cody felt a thud in the back, and heard his dad yell in pain. His mind raced and he pushed the gas further, rather than the break, rolling over his dad in the chaos.

"CRRRACK!" the haunting sound Cody heard as the car fully rolled over his dad and slammed into the mailbox, coming to a halt.

Jim lay in the driveway motionless, his leg positioned like a cruel game of twister as blood streamed down into the street. Diego hopped out of the car and went over to sniff Jim, his bloody pawprints leaving a circle around the lifeless body.

Cody sat frozen behind the driver's seat, his hands dripping sweat and his heart thumping violently against his chest. His mother's screams sliced through the silence, jolting him back to reality.

"Cody!... Cody!" a frantic Cindy yelled as she ran towards the car. Cody could not respond, he was a prisoner in his own body. He caught a glimpse of himself in the rearview mirror and could not recognize the face staring back at him. The yelling faded away.

"Cody... it's me. Cody," the voice said. Cody stared blankly at his reflection in the window, slowly turning his attention back to his mother, who sat across from him with tears in her eyes.

Cindy seemed to have aged twenty years in just five. She clasped his hands in hers.

Cody, who hadn't said a word since that horrific day, sat staring at his mother. The white walls and orderlies walking back and forth were now the place he called home.

"Cody, mommy loves you and daddy, too, okay, be good," she said, as the doctor came to let her know her visit was over.

He watched his mother disappear out the door, and then turned his attention to a small, wrapped box she had left him. He cautiously opened it, inside was a 1969 Camaro Z28 hot wheel. He grabbed the hot wheel and squeezed it into his hand, so tight that the metal dug into his skin.

"Okay Cody, it's time for your medicine now," said the doctor, as he put his hand on Cody's shoulder. Cody clutched the car tighter.

Hunter

By James Boyle

Like any good hunter, he was patient. He'd been standing in the shadows under the oak since darkness fell, more than three hours ago. Three motionless hours, waiting and watching students pass by, always in groups, all unattainable, all forgotten as soon as he saw her.

The young woman scurried down the sidewalk across the dark and deserted quad, moving from streetlamp to streetlamp the way a rabbit scurries across a clearing between briar patches. She seemed attractive, slim and athletic, with long dark hair. She wore jeans, white athletic shoes, and a dark sweatshirt on this cool spring night. She walked with her gaze lowered to the sidewalk ahead of her, arms crossed over her chest. The odd stumble was the only clue that she may have been drinking.

The hunter found it mildly odd that she was walking alone this late. Most women didn't walk alone after dark. But the area known as Greek Row lay behind her, well known for hosting parties most weekends. Perhaps her friends had hooked up and abandoned her. Now she was returning alone to her dorm across an empty campus.

It seemed perfect. For him.

The hunter watched her approach with coiled anticipation. If she was truly heading toward the dorms, she would pass within mere feet of his position in the shadows of a massive oak. He didn't move as he watched her draw closer; he scarcely breathed. He could have been part of the tree.

The woman had no idea he was there, didn't so much as glance in his direction.

She was less than ten feet from him when she walked past, separated by only an expanse of lush lawn. No one else was nearby. No voices sounded. The campus was silent, deserted.

When she was two steps past him, the hunter struck. He swept across the grass and pounced on her. One powerful arm circled her throat; the other covered her mouth before she could cry out. He dragged her backwards past the oak and deeper into the shadows. She struggled, flailing with her fists, but with no effect. He had her off-balance and totally under control. Her resistance was a waste of energy. They always resisted, though. They always struggled.

They reached the deep shadow at the base of the University Art Museum and he threw her hard against the aged brick wall. She grunted and crumpled to the ground.

"There's no point in fighting," he told her. "You won't win. Accept your fate and enjoy the journey."

The young woman climbed back to her feet, unsteady, stunned by the blow.

The hunter jerked her upright, pinned her shoulders to the wall. "Congratulations. You are about to learn a secret most people never do."

And he showed her his teeth.

"Oh God." Her eyes went wide.

"Yes," he said. "Vampires are real. All the legends are true."

She didn't say a word, just stood there looking at him. They often did this once he revealed himself. Their minds couldn't process the information and shut down like a computer with bad code. This usually ended whatever resistance they may have tried to mount.

There was no point in prolonging things. He pushed her head to one side and bit down on her throat. Her blood pumped warm into his mouth and he drank hungrily.

His mouth and throat caught fire, like he'd drunk gasoline and lit a match. He pushed away from the woman, spitting out whatever was still in his mouth and fell to his knees. His insides clenched and spasmed in pain. And such pain. He'd never felt such pain before, never even close. He wanted to throw up the offending liquid, but feared his internal organs would come apart in the process.

"Didn't like that?"

The hunter became aware of the young woman standing over him. "What...?" But it hurt to talk. It burned like fire.

"Corrosive, huh?" she said and shrugged in the darkness.

He still didn't understand. His mind seemed muddled, enveloped in thick fog.

The young woman tipped his head up by pushing up his chin until he was looking at her. "Guess you're not the only one with secrets, are you?"

The hunter tried to get back on his feet, but she lunged sideways against his chin. His neck broke with a sound like a carrot snapping, and he fell limp to the grass.

The woman looked around her. Their struggle had attracted no attention. There was no one around to give attention, period. The campus was truly deserted.

Satisfied, she pulled a device that looked like a smartphone from a pocket and tapped a series of buttons.

Seconds later, the connection was made. "Something to report?"

The voice spoke in her native language.

"I have made contact with the subspecies." She replied in the same, exotic, language.

"And the subject?"

"Neutralized. The subspecies is stronger than the dominant and faster, but still vulnerable to damage in the head and neck area. I have a specimen ready for transport."

"Very well. Activate beacon and standby for extraction."

"Yes, sir."

She disconnected and tapped another series of buttons to activate the homing beacon. Now she would simply wait until the extraction vehicle arrived. She took a deep breath and leaned back against the cool brick of the wall.

The specimen would provide valuable scientific and strategic information to their leaders. She, as probably the first scout to make contact and secure a specimen, would be rewarded. How much, remained to be seen. She might even earn a promotion before all was said and done.

She gazed up at the myriad stars above and smiled. It had been a wonderful night for hunting.

I Am Nicky Gaskill

By Matthew Harris

My woman Andrea Doria endearingly calls me Pookie.

We grew up together in Morrisville, Pennsylvania and practically considered each other like brother and sister.

Blissful innocence frequently found us trucking (in a makeshift flatbed) together in my Ford Mustang convertible on warm summer nights.

While hand in hand (with our respective fingers intertwined) strolling down the main thoroughfare, we felt the quasi laser beams of penetrating lip-smacking gazes.

Testosterone oozed from figurative bin Laden hormonally charged young bucks.

I could nearly grapple with the hungry stares of well-nigh every horny adolescent as skintight sateen stretched to the maximum threadbare limit outlined the hourglass figure of ma biracial, beautiful babe, inducing dog gone pants and lolling tongues with mouths agape .

Her hips swung back and forth (like a metronome, or a swivel door) in tandem with observant hotshot guys rolling tongues around moist lips.

I felt like the luckiest badass blessed Buster Brown in the world knowing that my gal spurred a collective orgasmic reaction in other healthy heterosexual males.

Me and ma babe sometimes hopped in my 2009 Hyundai Sonata, and drove the automobile to no particular destination, yet invariably went out to some secluded neck of the woods as our sexual appetites arose in sync with the speedometer.

The accelerator pedal oftentimes raced the engine, especially when this untamed, teasing tigress grabbed hold of my crotch, which gonadal gratification nearly found me as a crash test dummy.

Once on the road, impetuousness found nonverbal concurrence to take the paths less traveled, which made all the difference in finding our way back to the back door that housed a chamber of secrets.

Seclusion some distance from madding crowdsource.

Upon pointing a slender well-manicured supple finger (red hot nail polish akin to riling an angry bull to appease spontaneous playfulness.)

Thus once mutual of Omaha trust surrendered of prime place per foreplay (ideally at some yonder-secluded woodland possibly still inhabited by indigenous natives), my big feet gently pressed down on the brake pedal. Tires rolled to a standstill soon after the engine died down.

These big baby blue eyes of mine invariably became infatuated with the female physiognomy feasted on countless times before, but never tired of visually, experiencing an uber lyft sans the near physical perfection of ebony female gastronomic hors d'oeuvres inducing an immediate erection.

She knew how men became manic (than depressed—as if infected with an incurable strain of bipolarity) characterized by the primitive animal, carnal, feral frenzy at how biology and physiology genetically engineered this zaftig (au naturel—no plastic surgeon could ever duplicate) top-notch queen of Sheba doppelganger.

Many rumors circulated (most likely instigated by my significantly sexual sotto voce ululating swarthy goddess), that a direct line of descent could be traced back to Cleopatra.

Nonetheless, the blinding beauty of this statuesque model of feminine anatomical perfection always witnessed a trickle of drool from slack-jawed passersby.

Even when colder weather imposed umpteen layers of clothing to keep from becoming totally comfortably numbskulls traversing wintry wonderland, the native aesthetic, concomitant trademark quintessential imprimatur invited erotic fantasies.

Early in boyhood, this writer found himself immediately blindsided and seething with hormonal secretions the instant metamorphosis transformed a wallflower into a budding, damn stunning ingénue.

Although pals since... well while housed in utero waiting to be birthed from our respective mothers, a tingling sensation awoke at some indeterminate time.

Once present, this sexually hungry gamesome fellow made every attempt to communicate that natural animal desire gripping hard libido loosening the pent up tsunami forces to pop the cherry of this virgin.

While I gingerly stripped down until throbbing cock bobbed up and down (like a buoy in rough seas), she seductively slipped off her satin slinky attire.

Each twitching finger of mine itched to access her supreme qua sutured dark pubic outline pulsating with hormonal invisible licentious messages.

My probe boss diving rod hungered toward verboten fruits sans this private sultry thicket, per this johnny-cum-lately.

Fingertips touched coiled dark springs of pubic hair gently maneuvering over vaginal hill and dale.

Moist slurry lubricated lush self-cleaning oven (as fecund feature referred to by Doctor Memet Oz) beating out by a long shot slam-dunk, both Dunkin Heinz and Betty Crocker to bake a queenly muffin.

As if charged by lightening (use say in) bolt, the pang to plunge phallus headlong into the orgiastic abyss to find ferocious fabled "G" spot ferried phallus hither, and yon until Kingdom Cum found.

Closer to thee coveted penultimate primordial portal purse, my puny penis plied with prolonged plunge into the cove ala chamber of secretes where gurgles the goblet of fiery fluid.

The cramped quarters of bucket seats caused us to list precariously until nonverbal cues found us entering a patch of restricted ground marked with do not trespass nor transgress beyond this point.

Any thought of impropriety went out the back door. Come hell or high water, nobody stopped me from affixing mine seminal signature deep within the padded lip locked warm wet whirled wide miniature (kink key cure fur mi asthma) woolen web.

My dick ken zine maxim maws hay shuns, homage to Postal Service motto with a twist (neither snow nor rain nor heat nor gloom of night stays peppy cockiness from the swift shafted completion of appointed pollination viz zit upon two-lipped rounded rosebuds).

Thus, thru thick or thin, nothing deterred me from thrusting my spear-like shank to sink deep within the glistening glade drilling fervently into the mossy covered perfect portcullis of this jewel of the Nile.

Ah this gold digger located the motherlode stone exactly at the Cape of Good Hope.

Nothing short of scoring a perfect win of sixty-nine and a Herculean homerun at first bat spurred voluntary whim to slip this paw-sized hand along the inner left thigh of erogenous filled gal.

Both of us quickly undressed with birthday suits to whit.

I Am Number Thirty

By Michael Alan Niad

The sudden burst of bright light indicated that a new wave of assault was imminent. Bracing myself I looked to my left and then to my right to check that the others were ready too.

"Here we go boys... INCOMING!"

The first strike rained down all around, debris flying everywhere making it difficult to see, but we held strong in our formation, lined up all in a row like good little soldiers. Some have broken formation a bit, battle fatigued over the years. We have been fighting this battle as long as I can remember. I look around, shocked to find some of the boys missing! I suppose fighting against this seemingly eternal onslaught over enough time, casualties are inevitable.

The fellow in front of me I don't even recognize anymore. I just call him Number 29. Half human, half metal, he's had multiple surgeries to replace his battered and broken bits. Still he fights on, relentless. I'm proud to serve alongside him.

The valiant crusader behind me is a true warrior. He wears special golden armor that the rest of us don't have and it makes him nearly invincible so far as I can tell. I've seen massive amounts of shrapnel slam down on and around him, yet he shrugs it off as if it were less than a mere nuisance. I sometimes wish for battle gear like this, but to be awarded it you must first become among the worst of the wounded. I prefer to stay whole if I can. So far I have been fortunate.

The stark white light illuminates the battlefield again and I prepare once more for whatever barrage the enemy assails us with. This time it's hot like napalm!

The battlefield is scorched, but our formation remains strong as the light fades and what appears to be weaponized magma washes over the ranks and away, swallowed in the dark of night.

I'm not sure how much more of this I can take, but I know I will never give up. None of us will. Eventually there will be a ceasefire. There always is, even if it gives us only a modicum of rest. Sometimes it is just a few hours but we relish those moments.

I gaze at the scorched and damaged ground around me from that last assault and harden my resolve. What more can you do? I am a simple tooth. A molar in fact called Number 30, and it is hot soup and sandwich day.

I Hit Him With a Sledgehammer

By Tiaan Lubbe

The chicken didn't know this was its last day. It just hopped around, or whatever the chicken equivalent of walking is. It did its chicken thing, picking at the worms or whatever in the dirt, kicking and scratching at the ones that got away. It clucked or cooed or chicken-noised when other chickens came around. I thought that this would be easy, quick. That's what she told me when she gave me the hammer.

"We're out of knives," she said, which I thought was weird.

"A sledgehammer?" I asked, confused. It was heavy, too.

"Whatever gets the job done," she said. "Dead is dead. And we need to eat."

The chicken was still clucking when I stepped forward slowly. I think deliberately slow, stalling. The sledgehammer got even heavier. But I raised it.

Then a chorus of clucks or chicken noises came from elsewhere. Not from the chicken I was about to kill. Feathers and clouds of dirt followed.

I thought, "They're on to me!"

Then I saw it, why the chickens were clucking. A dog. Dinner on its mind, too. He ran through the clucking horde and headed straight for my chicken, the poor thing still unaware and picking at pesky worms.

He was going to kill it! His teeth brushed the innocent feathers.

I hit him with the sledgehammer. The dog went down. Silence.

"My God," I thought. "I chose a chicken over a dog."

At least the chicken was still clucking. Still doing its innocent chicken thing.

Then she came out of the house and said, "I found a knife."

In Your Head

By C'helle Griffin

Run a pipe from the exhaust in through the window of the car. Leave it running.

Drive off the overpass where the guardrail is down.

Hang myself from the tree branch in the driveway. Remember to kneel.

Lie down beside the hot water heater and blow out the pilot light. Send the baby to your mother-in-law first.

It's a litany I repeat daily, sometimes adding to it, but never shortening it. It gives me a fleeting sense of power, of hope. It could all end. I could make it all end.

The baby is screaming for the sixth time today Screaming, not crying, and it's only 10:00 am. The pediatrician (all the pediatricians, actually) has said it's colic, but temporary. My friend, an anthropologist, says that infants with colic are more likely to survive during famine; their mothers can't succumb to lassitude and allow them to starve to death as they might with more docile children.

Colicky infants are more likely to get thrown through a plate glass window, though.

That one, jarring thought is the reason I'm sitting in the doctor's office today. He ticks off boxes on a patient survey as the baby wails. He looks surprised when I mention the Edinburgh scale.

"Yeah, I mean, psychiatry isn't my field, but those are risk factors, not guarantees."

No fucking shit That's why my best friend is handling motherhood just fine, while I have intrusive thoughts about throwing my crying baby.

"So tell me about you. You working right now?" he asks.

I just had a baby. I was fired when I was eight months pregnant. There was no other newspaper in the region, so no, I'm not working, and furthermore, suicide and infanticide are definite barriers to future employment.

"How about you just refer me for a psych eval?" I ask.

He frowns. "No need for the big guns just yet. I'm going to write you a prescription, but I'd like to see you making plans for gainful employment and self-care. Even if that means giving up on your dream of being a writer."

I look at him, agog.

It wasn't a dream. It was my job. I lost it. You said you weren't a psychiatrist. Yet apparently you're a career counselor.

His smile oozes condescension. "All the medication in the world isn't going to help if you can't do some things for yourself."

"That's kind of why I want the medication," I reply, wearily.

His pen scratches across the prescription pad as the tears well in my eyes. I hate him. I hate him for wearing down my last defenses. I hate myself for being so weak. I hate my husband for being more concerned about our sex life than the fact that I no longer feel human. I hate motherhood. I hate life.

#

At the pharmacy, I watch the mother ahead of me. She glows with maternal pride, an archetypal mother figure. Her blouse falls stylishly off one shoulder. She tosses her long hair as she sways with her baby.

I'm an obvious failure at motherhood, with my frizzy hair and my sagging maternity clothes and my inconsolable baby. I wish I were invisible.

I'm relieved to finally hand my script to the pharmacist.

"That'll be $75.50," she says.

I cough. "I have drug coverage on my insurance, though."

"There's a $500 deductible for psychiatric drugs on your plan. There's not a generic. I'm sorry."

I hand my debit card over.

"I'm sorry, it was declined. Do you have another form of payment?"

"No." I numbly retrieve my script and my card and slouch out of the pharmacy.

#

My husband isn't worried. "We can get it when I get paid again."

"That's two weeks from now."

"Please, just try to make it through."

I don't think I can. I am afraid of being alone with my own baby. I'm disappointed every day when I wake up, because I'm still alive. I've thought of multiple ways of killing myself." I stare at my hands. "It keeps getting worse. I can't handle the thoughts about harming her."

"These are thoughts that are in your head," he counters. "You have to fight them. You know you'd never hurt her."

"Your epilepsy is in your head," I point out. "Literally in your head."

"That's a physical thing. You can choose whether to act on your emotions. I can't choose to have a seizure or not."

My eyes sting as I walk out of the room. I can't convince him, on my best, most rational day, that the mental is predicated upon the physical.

The baby sleeps through the night, a rare occurrence. I look at her and seethe, despising myself for resenting a helpless baby, my own child. Hating myself for being washed-up, unmaternal, unemployable.

I walk to the bathroom and open the medicine chest. My eyes alight upon the red bottle, sitting like a self-satisfied little despot among his serfs.

I know all the costs associated with this little bottle—how much it costs our bank account each month. How much it costs my husband if he misses a dose. I open it and pour its contents into my hand, cradling the tablets like a handful of jewels.

It's in your head. You can control it.

I can't, though. I know the costs of waiting. I fill my cup with water then choke down the medicine.

Jamming

By Ismael Parra

The music echoed sweetly and vigorously; he had discovered some new level of his craft, and his inner world became his guitar. Up and down, through the keys he seemed to flow; he saw how they connected like some language that until then he was unable to interpret, A through G, it all became apparent. Jazz, blues, folk, it did not matter. It all flowed through his forearms, which screamed with the golden fire of exhaust, it was joy, with the sweat and tears to confirm that he was in fact jamming out.

What fiend would be so cruel as to interrupt his metamorphosis; once a single-celled organism, he was now dividing from 1 to 2 to 4 to 8 all the way into a trillion-celled organism with a lightning-fast left and a coordinated right. No, the symphonic wards protect him from any fiend, demon, or devil. But the gods can be cruel as well, and no wards can help anybody from that.

In his hours-long session, the sweat tricked down his face, lending the hollow-bodied landscape salty rivers. An unseen force, immune to wards or prayers, plucked at the high E string. The force was too powerful; the string popped, and without a replacement set, his jaw fell, the shrill song spoke curses. His despair gave way to fury and the guitar that had once represented the unification of all inner and outer worlds was struck against a wall, sending splinters of wood darting through the air. It lay on the floor shattered, its hollowed body still ringing its despair.

Judgment Day

By Michelle Simkins

The girl waits in the church foyer, staring at the orange-brown-yellow indoor-outdoor carpeting, at her black patent leather shoes with straps and buckles and embossed flowers, at the frills on her dress, pink and frothy. Mother stands behind her talking in a low voice with the Reverend's wife and daughter. Sometimes Mother plays with her hair, smoothing the fine, wispy strands. The girl's stomach feels as ruffled as her skirt, curling and bobbing with excitement and worry.

Today is a Very Important Day at Abundant Life Full Gospel Church. Today's special service will, Lord willing, bring lost souls to Jesus. Today they will perform a play of the Apocalypse before a live sanctuary audience.

On the other side of the foyer doors, the shabby sanctuary—which usually smells of dust, carpet shampoo, and, faintly, of diapers once changed and left too long in the garbage pail—now smells of hot wax from candles flickering on the windowsills. The podium has been removed from the stage, replaced by white poly-fill clouds and clear Christmas lights to represent Heaven. To the right of the stage is a doorway, where red and orange crepe paper streamers blown by a metal fan mimic flames. Usually the door leads to the basement, but today it leads to Hell. Reverend Larry Stiles—a short, round man with a head-full of dark curls, a thick mustache, and a red plaid suit—will play the Devil. In rehearsals he has played his part with glee. She thinks he is funny and scary at the same time.

She is eight years old, so she doesn't get to play an angel like she wants to, but the Reverend says her role is one of the most important. She will play a child crying for her daddy as he is dragged to Hell by demons. This role could be the one to save a mommy's or daddy's soul, so she will play it with all her heart.

When she rehearses her line, the anguish in her voice is all too real, because she has a daddy at home who, Mother assures her, is going to Hell if he doesn't Repent and Accept the Lord as his Personal Savior. He will not come to the special performance because he doesn't want to feel Convicted in his Heart, Mother says. But they won't stop praying for his Soul to be Saved, Mother promises.

She has only one line. "Daddy? Daddy, where are you going?"

She has it memorized (even a baby could memorize a line like that), but she practices anyway, over and over. She asks God to make her one line count. She asks God to make Daddy show up unexpectedly at the last minute so he can see the play, so his heart will be changed and he won't go to Hell.

Daddy's heart needs all the help it can get; he has had a heart attack already, and that is why they drink skim milk and eat fake eggs and spread margarine on their toast instead of butter. Daddy could die any day, so she prays every night for God to save him.

Besides, even if his heart holds out... there is still Judgment Day.

Which is what today is all about. And which is the reason her stomach churns.

There are two plays happening today, one put on by the church, and one put on every Sunday and every holiday and every time there are visitors. The first play, the church play, is a story she believes is true. The second play is a fiction performed with her mother, a fiction in which the mother dotes and adores, and the girl is a perfect daughter. It's a lie, but she masters her role each time because while the performance is on it feels real. Real enough that when people tell her how lucky she is, how spoiled she is, she smiles and says "Yes." Real enough that she almost believes she is Such a Good Girl, like everyone says.

The truth is, she will probably go to Hell with her daddy because she's a bad daughter. She's afraid of Hell, afraid of the flames; but she's more afraid of the humiliation she will feel when she is declared unfit for Heaven and carted off by demons.

"She seemed so good," they will all say. "We thought she would come to Heaven with us. We can't believe she was really bad all along."

Someday everyone will know the badness in her heart. She is trying to purge away the badness before Judgment Day. She knows it is All Her Fault. She knows the belts and switches are Consequences for Her Mistakes. She prays for forgiveness every day, many times a day. She invites Jesus into Her Heart over and over. She asks God to make her love Mother the way she ought.

But every time she is punished, she feels the hate in her heart. She hates her mother, and she is going to Hell.

Piano music reverberates through the sanctuary, signaling the beginning of the play. The church ushers open the foyer doors, and she proceeds up the aisle with the rest of the souls Approaching the Throne for Judgment. Her vision blurs, and time accelerates: one soul, then another, is judged, and then her fake daddy struggles against fake demons and the time has come to deliver her one precious, potentially soul-changing line.

"Daddy? Daddy ,where are you going?"

And she cries a little bit for real, as she ascends the steps to fake Heaven with her mother. But her tears aren't for her fake daddy, or even for her real one.

She cries because she sees the glowing orange flames of Hell, and knows they wait for her.

Karma Speaks Up

By Louise Frager

Crash! Bang! I jerk awake, heart hammering. A commotion outside. Footsteps running away. Someone tried to climb in the screenless, open bedroom window. The rolled-up, dried-out shade above it was knocked down.

I hurry to the living room and awaken Donny. He walks me back to my room, which is separated from Grandma's by a thin wall. I crawl into the squeaky bedstead. Donny tells me to go to sleep. He sits on the edge of the bed until dawn, then goes back to the couch. We don't tell Grandma about the intruder. It would scare her. She's lived alone for years in these backwoods. She secures her door with a butcher knife. The windows are usually shut and locked. I figure the culprit is after me, a young college student on vacation, not an old woman.

I arrived two days ago. Yesterday, Donny arrived unannounced, having followed me from Colorado to Hamilton, Montana. He took a bus like I did. Upon arrival he called Grandma. She thought his tailing me was cute and, to my dismay, invited him to stay. Cousin Bob drove Donny to Grandma's place. Grandma doesn't have a car. I didn't tell her that part of my coming here was to get away from Donny. I'm trying to figure out how to gently break up.

Grandma's place is in disrepair. The grass in her yard is taller than my knees. Donny and I took a sickle and cut a path from Grandma's porch to the gate. Today, he and I walk around the house, finding smashed-down areas outside most of the windows. Someone was watching our every move. We decide to leave the growth because it will be easier to see if someone spies on us again.

Not wanting Grandma to hear, Donny and I walk three miles to Corvallis, a small bump in the road between her place and Hamilton. We use a payphone and call the county sheriff. Sheriff Blake says he can't be bothered, that I should just close my window while visiting. He says the odds of catching the creep are poor, that the peeping Tom would see a car coming and be gone before he arrived. Sheriff Blake figures Grandma is safe. When we return, Grandma comes outside and sees that a stray brown mutt has joined us. She chases it away by repeatedly striking it with a broom. It sneaks back the second Grandma goes inside and I slip it an old pancake.

That night the mutt starts barking and chases after footfalls running away. With my heart pounding, I go to the living room and wake up Donny. Though Grandma forbade us use of her TV, we decide to watch it to get our minds off the predator outside. We sit on the couch, without lights, sound low. I hear Grandma coming and quickly switch the TV off. She thinks we were making out and doesn't believe I turned off the TV to stay out of trouble. She sends Donny to the guest room and relegates me to sharing her bed with her.

Before going to bed, Grandma calls my parents in California. She says Donny and I were on her sofa making out and that I lied about it. She said she heard the two of us on my bed the night before. She says she doesn't trust Donny and is scared to have him in the house. Mom and Dad pack their suitcases and start driving to Grandma's. I wonder if any of the thirteen families that share the party line are still awake and listening. Knowing Grandma's feelings, I didn't even hold Donny's hand when we were walking, let alone kiss him or do anything she would consider inappropriate.

I'm so angry I feel like I'm about to boil over. I tell Donny that Corvallis has a church and we should go find the reverend and have him marry us. He looks taken aback, after all he is the one following me and I've been the one trying to build barriers between us. He agrees and we walk to the church. The door is open, but there is no minister about. We wait a little while, but reality is beginning to take over, and I'm glad there isn't a reverend available. I say we should go back and Donny looks relieved.

When my mom and dad arrive, I ask my father to let me explain. He won't. He says he has the facts. Grandma tells him I would lie to him anyway, that I had lied when she caught me and Donny in the living room in the dark. My mother says she'll believe me if I say white is black or black is white. In my anger, I think that means Mom expects me to lie, but she'll force herself to believe that I'm not. I refuse to say anything.

My dad takes Donny to the bus station. He discovers Donny is broke. He sold an electric toothbrush and something else to buy a ticket to Hamilton. There is no bus stop in Corvallis. Dad pays for his ticket. He doesn't want Donny anywhere near Grandma or our other relations. I'm packed when he gets back and we immediately leave for our home in California.

Summer vacation ended. I'm back in Greeley, going to school. I just learned that Grandma was put in a nursing home four months ago. None of her kids believed her when she said someone had been watching her and had chased her down the road. They thought she had the onset of some kind of dementia. I believe karma has spoken.

I'm not sure what to do. Grandma's predicament seems fitting to me. She is a mean old lady, not nice at all. To speak up or to not speak up, that is the question.

Lime Gold and Four-in-the-Floor

By Hannah Cole

Lime gold, four-in-the-floor, a 1968 Chevy SS 396 that was every young boy's dream. The question is, "Was it every teenage girl's dream?" Well, since I had turned twenty by the time we bought that car, I guess that I was no longer a teenager or a "girl," but it was a sexy car.

My cousin Robin posted on Facebook about learning to drive the SS cars versus the '57 Chevy. I, too had to learn driving in, shall we say, "challenging cars." By the time my parents allowed me to learn to drive— "How old are you?" "Fifteen." "Sorry, not old enough." End of conversation—my mama had traded a '49 Chevy for a yellow and white shark-finned '57 Chevy. This car excited most of the boys I knew, but I hated it with a passion. It had the stick on the column, and NO power steering. I once drove it into my classmate's front yard attempting a sharp right turn, but couldn't get the steering wheel to conform to my wishes. My other option was to drive Daddy's car. He had traded a 1951 Pontiac Chieftain with 250,000 miles on it for a real "family car." Welcome to the '60s. It could have been a Sherman tank, but it had four tires instead of tracks on the bottom. This monster had three seats, the rear one facing backward. Seats two and three would fold down flat, essentially turning it into a pickup truck. It had power steering, but I couldn't see over the hood driving up a hill. My skills improved later to a 90 mph race across Knoxville's Henley Street Bridge. Thank God nobody told Daddy.

By the end of 1966 I was a married "woman," college postponed indefinitely, awaiting the birth of a sweet, beautiful baby girl. Since Hubby drove our vehicle to college, I was wheel-less. That '54 Ford became too tired to back up our down-sloped driveway. After many mornings of pushing her out of the driveway, she finally refused to go anywhere any more. There were no repair funds, since his part-time work just kept us in food and rent. My father-in-law gifted us with a blue and white '53 Chevy, and we held on until May 1968 when Hubby graduated from UT-Knoxville.

With graduation came a real job, some financial solvency, and a move to South Georgia. Of course, we needed a car that could actually make it to the Peach State. We were two shoppers with a baby who had never had their own brand-new car. The finalists were a 1968 Dodge Charger and a 1968 Chevelle SuperSport. Remember the part about having a baby. The Chevy dealers wanted to sell us a car. The sexiness outweighed every bit of common sense in this purchase. She was lime gold—a beautiful mix of green and gold—with vinyl bucket seats, four-in-the-floor, a powerful 396 engine, and only two doors. Remember the baby. Car seats in 1968 were made only for bench seat cars, so we found a harness that could be anchored by the rear seat belt—standing baby riding in the sporty car! But oh what a car. It took practice to master it, even though the clutch was a dream after driving the '57, and she steered easily. Actually, she purred like a just-fed feline. The 396 couldn't be patient behind a Georgia blue-hair even in first gear, requiring constant braking.

She had adventures, like the time she took us to Memphis to see my sister. She raced on, but somewhere near Corinth, Mississippi, baby decided she was done with the car. Baby fidgeted, and she was burning up. Wait, as Tennesseans, we didn't get air conditioning in the car before moving to steamy South Georgia. This mistake convinced us to add a non-factory air conditioner as soon as possible. Soon, every turn of the wheel was accompanied by a plaintive and monotonous wail, "I'm so hot. I want a drink." I climbed back beside her to mollify her by telling her favorite "Little Red Riding Hood" over and over until the Tennessee Highway Patrol stopped us just outside of Memphis. Instead of stopping to get his precious girl a drink, Hubby kept driving, faster. Lucky for us the patrolman was a father, walking up just in time for a renewal of "I'm so hot." He let us off with a warning, and a reprimand to "get that baby a drink."

That car was a dream car, but not for people who soon welcomed a second beautiful baby girl. This one, who started as a tiny preemie, was scarily strong and scarily adventurous. When the car rolled down the hill and across the road, I was petrified that adventurous baby had somehow managed to knock it out of gear. When I found her safe inside the house, it was merely a relief to know that whoever drove last had failed to put the car into gear. When a crawling baby is able to scale to the top of the refrigerator, you never underestimate what a tiny girl can do.

My adoration of the car soon came to an end. When adventurous baby turned one in March of 1971, we had been living in North Carolina for almost a year. Adventurous baby fought the harness with supreme gusto. Unlike sweet baby, she did not talk to us until she was three, so she managed to communicate in other ways. It required way too much energy to battle this willful little being who wanted to sit alone in the front bucket. I agreed this time, and as I began to park the vehicle, she opened the passenger door and dived head first to exit the still-moving vehicle. On this day, my mom radar was quick, and I managed to grab her foot as the door swung open. Needless to say, this would be the end of my infatuation with that car or any car. This event also engendered a new rule—nobody opens my car doors while the motor is still running.

We actually kept the car for another couple of years before we purchased a family car. Ironically, it was a huge used Pontiac that had three cigarette lighters, and I am a militant non-smoker. The two lighters in the rear had to be removed so that Miss Adventurous would not get creative with fire.

And Miss Lime Gold SS 396? We sold her to a young man who loved her almost as much as we did—except that he tore out the rear seat for some reason, and he couldn't control her speed. A month after we sold her, I found her crumpled and forlorn at the gas station. He had ended her life on a sour note. It made me sad, but it also made me realize that my car needed to be functional and not necessarily a thing of beauty.

Loathing Life through Opiates and Beer

By Tyrone Townsend

It was a simple plot: Obtain Percocet from Emmanuel for a drug-induced misadventure. Matthias called Emmanuel to let him know we were on the way. Matthias was my partner in crime and longtime friend. We always managed to survive countless fiascos, and his 4'11" wife, Jessica, allows our friendship to continue. I hoped she would pardon this endeavor as well.

I gazed upon the dingy, grimy apartment building. Freaks, deviants, and junkies roamed throughout searching for their next fix. We kept our heads low, bolted upstairs to Emmanuel's apartment, and waited for him to answer. At least five minutes passed by.

"Didn't you just call this jackass?" I asked Matthias.

"Uh. Yeah," Matthias said.

I hammered on the door. Maybe he was on the toilet.

"Call him again," I said.

Matthias pulled out his phone to redial the number. I heard a faint ring come from inside. I hammered my fist on the window. "You son of a bitch!" I yelled. Matthias just shook his head. I peered closely at the window latch and realized it wasn't secure. I looked over at Matthias; I could see the anticipation ooze off him. He knew our luck had changed in our favor, yet consequences burdened our shoulders. I'm black and he's Mexican. If we got caught, we would be the breaking news story.

I raised the window open, crawled through, and opened the door for Matthias. Emmanuel's desk was a filthy mess of unnecessary papers, pizza crust, and fast food bags. Where was the bottle of Percocet located in all this muck? "Let's go," Matthias said. Before I could retaliate with an argument, I followed him out the door. I should have realized Matthias would see the ignorance in this situation.

"By the way," he said. "I found the bottle."

I stared at him in awe like he was a superhero, but he was my accomplice in breaking and entering.

Our journey had only begun.

We ingested 30 mg of Percocet before we left in the late evening. About 30 minutes after arriving at the bowling alley, the opiates began to take hold. Too many sensations flooding the brain at once. Time was moving too fast and my reaction was too slow. I needed my mind to focus. Matthias was talking with our friends; they had already ingested three of the five beer towers on the table. They noticed me and summoned me over to join in the drinking ritual. We each got a plastic cup of the golden nectar and then made a toast. The beer traveled down my throat into the depths of my bowels. A Percocet high is an unbelievable experience, seducing the body and the mind. It's an intimate affair with a toxic lover, because the two of you satisfy each other. The raw, sensual pleasure generates throughout your body as you enjoy the climax. If you add beer to the mix, you're in for an absurd experience. We set ourselves up for failure. Matthias turned to Jessica and squeezed her tight. He professed his undying love for his wife while she looked bewildered. At that moment, I realized no bowling would be done between Matthias and me. After he released his wife, we stepped out of the bowling alley for a "cigarette break," and we popped another 30 mg before walking back inside.

"Wooooooo!" Matthias shouted. I laughed uncontrollably. Jessica seemed to know there was more behind our behavior.

"Are you two okay?" she asked.

"Are you okay?" I replied. She wasn't buying whatever product I was trying to sell. Another beer tower down and the rest of our friends filled the atmosphere with obnoxious savagery. I was thankful the bowling alley was nearly empty. From an outsider's perspective on our motley crew's area, it was deplorable. Scattered plastic beer cups, five empty beer towers, numerous bowling balls for a group of eight, only one frame played, and two of the eight acting too jovial for their own good. I was too high as a kite to understand the other deviant behavior going on. When did the lights get brighter? When did the music slow down? A tingling jolt surged through all the crevices of my nerves. Matthias and I knew that we needed to continue the high. One more "cigarette break" included another evil eye from Jessica. We knew she was onto our scheme, but we had zero fucks left to give. The last pill pop put us at the 70 mg marker. Success! We strolled back in.

"I feel so happy!" Matthias said. He was right. This was genuine, intense happiness. I had officially reached nirvana. As time passed, the increase in happiness overwhelmed me following a feeling of warmth, but I started to float in and out of consciousness. Somehow, Matthias was stuck in a placid euphoria.

My eyelids began to feel heavy, reality was distorted, and objects seemed farther away. I began to nod. The nod was like a time slip. What I thought was two minutes was actually thirty. Once your eyes close for a split second, everything instantly changes; you forget where you are, what you're doing, and who you are. I blacked out and couldn't remember anything from the last ten minutes. However, during the nod, I drifted off into dreaming. I vividly dreamed I was driving through a futuristic city. The city glowed with strange, neon colors I had never seen, it was rather psychedelic. Jessica's loud rant managed to wake me up; she was fussing about our stupidity. We were back at their house. My vomit filled the downstairs toilet. I hear Matthias, in the upstairs bathroom, puking his brains out.

I began to drift...

"WAKE UP!" Jessica yelled.

I vomited again.

Madness

By Kathryn Mattingly

I live in the shadows of the art academy. Come and go at my leisure. Like a gust of wind I enter the stuffy rooms. Sometimes heads turn when I breeze past sweaty faces in the painfully warm spaces, harboring half-decayed crickets in dusty corners. Day after weary day I watch youthful energy pour onto pages in spiral sketchpads. Charcoal swirls in the air and leaves a gray mist that settles on the desks.

In the dead of night when students have long gone home I contemplate the soft glow of their creative energy, still hovering over each chair. It always stuns me, as I watch, mystified. If I sit in one of the seats a warmth tingles through my being and these fingers, ghastly white as death, itch to hold a pencil or pen one more time. I don't hold the secret to life, but certainly, I can mold it. Just as I might shape clay or carve marble. Since what feels like forever I have labored over this treasured piece of work or that in those silent hours when the forsaken play. Even knowing that every coveted line of perfection will fade with morning light. Vanish completely, leaving once again blank page or naked canvas.

This is when I become riled, like a suitor having caught his cherished lover with another. I begin to pace the high-ceilinged halls of my hallowed institute. Students, still lurking about somewhere, driven to finish a piece or meet a deadline, have been known to flee witlessly at the hollow echo of my feet on the oak stairs. All too often, I must confess, I run dizzily throughout the cathedral-sized structure, intensely distraught over the injustice of it all. No matter really, for by the time dawn arrives, my masterpieces have faded beyond redemption regardless of my outbursts.

This agony has often nearly defeated me, made me groan with eerie wails that rattle the heavy-framed paintings on the thickly plastered walls. It is legend—my frustrations crying out through the classrooms. Many students refuse to reenter the premises for fear they might meet the crazy spirit of the art institute. This is how they refer to me, as a crazy spirit. It is so unfair. For I have not assaulted them in any way, not touched a hair on their young thickly maned heads.

Quite the contrary, I enhance their visual perception. You might say I AM their visual perception. For it is I who breathes life into their naïve thoughts, their nearly completed notions needing a push up and over the creative fence, so to speak. I woo them carefully, watch them mindfully, and choose them discreetly. Only the best of course—the most determined, most obsessed, most like me for complete and utter betrayal of reasonable thinking—will do. Yes, I know reason is our guide, but fancy is what reason feasts upon when scrambling to a higher level.

Carefully choosing my prey, I play with the ends of their hair and widen their youthful pupils. Lustfully they stare at the blank page until attacking it with all the gusto never known before. I am the anointed one who opens their shaded eyes. You might say I gently bridge the gap, even occasionally shove them roughly into territory not yet charted, where they fear to go, yet long to explore. I am the *art* of making *art.* I breathe life into a piece of work. Elevating it from biological sex to seductive lovemaking by causing emotion. True art allows intimacy. It draws you in, and you are taken aback. The students feel a tingle up and down their spine as they raise the spirit of their creation above the restraints of mortality.

I am the angst that drives them. Some call me creative genius. What do I care? Intangible talent, guileless giftedness... no matter the title, for it isn't explainable and isn't in their power to command or control. It just IS. I just AM. And whatever I am, I am fleeting. I come and go. It's a big world to color after all, even with broad strokes. And furthermore, as for pinning me down to mere talent or lofty gift—I say pish-posh! Creative energy? Damn them all! I am nothing more than madness! And what a bane of existence this all would be without me. Can you imagine a world without creativity? Written, sung, played, acted, chiseled, drawn, painted—however envisioned—not created?

Fear me if you wish, when I stomp around the empty rooms in the wee hours of early morning, or scream through the rafters above the silent halls, or play wistfully with locks of your hair like a breeze through the window. But hear this: Without my presence there would be no betwixt and between. There would be no turmoil of creativity fighting to form, no unresolved imagination, nothing to fancy—but facts! So be thankful for creaking walls and howling wind, fairy dust and ominous feelings, without which, canvas will lack for color. Paper will hunger for musical notes and whimsical fiction.

If you want to fear something, fear imagination dying, squished beneath the beast of conformity, rationale, and routine. Dread an ending to the dance—the embrace of shared emotion through absorbing a sonnet, touching a sculpture, inhaling a book, movie or play. Dread that I might ever be stilled, leave the halls, silence the moan, numb the tingle, put down the pen. Hang on to glorious madness and never let it cease. I am what powers the wings of truth through artistic impression.

Like faith—what you can't prove exists, makes all the difference!

Madness

By Natasha Kelly

"I love you." The words came out without my permission. They were meant to be thoughts, not words for him to hear. I wish I would've said, "I love pasta," or "I love Lilo," the cat, but no, the words came out crystal clear, "I love you." There was no deniability when you made a statement like that, put all three of those words together so they sounded like one.

I lay comfortably on the bed, without any sheets or covers to hide my nakedness. His back was to me, he was looking for the shirt that had been flung somewhere right before we had sex. He paused when he heard those words. It was a noticeable pause, an obvious pause. His movements were slow as he straightened up and came over to me. He smiled at me, a tiny smirk as if he was letting me know it was okay. In a soft, sincere tone, he said, "I love you too."

I looked away from him, focused on his newly well-defined abs. I didn't want to look into his eyes, didn't want to look into masked sincerity. I was not going to fall into his trap. No, I was too smart for that and believing him would only dismantle me. I forced my head back up in his direction, avoiding his eyes, and smiled a sweet smile.

He placed his hand on my cheek, leaned in and kissed me, softly, not rushing. I gave in to the sweetness of it and ignored those lingering thoughts in the back of my mind. The ones that told me his kiss felt like I love you. I tossed those harmful thoughts aside and focused on the smoothness and softness of his lips and the sweetness of his tongue as it danced with mine.

Soon his body was next to me on the bed, pressed up against mine, lips and tongues still communicating in the language of lust. My arms wrapped around him, clinging to him, wanting him to rescue me from the hurt and pain that lived inside of me. He shifted his body until he was on top of me. My legs automatically wrapped around his waist and I could feel how much he wanted me. I wanted to erase the past and live only in that moment. His lips and tongue made a path from my earlobe to my neck, down to my nipple, licking, biting, sucking my flesh along the way. His hand squeezing, massaging my breast, sending tingling sensations up and down my body. Soft moans escaped me as he took me away to a better place, back to beautiful views overlooking white sandy beaches, back to happiness.

I felt him teasing me, wanting me to beg him for it. I shuddered, moans growing louder, my body telling him things I refused to speak. I moved my hips, blindly searching for him, needing him more than I needed air. Without warning he filled me up, pushed in and out of me hard, making me call out to the heavens. Feeling him, feeling his passion, I was in love. I struggled to keep my sanity but his movements were sexy and raw, driving me close to the edge. I held on, fought that feeling for a while, basked in the pleasure he was giving me. Every sensation was magnified. Each touch, squeeze, scratch, and bite felt like it was on fire. My body was weak and his determination was strong. I gave in, let him win, my body trembling as madness took over. My conversation with the heavens continued until calmness and clarity returned, but he wouldn't let it last, forced madness to revisit me over and over again. My body trembled and I cursed each time that euphoric feeling took over.

When I finally caught my breath, I looked into his eyes. I could see his pleasure was near. I whispered in his ear, urged him to let go. I could feel madness taking him over and I joined him once again. He yelled, screamed crazy words, professed love over and over again until everything he had was released, until exhaustion settled in and tranquillity came with it.

He lay next to me, holding me as I drifted off to white sand beaches, inhaling crisp fresh air, looking out into deep blue ocean water, sipping on apple martinis. It seemed every time I closed my eyes, I was dreaming of where it all started, those wonderful moments when everything was fresh and new and perfect. I was awakened from my island by the chimes of his cell phone. He got up, silenced it. He said, "It's just work." I knew he was lying. He came back and lay next to me, held me again, as if he would stay here forever, all the while thinking of his exit strategy. Moments later we heard the chiming of his cell phone again. Again he got up and silenced it. He came over to the bed, kissed me, whispered, "I gotta go," a fake expression of sadness on his face. I said, "I know." I watched as he got dressed, the plain black T-shirt now recovered. He looked over at me, kissed me again, slowly, as if nothing else was more important than me.

I watched him leave, knowing tomorrow would be different. Tomorrow would be February 15 and our day of romance would be over. Things would go back to the way they always were, but today we laughed and reminisced. Today brought out the side of him that felt like my husband again, the side of him that made me want to believe that I was the only one.

Mama

By Heather E. Hutsell

Baby twisted her lips into a contemplative frown, a needle poised in one hand and a little wig of long cocoa acrylic tresses in the other. The task of adding silver strands to it, one at a time, was proving tedious.

"It'll be worth it, Mama," she said. "You'll see."

The porcelain doll on the tabletop where Baby worked sat complacent, bald, and unblinking. It had the body of a young, proportionately endowed woman, though something about its feminine face was mildly childlike—a contradictory quality to the wisdom in the bright emerald glass eyes.

Baby threaded another sterling strand through the needle's equally glinting eye.

"It won't be long, though I know it *seems* like it will. But nothing takes long when it's meant to be forever. *Right, Mama?*"

Another dozen hairs were woven and knotted with slow and careful expertise, while Baby occasionally afforded a glance to the doll. She wasn't at all slighted that not a single response followed her question or commentary. In fact, Baby could almost certainly imagine what the doll would say if it were able.

She paused to clip the end of a hair with her filigree brass embroidery scissors while holding the needle between her teeth, and then set them both down. The wig was not yet completed and the doll's chemise of antique lace was simple and without additional adornment. Baby had used scraps to construct the delicate gown from part of an ecru canopy ruffle, and an eggshell corner snippet from a wedding handkerchief made off-the-shoulder flutter sleeves. It was a delicate ensemble, and much more revealing than Baby had intended, but she was quite happy with it thus far.

"You're happy with it too, aren't you Mama?"

The doll's eyes remained wide, staring straight ahead into oblivion. Baby settled the wig on the doll's head, tipped the center part just slightly to the left, and then sat back in her chair. She studied every detail of the doll from where she sat, her recollection of its creation something she'd pondered more than once. After sculpting each piece of the doll with painstaking precision, Baby had baked them, sanded them, and carefully connected them with pins to create working joints. She had pierced the dainty ears just before firing the porcelain, and had since inserted miniscule chandelier earrings bearing freshwater pearls. The face had been painted with no less care, and Baby was rather proud of how realistic and alive the details had made it, even if, at first, she'd found the deep red of the doll's lips to be a touch too dramatic.

Baby smiled and stood.

"You look beautiful, Mama. I'll be right back." As usual, there was no reply.

Baby went to the garage where a kiln sat, already hot. With her molds open beside her, Baby donned a simple white mask to cover her mouth and nose, and carefully poured a mixture of ground feldspar, silica, and kaolin into a bowl. She stirred slowly, pausing when a puff of the powders would cloud up from within the bowl. When it dissipated, she continued.

She left the blend on a bench and removed her mask to return to the craft room.

"I think the delivery is supposed to be here this morning, Mama..."

Baby froze in the doorway, her eyes immediately falling on where the doll now sat—a foot away from where it had been—and with its head slightly cocked. The initial sting of shock passed and Baby sighed, saying nothing. It wasn't the first time, but she was sure she'd never get completely used to it.

Baby picked up the doll's sage velvet headband and placed it back in its hands. She couldn't wait to get the wig done so the headband could crown the doll's head. *Soon.* Her eyes fell on the doll's feet. The stockings it wore were lacy striped thigh highs, one tint pinker than the dress.

"*Shoes,*" Baby said. "I should make your shoes."

She went off to her bedroom to retrieve a wide satin ribbon in dark olive. It would perfectly complement the headband.

"*Mama!* I have something for your slip..."

Baby's words evaporated from her tongue and she again stopped on the threshold. The doll had moved another few feet, and seeing the ornate scissors on the doll's lap made Baby's heart give a hard thump. She was slow to approach the doll and slower to carefully remove the scissors. Baby placed them in her pocket, before retrieving a jeweler's screwdriver. She sat at the table with the doll on its back, and took up its left hand. Baby's heart continued to throb. She began to twist the screw in the doll's wrist.

"I'm sorry, Mama. Just for now..."

Baby removed the graceful hand, taking a glance at the doll's face as she set the appendage into a little glass box.

"Please don't be angry, Mama. Crinkling your brow like that looks painful! I promise I'll put them back on soon..."

The right hand joined the left and Baby stood, glass box in hand, to return the screwdriver to its place.

The doorbell rang and Baby started. She beamed.

"*It's time!*"

She raced to the door and flung it open, startling the man on her porch. She snatched a small parcel out of his hands before he could so much as say *Delivery, miss*, and the door slammed between them.

Baby was tearing open the brown wrapping as she rushed down the hall, then paused to carefully reveal a wooden box. She gave the box a little shake, knowing that the gold token of promise knocked about from within. She ran her thumb over the rolling corner of the peeling label.

Bone Ash, S. Dexter, Sr.

She slid back the lid to reveal the contents. She could now finish blending new porcelain to make a new doll.

"*Mama!*" Baby merrily poked her head into the craft room. "Daddy's here!"

The Triumphant Return of Caleb A. Hughes

By Mike Mavilia

*We've traded whimsy and imagination for a life of
comfort and stagnation.
As the years go by, the heart inside starts to
wilt its leaves and die.*

The driving rain made it difficult to see past the next house. Back streets have the tendency to elicit a feeling of solitary existence on a moonless and starless night like this, in this land foreign to street lights. Soaking wet and cold, he trudged on, head down, save for the occasional up-glance to check the house numbers. All their inhabitants had been long asleep and comfortable in their beds, decidedly not lonely, highlighting the disparity between them and him.

As he ghosted past each well-manicured home, he couldn't help but wonder about their residents. It would be easy to think of them as sparkling portraits of achievers of the American Dream. But, as his recent years of wisdom had elucidated, he knew that this image was but a blurry snapshot from afar. To have: a concept, a desire we so fondly and readily accept. And yet, once in our grasp, what do we "have" in our hands? Is it security? Is it a sense of accomplishment? Likely. But it is no bulletproof vest, making us impervious to the disasters of human emotions. There is no protection from that, and it's what makes life, within or without the Dream, so utterly, magnificently, depressingly "life."

His shoes had long ago been sogged to the point of saturation, making him feel as if he had strapped large sponges to the soles of his feet. Scrubbing the sidewalk so nicely, he looked forward to the end of his long trip. Not out of weariness or the end of discomfort, but for its promise of closure. Like finishing a book and then, with finality, closing the back cover and thus sealing the story shut in its own little world. He was anxious to place this journey firmly in the past and place it on a high bookshelf to, undoubtedly, collect dust in the library of his mind for years to come until the day he bravely and with the utmost conviction took the book down again, brushed off the musty film of debris, and reopened it to let out the old spirits and memories trapped inside, suffocating, for so long.

Hannah had left the porch light on—the proud and singular firefly hovering defiantly amongst the berating of the falling sky morsels. When he got to the doorstep, he paused, as one might expect, to take a moment to collect the swirling thoughts and fragments of his journey and stuff them, rather hurriedly, into his back pocket—out of view—so that it would appear as though he were merely a wet cat, and not a withered and beaten one.

Out of the corner of his eye, he caught a glimpse of the tree in the yard bending and groaning under the weight of the wind and rain, making him feel as if he had just met his own soul incarnated as a great elm. It affected him so much that he abandoned the stair on which he once upon a time spent hours sitting with his good friend, talking and passing time on so many summer afternoons.

He glided over to the tree, all the while staring up at it, like it was some great being of vast beauty and allure. For several minutes he just stood there, looking, as the smell of damp wood permeated his goose-bumped skin. There were no thoughts, no wonderings, no imaginings, none of those mind sparks that had accompanied him on his lone trek toward the present.

He watched the branches and leaves dancing about, not wildly or fiercely, but emphatically, as if his elm was now communicating to him in its own sign language. Perhaps many years ago, when he was still a child with dirty pants and whimsically messy hair, he could have signed back, could have understood. Now, he knew, he was much too old to speak the language of youth that fostered greater wisdom and connection with the entities around him. Growing up has its way of bringing our head and, hence, our point of view, upward and away from the ground with which we used to have such an intimate relationship, snuggling and caressing with hands and knees.

With a heavy sigh, he closed his eyes, still fixed on the tree, and wished for a moment that youthfulness to return to him so he could converse with what he was now convinced was another form of his earthly self—to hear this message that was being transmitted so urgently from the sad and lovely dance of limbs and leaves.

Lingering in this manner for ten seconds or perhaps ten minutes (he couldn't be sure), his trance was broken by a clap of thunder and a flash of lightning. Opening his eyes, not startled, he saw the tree lit up against the backdrop of the cloudy and raindrop-perforated atmosphere. He swallowed hard. The snapshot was now embedded in his mind, like the spots one sees after a camera flash. And with this final image now engraved on the back cover of his book, he reached forward, took hold of a leaf and kissed it tenderly, softly, then peacefully walked back to the house and up the steps.

Neighborly Notes

By Kristin Owens

Greetings Mr. Needs-to-Reprioritize,

Congratulations on making the big decision to redo your deck. That's fantastic! It will raise the value of your home and provide outdoor seating on lovely days. I see you got an early start in April. Always the eager beaver. But now that it's September, it's still not complete. What's wrong? Not enough materials? Run out of nails? Now that football season has started, I see you through the living room window watching games every Sunday. Meanwhile, an assortment of lumber, ladders, and power tools decorate your backyard. In another month, you won't be able to find them because of snow. Just some friendly advice—please finish it already. It may not be perfect, but at least it will be done.

Sincerely,
Tired-of-Watching-Slow-Mo-Progress

Dear Busy-Bunnies,

Howdy neighbors. When you first moved in, you looked like a nice family. Two matching minivans in the driveway and a cute front door *Welcome* sign. At first, I thought you were running a day care, but realized after a few weeks—all those kids are yours! Gee-whiz! Can't you find anything else do on a Saturday night? There's some good TV on. Or maybe that's what got you into trouble in the first place? But seriously, where do you find the energy? You must be too exhausted to do anything else because toys are constantly strewn across the backyard. A trampoline, play fort, sandbox, plastic balls of varying sizes, nerf guns, bicycles and tricycles. It looks like Toys-R-Us threw up. Please stop procreating or at least teach your brood how to pick up after themselves.

Love,
Childfree-and-Loving-It

Dear Mr. Christmas,

Happy Holidays! You must really LOVE Christmas because your holiday lights are still up. Are you getting an early start for this season? (Now, before you get all "War on Christmas" with me, I'm just trying to gently remind you it isn't necessary to celebrate all year long. God will still love you.) Sometimes less is more. Also, those pretty solar lights you have placed two feet from each other? You know the ones that encircle the entire yard and driveway? You must have a hundred of them. Good sale at Costco? Well, they are SUPER bright. Honestly, it looks like an airport landing strip. If we ever get invaded by aliens—I know just who to blame.

Best,
I-Hope-They-Abduct-You-First

Dear Wishful-Thinking,

I applaud your enthusiasm but dreams don't fall from the sky. Let's be honest, your kids will never play professional basketball. How do I know this? Well, they have NEVER played basketball. Ergo, your basketball hoop outside is obsolete, just like their chances for a college scholarship. Playing basketball on a Nintendo or Gameboy doesn't count. Think about it. Would you have a bowling alley in your driveway? No. So, just get rid of it. I promise you, they will never notice. In fact, I never see them at all. Do they live in the basement now? I think one of them delivered my pizza last weekend.

Cheers,
Please-Lower-the-Bar

Dear Richest-Person-on-the-Block,

You really have it all. And yes, *everyone* in the neighborhood knows. We see the Porsche tucked sweetly in the garage under a protective cozy. We watch the maid service arrive weekly making your home sparkly and squeaky clean. We notice the yard crew mowing, trimming and mulching your landscape to perfection. Yes, you got the bucks to hire people. But answer me this: Why do you have 200 pink plastic geraniums? Every spring, we see your housekeeper carefully stick them in the ground to circle your mailbox and shrubs. And (surprisingly) they aren't even the *good* silk kind from Michael's, but the cheap plastic ones from Dollar General! Even my dog can tell they're shit, because he pees on them during his walks. I may clean my own toilet, but honestly, even I know those flowers look like hell. Money doesn't equal taste, but please try to buy yourself some.

Sincerely,
Being-Blue-Collar-Is-Just-Fine-with-Me

Hello Dead-Person,

I saw you a few years ago and we waved friendly-like to each other. I haven't seen you since. Your lawn isn't mowed, the trees are untrimmed and the weeds are overtaking your driveway. Squirrels have set up camp on your patio. Bird shit covers your windows. Once in a while, the Fed Ex man comes to your door, but other than that there's no activity. Just wondering, are you dead? Or have you given up all hope of maintaining your house? Crap. In either case, this is really going to bring down our house value. If you are deceased, can you notify your nearest relative?

Best,
Concerned-about-the-Smell

On We Who Burn

By J. Andrew Killian

I look at her, and feel the weight of her smile on my soul, and wonder how I will tell her I am leaving.

In the end, I am a coward. I tell her nothing as I peck her cheek and turn for the door. Her hand on my arm stops me. The years have painted wrinkles across her features, shallow gullies carved into flesh by the river of time. But there beneath the surface is the girl I fell in love with, similar but not the same. Her lips thinner than at our first kiss but full of the promise of future embraces. Faint crow's feet form at the edges of her eyes like the fragile strands of spider's silk in which the fly is entangled. Those eyes hint at some doubt, some suspicion. She must have noticed something in the way I looked at her, pausing a second longer than usual as I drink in her image for the last time.

Something broke inside her that day at the clinic, some small spark in her eyes extinguished forever with the news that she was barren. A curse she bore in stoic silence, giving voice to those dead dreams only in the dark of night, as we lay side by side in our marital bed, her stifled sobs wracking her slender frame. And I lay next to her in the midnight hours, with no urge to console her, no desire to wrap her in my arms and mouth pleasant promises in her needy ear. Just the two of us, wrapped up in solitude and suffering, miles apart but only a touch away. A touch that no longer matters.

I wink, turn, and scoot out the door. I've found someone else, but not in the way she thinks. Not in the way anyone thinks. Thinking has little to do with feeling, and even less to do with living. I am a coward to my wife, but I have found my greater courage.

The leather interior of my F-150 bakes like an oven. Damn Texas summers. Rivulets of sweat course between my shoulder blades before the air conditioning takes hold. I pull out and turn towards Austin proper. The award hangs from my rearview mirror like an albatross, a circle of gold on a navy loop of ribbon, reflecting the bright sunlight into the corner of my eye. A subtle reminder of my success. They gave me a medal for the child I saved. No one talks about the one I didn't.

He looked out at me with tearful, pleading eyes as I made my choice and carried his sister to safety. She screamed for him, for me to go back, but he never made a sound as I hefted her over my shoulder and sealed his fate. He never asked who I was to play God with their young lives, deciding who would live to see cars and college and children, and who would burn to ash and blow away on the wind. His eyes begged me for his life, but his lips stayed silent, even as I surrendered him to the fire.

I drive past my new station house, not even slowing down. It's a day for new beginnings. Engine 33/Ladder 15 was my baby. Decommissioned is how machines die; humans are reassigned. It doesn't matter.

Last week at the bakery fire in Round Rock, I saw an image of the boy in the flames. Not among them, not surrounded by them, but in them. Part of them, his figure as wispy as the fire, as swirling as the smoke. His short hair was flattened on top, pressed into spiky protrusions on the side of his head, as if awakened from a sound sleep. His eyes stared out at me, wide with wonder as he gazed on this new day. Then his thin face broke into a beaming smile, his nose wrinkling as his eyes slitted nearly shut with joy. The boy laughed, his high melodic tone cutting through the roar of snapping flames and groaning timbers.

Every movement of his incorporeal body screamed, not with the agony of death but with joy. He was the playground child, lost in his own delirium in the world he created out of swings and monkey bars, running back and forth with wild abandon as he cruised the fertile seas of his imagination. His eyes wept now with pleasure as he saw me, filled with the promise of adventure, not judgment. He waved with his perfect, tiny hands. An invitation for the man whose choice had set him on his path beyond family and friends. The boy understood that which I could only imagine. He beckoned and I rose from my crouch to follow, only to find my feet had turned traitor and would not obey the order to plunge into the maelstrom.

He clapped his hands before him, then turned and raced away. There was nowhere for him to go, standing as he was in the sheet of flame spread over an interior wall, but run away he did. His image grew smaller, dwindling away to nothing until he was gone from my sight, though he hadn't actually moved. His laughter faded with his form until only the cacophony of the blaze filled my ears.

I park outside the old warehouse, slip my favorite Bradbury novel in my back pocket, then lift the cans from the pickup bed. Inside the shade drops the temperature from hell to purgatory. I consider this as the cans empty, liquid sloshing against dilapidated walls and my Red Wing boots. Maybe that's where I'm headed. It doesn't matter.

The match pops against my thumb, then arcs into a pool. I sit on a discarded crate, open the book, and read the first line. An old familiar thrill courses through me, like a lover's touch.

Performance

By John Houlihan

Even the three layers of cardboard she had taken from behind the supermarket and placed beneath her could not totally prevent the chill of the pavement creeping up and into her bones. Dusk began to overpower the sky, like ink staining water, bringing with it a bleak blue-greyness that made the shop lights burn even brighter. The neon signs began to glow, coming out like terrestrial stars.

A man came striding along the pavement towards her, heading for the dilapidated station up the road that would transport him away from his humdrum job and to whatever life he dreamt away in the distant suburbs. He saw her there, sitting propped against the bin, and she tried to catch his eye, held out the battered plastic cup and rattled her few coins. But he had already fixed his gaze straight ahead, deliberately unseeing her, and when he had passed, his footsteps echoed, diminishing hollowly along the pavement slabs.

She slumped a little and pulled her layers closer around her, peering into the lights that filled the vast shop window opposite in the December gloaming.

Despite the faded grandeur of its imperial glories, the thrust of its bustling new skyline, and its people's reputation for tolerance and fair play, she found the city a harsh and unforgiving place, far removed from her memories of home.

Her gaze dissolved into the lights and she recalled again the warmth and heat of her homeland, the deep azure skies that stretched from horizon to horizon.

There, a lifetime away, she had been a player of music, a singer of songs, a reciter of poetry, a teacher. She had loved to see the children's faces, eyes upturned, rapt with wonder as she had imparted the joys of rhythm, melody and harmony—the wonderful mystery of music.

That was before the war came, the terror that had riven her homeland, turning brother against brother, sister against mother, father against son. Some had said it was a duty to stay and fight, but she was no fighter. As the shelling came closer, the advancing terror more imminent, she had been offered an opportunity to flee and she had taken it, handing over her bundle of dollar bills, which represented nearly everything she had.

She did not care to remember that terrible journey, the fear, the smell of unwashed bodies in close proximity, the hand in the dark. She did not care to remember those untold miles spent hidden, bumping against the metal floor, cold and hungry, smuggled across the unseen borders outside.

Abruptly the lorry door had been flung open and her fellow travelers had streamed out, scattering in all directions, fleeing into the anonymity of the back streets and the indifferent city night. She alone had stood, looked around, marveling, until the driver had said, "Quickly! Lose yourself woman, you can't stay here, go, or you will be taken!" But she had not moved, even long after his red tail lights retreated into the dark.

She rubbed together the fingerless gloves that she had found, imparting a little warmth, but they left the tops of her fingers exposed and made the tips numb. Now, those hands, which had been capable of drawing the most enchanting music from a variety of instruments, were becoming dirty and coarse and thickened. Her voice, that voice which had held her young charges in such rapture, was also silent, as yet unable to master the intricacies of this foreign tongue.

A young couple came along, arm in arm, laughing and chatting, wrapped up in their warm winter coats. They swayed a little, intoxicated by drink and each other. In that she saw an opportunity.

For a moment her pride rose up in rebellion and the course that presented itself vaguely disgusted her, but she quickly suppressed her qualms. She had learned that the first thing, the easiest thing to sacrifice was her dignity, and once that particular Rubicon had been crossed, it became a little easier every time.

They were close now, almost upon her, She began to rock and wail, moaning piteously, her eyes pleading, holding her arms outstretched, putting all of her self into that little performance, as she used to when drawing out the most exquisite notes and phrases. She was correct, a chance to impress his *inamorata* or the effects of the drink, perhaps both, made him smile benevolently.

"There you go luv, don't spend it all in one place," he said bending and placing something in the cup.

"Oh you shouldn't, Dave. She's probably already scrounging off the social. She'll only use it to have more kids or something."

She didn't understand the words, didn't understand his clumsy attempt at humor, didn't understand the woman's unthinking prejudice, but she saw the note and salaamed and spoke the only words in their language she had.

"Tank yu, tank yu, gud bless yu."

It was enough for another day.

Pay It Forward

By Andrew J Lucas

I'd always wondered how vibrations at certain distinct frequencies could access higher tenuous dimensions.

I wasn't a scientist, just a stevedore, a simple cargo carrier, a loading bay ape, but I wondered how every shipment rose then fell through differing planes of reality.

That each package could tele-locate, from here to there, then from there to here and back, dragged back from the potential infinity of universes.

Instantaneous transportation of small packages through dimensional rifts across the world begat larger and larger endeavors.

Vehicles winked out of our space-time, traversing unknowable realms to reappear back on Earth unchanged, then the Moon, Mars, further.

Our starships skipped across the expanses of space, rising on plumes of fire, before winking into other dimensions before falling lower, slower, on target, on schedule, on time to planet-fall circling other stars.

But I wondered: Was the package sent the same package received? The vehicle sent the same as the vehicle received?

Who was to say our starships were crewed by the same colonists or visitors from the fringe of a parallel universe, like our own in every detail?

How can we know? Can we be sure?

Or are we dependent upon the kindness of strangers?

School District 375

By Tahni J. Nikitins

Three weeks after I started working as a paraeducator in School District 375, a boy with a shaved head came in smelling like a meth lab. The teachers, eyes watering, opened all the windows and doors to air it out. I volunteered to escort the boy to the nurse's office. I wanted to help. That's why I took this job—to help.

The nurse, shared between three equally poor school districts, was not at our school that day. The poor kid sat in the nurse's office while I looked through shelves to find him a change of clothes. He was on the verge of tears himself.

That evening I called Child Protective Services. Nothing happened, not even an investigation. Apparently having your kid living in a meth lab only constitutes neglect, and CPS rarely investigates neglect because they're overloaded with abuse.

I didn't realize it then, but I would soon start keeping a reader board in my head that said DAYS WITHOUT A CPS CALL. Today my reader board says twenty-nine.

A girl with red hair and an abundance of freckles comes in. She, like two out of three kids in the classroom, is wearing badly fitting hand-me-downs.

Her hair is in a ponytail on top of her head. There's a strange new bald spot on her scalp, just above and behind her right ear. She carries a binder overflowing with long-overdue homework and random scraps of paper with no discernible order or purpose.

I cross the room and sit on her desk. "What happened to your hair?"

"My mom tried to shave a heart in it," she says. Her eyes are almost the same reddish tinge as her hair, fringed with naturally thick, long black eyelashes. She leans toward me and motions for me to lean down, and when I do she cups her hands around her mouth to whisper into my ear: "She messed it up because my uncle scared her when he came in—he was shouting and waving a bag around. Then he stuck a needle in her and she fell asleep."

I look at her and I blink. A chill settles on my skin while my bones start burning. "He stuck a needle in her arm?"

"It's okay." She keeps her voice to a whisper and darts her eyes around to see if anyone is listening. "She wanted him to, she let him. She went to sleep and..."

"And?"

"I shouldn't say." She drops her hands and opens her binder, rifling through it as though she had some purpose. I think she's just rustling the papers like leaves to make noise.

"You know if you want to talk to me about anything you can, right?"

"I know," she says, but as she says it her proud little shoulders slump and deflate. She doesn't look at me. "I think I'm just cranky. I didn't sleep much. And I didn't have breakfast."

"Why not?" Leave it open-ended, let her pick a part to answer. Let the kid lead the way and they're more willing to talk.

But instead she shrugs. I shouldn't push. If I do she won't ever tell me. I get a sick feeling in my gut, like I've swallowed too much tequila and am only now discovering that the worm in the bottle was still alive.

"I went to my room," she says when I'm about to change the subject to something safer and more comfortable, and she looks at the binder in her lap. "Or... I mean... it's not our house, it's my mom's boyfriend's house. But Mom was on the couch in the living room, and I just went to the bedroom and... her boyfriend was in there, I didn't know he was home. And I didn't know, but my uncle followed me, and he picked me up and put me on Mom's boyfriend."

All that can be done is to listen.

"He woke up and—I don't know." She shrugs again, her shoulders coming up toward her ears and cinching tight. She doesn't lower them. I can see by how her elbows move that she's wringing her hands under the binder.

"Are you okay?"

Her whisper changes, so it sounds hollow rather than secretive. "I don't feel good today. But I don't have anywhere else to go." She still doesn't look at me. "I don't want to go home."

The nurse is not at school today. She never is when we need her. Not for the kids who come in smelling like a meth lab, not for kids who accidentally drank their father's coffee for breakfast instead of their own and show up drunk to school, and not for the kids who've been raped by their junkie uncle and their mother's junkie boyfriend.

I want to hug her. I want to hug her and ask if she wants to go for a walk, to get out of class and go somewhere else, and then run away with her.

I don't want to be here anymore either. I'm tired of hearing these stories day in and day out. I'm tired of having a reader board in my head, that now says zero, by the way. I hate this place with over half of its residents on EBT and a principal who voted for a Republican who is pushing to cut funding for free school lunches. I hate this place with its meth and its alcoholism and its poverty and its hunger, homelessness, and abuse.

I hate this place.

Twenty-nine days made me almost forget what it's like to have an incident.

It'll make her forget, too.

Within the week I'll be counting on my reader board again, and she'll be fantasizing about moving to Hawaii with her mom when she's supposed to be doing her math.

Everyone will move on, as though nothing happened. CPS will take my call, make their report, file it away, and the file will collect dust while my reader board collects more days.

Nothing else could happen.

Self-Summary

By Sandra Valmana

Beauty. Harmony. Red. Nest. Nature. Body. Dance. Love. Rhythm. Flow. Smiles. Soul. Words. People. Pictures. Dreams. Air. Moon. Magic. Beams. Islander. Waterbearer. Rebel. And. Or.

Shimmers

(A Short Scene)

By Lindsay Partain

THE CHARACTERS

>Amanda...20s, sincere, blind.
>Ryan... 20s, in love.

THE SETTING

>Tonight. In the middle of a forest.

>"Meet me at midnight in the forest of my dreams
>we'll make a fire and count the stars
>that shimmer above the trees"

>*Christy Ann Martine*

>*AMANDA and RYAN, new friends, take a very
>important walk through the forest on the darkest
>night of the year. AMANDA walks hesitantly but
>RYAN gently holds her linked arm and leads them
>both through the trees and the darkness.*

AMANDA

Ry- wait, just, hang on a minute.

RYAN

You okay? Did you trip?

AMANDA

No, I'm fine. I just- it's nothing.

>Is it time yet?

RYAN looks up into the night sky

RYAN

Almost. Are you cold? You're shivering.

AMANDA

Hm? Oh, no. I'm alright.

RYAN

You can have my jacket if you like?

AMANDA

N-no. No thanks. Really, I'm not cold.

You remembered to bring them didn't you?

RYAN

I remembered. I've got them right here.[RYAN touches his pocket.] You're sure you're alright?

AMANDA

I just, I really don't like the dark.

RYAN

But you're...

AMANDA

Don't.

RYAN

But if you're scared...

AMANDA

...I never said I was scared...

RYAN

All I meant to say is that, if you don't like the dark, it... well, it must be awful for you.

AMANDA

Is it time yet?

RYAN

Nearly.

AMANDA

Don't let go of my hand, kay?

RYAN

I won't.

                              AMANDA

I remember this. I can see it in my head perfectly.

                               RYAN

How's that? Watch your step, there's a fallen tree. Here, let me help.

                              AMANDA

I- thank you- I know it by the smell. The pine and the wet rock and the lemon balm. The feel of the moss on my palm. It must have just rained.

                               RYAN

It seems that way.

                              AMANDA

What can you see? Would you tell me?

                               RYAN

Not much I'm afraid. It's very dark. The darkest night of the whole year, I think.

                              AMANDA

Certainly seems that way.

                               RYAN

But you remember this place? It wasn't always like this? You didn't used to be-

                              AMANDA

No. I used to be able to-

                               RYAN

Did you get sick or something?

                              AMANDA

I gave it to someone.

                               RYAN

I don't understand, what do you mean you gave it to someone?

                              AMANDA

I gave it to someone... it was a very special gift.

                              RYAN

But you're afra- you don't like the dark, though?

                            AMANDA

It's not so bad. You kind of get used to it after a while.

                              RYAN

I guess you have to.

                            AMANDA

I don't have to do anything. I chose this.

                              RYAN

So, who did you give it to?

                            AMANDA

Her name is Amalia. Is it very nearly time?

                              RYAN

Soon. Did she ask for it?

                            AMANDA

No. No, how can you ask for something like that? I simply gave it to her.

                              RYAN

I don't understand.

                            AMANDA

Perhaps you weren't meant to. It was her wedding day. She was looking
right into the beginning of her forever, if you believe that something like
that can be a kind of forever, and the way he looked at her, with such- joy.
Swelling in his eyes, choking up in his throat, making his fists tight around
her little hand. It was a very special gift. She deserved to see how beautiful
a thing she had. It was then, during the ceremony. He was looking at her,
both of them holding the other so tight. She was crying and he- he reached
up his hand [AMANDA shows RYAN.] and, with his thumb, gently wiped
away the tears from her eyes. The last thing I saw was the look on his face
when the clouds left her eyes. Afterwards I could hear their beating
hearts, loud as drums.

                              RYAN

But why would you...

                            AMANDA

I forgot to bring a gift.

RYAN

But that doesn't mean that you...

AMANDA

It was mine to give to whoever I wanted. And I wanted to give it to Amalia.

RYAN

It's nearly time.

AMANDA

Have you ever been in a position to give someone something of great importance? Something of great beauty? Something, greater than yourself?

RYAN

We're nearly there.

AMANDA

There are always doubts. You can be staring it right in the face. The most. Perfect moment. Perfect person. Someone who deserves it so completely. And you'll want to keep it for yourself. Keep your gift. You start to wonder, do they really? Could they really? And most of the time, they do and they could, and there will come a moment where you will see your gift again. You always hope you will see it often enough to enjoy it. Pretend that it's yours. So that you know perfectly well that you made the right choice. That you chose the right person. A worthy person.

RYAN

We made it. [RYAN lets go of AMANDA and walks away.] Now just, cover your eyes and stay put. [AMANDA covers her eyes with her hands.]

AMANDA

This must be something special if you're asking the blind girl to cover her eyes. [Nervous.] Ryan?

RYAN

I'll only be a moment.

[RYAN reaches into his pocket and pulls out millions of little stars. He begins to walk around the clearing and throws them into the sky, which begins to light up in shades of pink, purple, and blue.]

AMANDA

Ryan?

RYAN

Amanda?

AMANDA

Can I?

RYAN

You can open. [Slowly AMANDA opens her eyes up to the sky, she can barely breathe.] Can you-? Do you see them?

[AMANDA nods stiffly, not wanting to move her eyes for fear of losing sight. RYAN goes to her, takes both her hands, painting them the colors of the Northern Lights. RYAN lifts her hand into the sky and paints the skies with green and violet. He's watching her face light up with the stars. Hands painted with stars, AMANDA watches the night sky, RYAN watches her. Lights out. End of play.]

Signifying Nothing

By Dan Repperger

May 22, 4118

Cross Vale Entertainment, Inc.
117 Broad Street NW
New Andelin Province
Salazar II, Vengedi Republic

Commissioner Howard Boone,

Your organization disgusts me, and it pains me to write to you. Unfortunately, the Republic feels my husband's story is of such significance that they've demanded I send you a statement for the public inquiry. So here it is.

Nearly two centuries ago, Dr. Collier famously quipped that mankind had cured death. Seven years ago, my husband, the now-infamous Joe Lancaster, not only knocked Reggie Houston unconscious in the second round of a boxing match, but Reggie hit his head on a defect in the corner post that caused his brain to—well, it's something so graphic they won't show the replays. But I was there in the front row. Even with immediate medical attention, it was determined any repairs would effectively create a new person instead of reviving the old one, and thus Reggie was declared dead.

As Joe was being hustled from the arena, someone in the audience said my husband was truly frightening. A reporter either misunderstood him or didn't like the headline, so from that day forward, he was known as Fighting Joe Lancaster. It was a stupid name, but I suppose I liked it better than Frightening Joe Lancaster.

I know the archetypical boxer is supposed to be a tortured soul, raising a broken family, but that's not his story. We were living happily by modest means until Joe killed Mr. Houston. The fight made him famous' Your organization snapped him up and then rushed him off-world to bigger ordeals. The spectacle, the sudden fortune—it was all a bit much for us.

Most of that money never got spent. The glamor was just props to make him the man fans expected him to be, and after each fight we went back to a simple home and our two sons.

His "arrogance" was no less a lie. Promoters made up the vulgar quotes, scripted to get people excited, but he never meant a word of it. "God hasn't made a man I can't beat," wasn't something Joe would say on his own.

Then the war came. Sirini attacked the frontier worlds of the Republic, and we weren't winning a single battle. Thousands of people were dead. Millions were now in the "dark worlds," cut off from their families.

My husband wanted to do something. He paced the house night after night. He wouldn't come to bed. He stopped eating and drinking. He wouldn't answer calls. He missed two fights, sponsors were pulling out, and your league was ready to drop him. He woke me up one night, repeating the phrase your people had given him. "God hasn't made a man I can't beat." I asked him what he was talking about, but he just kept saying that over and over. I called our family doctor, who rushed to the house and sedated him.

When he woke up, he ate a big breakfast. I kept cooking, and he kept eating. I couldn't have been happier. I thought we'd finally turned a corner. But the moment he was full, he called his agent. "Do the Sirini have martial arts? Do they have a sport like boxing?" I thought he was still delirious, but he was almost frighteningly calm about it. He had found the solution he was looking for: He couldn't defeat the Sirini fleets, but he could at least make one bleed—show our people that they could be beaten by a mere man. Or as he told me, "Maybe it isn't men God made me to beat."

It was insane. Surely the Sirini had no such thing. Even if they did, why would they send someone to fight Joe in a boxing match? Then, two nights later, the response came back. The fight was on. I was never told why they accepted. My only guess is that the Sirini wanted to do the same thing Joe did: Use the fight to show us whether a man could beat them. One more defeat to drain our hope.

Fight night came. I was in the front row, and for the first time, I was afraid for him. The Sirini was already in the ring. It was nearly twice my height, like a spider with only four legs and a human torso hung upside down in the middle of them. Hideous, distorted, and muscular. I'd seen them on the news, of course. Even been near one before the war, passing by at some port. But this was the first time that I'd seen one in this way. It was a nightmare come to life.

When my husband walked to the ring, the crowd went crazy. They knew what this fight meant to both species. And when I looked at Joe's face, I saw him smiling like I'd never seen before. For the first time, I think he felt like a hero.

I don't know how long the fight lasted. I just know it was fast. Joe stepped out of his corner, gloves up, and the Sirini hit him with one of those massive legs. It struck him somewhere around the stomach, tore him open, broke his ribs, shattered his sternum, and smashed his skull. I still have nightmares about what I saw hit the mat.

Just like Reggie Houston, he died in the ring. The brain damage was too severe to reconstruct him. They yanked the Sirini from the arena before the riot broke out.

Then the decision came down. Apparently no one told the Sirini you can't kick in a boxing match. Was that an intentional oversight by your organization? I've been told their arms aren't all that strong, so that's how they fight. But that meant Joe would win by virtue of his opponent's disqualification. So he was right. All I have is an empty spot at the dinner table, but maybe God did make Joe to beat something other than men.

Sincerely,

Ellen Lancaster

Revelation

By Clark Zlotchew

By age five, I was curious as to why my older brothers were so interested in the *big girls. Big girls* is what we kindergartners called the female teenagers. We little kids were not interested in girls our own age; they were just annoying. They were always trying to kiss you or show you their underpants, or get you to play house with them. But, looking back now, there was one day when I began—just *began*—to understand, to get some inkling of what it was all about, on a kind of subconscious, instinctual level.

It was a steamy day in summer. The kid's clothes were grimy and splotched with mud, and his arms, legs and face were encrusted with dirt. He was sweaty and you could see trails of almost-clean skin on his forehead and cheeks and neck where the sweat had run down. He showed me a pink rubber ball. "Wanna play catch?"

"Okay."

We started to throw the ball back and forth when these two girls came along. I don't mean little girls, girls our own age. No, these two were *big girls,* about fourteen or fifteen years old. They were eating ice-pops. I think they were Popsicles, the kind that were double and had two wooden sticks as handles instead of one. The kind you could split in two. I remember they were orange. Funny how you remember these details...

It was hot and the ice was starting to melt and trickle slowly down the sticks onto their hands and wrists and drip onto the ground. The girls, all smiley and kind of loving, bent down to get closer to my face and began to talk to me. They asked all kinds of questions, laughed good-naturedly at my answers—even though I didn't think I was being funny—and patted my head. And when they would touch my head, it would send a soothing feeling all the way down my spine.

There was something about them... I had never before noticed the *big girls;* at least I don't remember ever having noticed them. But this time they made me feel really strange. They were so friendly, and they had such pretty faces. It gave me a good feeling to look at them. I couldn't get enough of looking at those faces. And their tanned arms against the light colors of their summer dresses—one was blue, the other yellow—their curvy legs, the outline of their bodies—narrow in some places, full in others—even the texture of their skin, which seemed to gleam... One of the girls, the one with the chestnut hair, kept slipping her foot in and out of her sandal as she spoke to me. Her foot was so graceful, and the instep was tanned but the arch was a lighter color. And the toenails were painted red.

I understand it now, of course, but at the time I was only five years old and didn't have a clue. They were just ordinary, everyday girls from the neighborhood, but there was something magic about them, something unfathomable. They radiated a kind of glow, a force...

There was something in their speech too. The way they spoke to me, the caressing tone of voice, the lilting intonation, even the quality of their voices: like silk or velvet. Listening to the music of their voices as they spoke to me made me drowsy. It was soothing, like when someone strokes your temples. I was enthralled, hypnotized. I couldn't move from the spot, from their magnetic presence.

I felt a sort of pleasurable irritation. I mean I experienced pleasure, there's no denying it, gazing at them and hearing their voices and having them touch me... But all that produced a kind of irritation as well, an itch in my soul that I couldn't scratch. It made me want something to happen. Something, but I didn't have the remotest idea of what that something might be.

And as they spoke to me—it was mostly to me; they seemed to avoid contact with Joey—they were touching my head, my cheek, my arm, and smiling so warmly. And through all this they continued to lick their orange popsicles, and suck on them, moving them back and forth between their pursed lips. At times they noticed the sticky melted ice dripping down their wrists, and they raised the popsicles to a point higher than their mouths, turning them so that the wooden handles were higher than the ends, in order to catch the drippings on their extended tongues, and they applied those pink tongues to their wrists to lick the sticky-sweet orange liquid so it wouldn't run down and drip onto their bright cotton dresses.

One of the girls noticed me gazing at her mouth as she held her Popsicle to her lips, and, thinking it was the Popsicle that held my attention, offered me some. I let her place the end of the tart-sweet ice against my lips and then I bit off a piece, the piece that she had just been licking and that had just been in her mouth. Then the other girl did the same for me. I was elated. It wasn't just that the Popsicle tasted good and felt cool. It was something else, something I didn't understand, something ineffable. I felt a mysterious connection between myself and the girls, between them and myself and something invisible but immense and powerful.

Joey asked if he could have some too, but the girls screwed up their faces and said "*No!*" in unison, in a nasty tone of voice. They said he was too dirty, that his mouth had germs. He stared down at the ground and clenched his fists. And you know, it didn't even bother me. I guess I was too young to sympathize with him. I just felt happy and proud, immensely proud, that they had liked *me.* That they had chosen *me.*

Strange Coincidence

By Belle Schmidt

I wandered slowly down the graveled path away from the newly covered grave, lost in thought. His burial in the town of Ketchiwawa, in the far northern bush country of Ontario, was fitting. It was there he had spent most of his life working underground as a hard rock miner in the Golly-G gold mine.

The first time I entered the living room of his rented home, a wooden plaque, prominently displayed in the kitchen, caught my attention. It read *"Everything I like is illegal, immoral or fattening."*

He pointed to the words and half-jokingly said, "That's my motto."

And, it showed in his puffy face and the road map of broken veins on his bulbous nose. His lifelong pack-a-day habit had painted his thumb, forefinger and middle finger tobacco brown and a cancerous-looking lesion on his lower lip held my fascination as he spoke. His overall pasty pallor confirmed his overindulgence in fatty foods, as did his girth. Two hundred and fifty pounds on a 5'9" frame qualified as obese. It was a lifestyle that guaranteed an early demise, and it came at forty-three.

"I've never seen such a severe case of atherosclerosis in all my years of practicing medicine," the cardiologist told the family.

The small gathering of mourners remembered good times.

"He loved music, dancing, drinking, women and gambling," his brother George said.

"Also, loved a good barroom brawl," his friend Mike added.

Years later, I visited the cemetery again. His statistics were chiseled in black on a block of grey granite:

Wasyl Stefanyk
March 1911 - May 1954

But that is not the end of my story. During recent travels, I found myself in a remote area of Vancouver Island in a village called Rainy Cove. As I trekked through the nearby rainforest, I came across a small wrought iron enclosure with a single headstone marking a grave. I stopped dead in my tracks. The name engraved on the grey granite sent shock waves through my befuddled brain.

Wasyl Stefanyk

The inscription didn't make sense. What a strange coincidence! How could one man be buried in two places? What was the connection between these two geographically diverse areas? Was Wasyl Stefanyk's body exhumed and reburied? By whom? And for what reason? Was this some bizarre clerical error? Or was something more sinister afoot? Did Wasyl Stefanyk have a doppelganger? More questions popped up, but no logical answers surfaced.

When I returned to Ketchiwawa to research the mystery of the duplicate graves, my inquiries were met with silence, shoulder shrugs and obtuse glances. In a day spent flipping through the archives of the local rag, *The Northern News*, I found a two-inch column buried in the "Blasted News" section about a fatality in 1954. It reported miner Wasyl Stefanyk died when he was overcome by toxic fumes in the Golly-G gold mine. Six other miners were affected, but recovered. No obituary appeared.

Sugar of Life

By Sandi Olson

I'm obsessed with touch—even just the touch of the workers' cane knifes as they strike the sugar canes. I miss touch. I know I'm dangerously close to them. One can never tell for sure who from the living can sense us and who are oblivious.

Last week I spooked a boy, only six years old. I'd closed my eyes, immersed in the steady beat of blades on stalks. All the workers were exactly in time. But then that boy. He came up so fast right behind me I didn't have time to move.

Layering into a live body is both exhilarating and exhausting even when I mean it, but this boy surprised me, like I said. He passed right through me and skidded to a halt behind one of the women. Like every mama who's ever been, she halted mid-swipe at the feeling that a child—her child—was too close to the blade. Just as she turned to scold him, he burst into tears.

I silently wept along with him. I can't give back what he left in me. And I don't want to anyways. The boy'll recover. His soul can grow back the pieces ripped away as he passed through my hollow, jagged vessel. I stayed put till he calmed down. Whatever dismissals they feed themselves about a still shadow get blown apart by a moving one.

But now, this week, I'm back. The boy had been running to his mama because his very pregnant older sister had taken a fall back at the house. She was fine. The baby was fine. And now I am staying until I have my fill. I know it's cruel, but I don't care. I want it more than I want to be the type that refrains.

The workers are at their evening meal before the activity of birth takes over the living quarters. The boy excitedly runs from hut to hut to inform everyone that his sister's water broke, though there's some doubt that he knows what that means.

Tasha, the pregnant sister, is about my age. Well, my age when I was killed. Her story seems like mine—except that she is here, giving birth. And I am here—staining the shadows. Waiting.

Tasha mewls like a stepped-on kitten. I move slowly toward the bed. A towel finds its way across her brow to wipe the sweat away. She groans. It's almost time. Even though he's long asleep in the corner, I watch Tasha's little brother. I'm mostly cleaned out of him, but sometimes a live body can recognize remnants of themselves in me.

The old woman at the foot of the bed braces herself. A fresh contraction strikes Tasha and the old woman commands her to push. I'm too far away for that one, but I'm there to layer over her just as the next one starts. Her horrified scream breaks to another moan. I adjust—I'm slightly taller than her—and open my legs. The next contraction hits and I feel her and her baby's life juices in me. She tries to shake me off but I am stronger than her. My desire to push seeps into her. We push. The hand holding the sweat cloth notices that Tasha is straining but not sweating. It will be mentioned later in passing but never resolved.

Tasha clenches inside me. The baby is leaving us. We push again. The baby's head crowns. I soak up this succulent new life. We push again and the baby's head and shoulders are released. It's almost over. Another push and the baby is free. A boy. A healthy boy. One last push. I tear myself away, down under the bed as the heat of the placenta scalds my frigid legs.

I stay under the bed, phantom birth juices slowly fading from my legs. I swallow a sob at the baby's first cry. I wonder if my baby would have been a boy, if he'd been allowed to live.

I savor the sounds of new baby busywork above me through the night and well into the next day, grasping at the last remnants of Tasha's and the baby's souls as they drain from me. I wait for sundown before I depart my hiding place. Tasha, the baby, and Tasha's brother are all asleep in the bed. The boy, sprawled protectively across his sister's still-swollen belly, rustles. His hand grazes the baby and I ache to reach out and touch them all. The boy's eyes flutter open as I pass through the open window toward the cane field. I hear him gasp in horror but I am far away before he finds his mouth and even farther before he can make the terrified words come out.

Texted

By Dee Horne

They sat opposite each other at the restaurant, heads bowed, and texted.

"Dish." Damn autocorrect. "Fish," she punched the letters on her cell again.

"Vegan," her screen flashed.

She went back to her online game of scrabble with her sister. He always wanted the vegan dish. She had weaned herself off red meat, pork, chicken and now only ate fish, but she was damned if she was going to stop that, too. Her doctor told her to cut down on wine, stop eating sweets, and ever since menopause, her libido had died, too. So she was not going to cut out fish. Not yet, anyway.

"Share Greek salad?" she texted.

"N," he texted.

She looked up, surprised, but he was busy scrolling through his messages. Or was he looking at pornography? She used to care, but now just took it as par for the course. She couldn't really blame him. Her libido had crashed. Truth be told, she probably missed sex as much if not more than he.

"VIXEN," she filled in, glad to be able to use the X at last.

"U fox," her sister texted.

She wished she were. She sighed and reached for her glass, then noticed it only held water; rarely did she drink wine anymore. Still the idea appealed to her. She wrapped her fingers around the stem of her water glass and slowly sipped the water, pretending it was wine. It wasn't.

Wasn't there something in the Bible about turning water into wine? She took another sip. No, it was definitely water. Heavily fluoridated at that. She looked around the restaurant. There were mostly middle-aged people, few young people could afford this place, and just about all were engaged in conversation. A few techies, like herself, were texting, but they were definitely in the minority.

What were they talking about? What could possibly be so interesting?

"Quixotic," she typed, pleased that she had landed a triple word score.

"N1," her sister texted back.

Her younger sister had always been a sore loser. She used to try to placate her by turning the board game (back when they still had board games) around to give her sister another chance. No matter how many times she turned it around, though, her sister always lost. It was like rubbing salt in the wound.

"ILY," she texted, but then her phone went black. It had been shutting down a lot.

She looked up from her screen and blew him a kiss. He wasn't usually needy, but for the past six months he'd been edgy. He needed to know she desired him.

Her feet found his and wrapped around them invitingly. He studied his screen.

"RUH," she texted.

He flipped his phone over and glared at her.

Definitely not his usual response. He'd been flipping his phone over a lot. He was probably having an affair. She'd even asked him, but he'd just said, "No."

She'd felt guilty about not meeting his needs but then got angry that she felt guilty. Hell, her own needs weren't being met much these days, either.

When the fish came it was overcooked. The chef had ruined it by slathering it in butter and peppering it with capers. It was the worst piece of fish she had ever eaten. Her one luxury left in life and this chef had to steal even that? She made a mental note not to ever come to this restaurant again.

"G1?" she texted, watching him devour his food.

"K."

What more was there to say? She wanted to reach over and try some of his meal, but lately he didn't find sharing fun.

That New Unfelt Thing

By J.B. Pravda

===
Memorandum

TO: Chief of Police
Re: John Doe #16/Suicide & Related Homicides Involving Clown
Shoes, Costume, Mask
From: Det. August Kingsley

"After months of litigation, I've finally gotten it, the reason for my
resignation. I figure that after ten years on the police beat it's time to
capture some new as yet unfelt sensation, maybe this damn novel can help
me find it." That was his suicide note, these few pages of historical fiction
and a research file on 'The Clown Shoe Murders.' Swanson, G., deceased,
quoted somebody, I think it was Doctorow, about historical fiction: 'Is
there any other kind?'

A. Kingsley

Attachment: Unfinished Manuscript of Police Reporter/John Doe #16
Cases

MANUSCRIPT

His lithe pianist hands must have literally aggressed the keyboard,
muscle memoried through the red ribbon in ALL CAPS the name of a
father whose 'love' had deformed him.
'Rap-a-tap-a', enough to unnerve the proudest quality control
veterans back at the typewriter factory, made in Taiwan with the doubly
famous name 'Remington.'
The noise must've registered in his sensitive ears like the report
of the shotgun he'd used with that same name. Tintinnabulation—his
addled brain's outcome from hitting his head against his foster home's
walls—the doctors named it, imparting the sound poets call
onomotopoeia, as if that somehow made his sanguinary clamorings less
felonious, though his 16th birthday party guests lay indifferently dead.
I wonder if he'd planned on pounding out the last part of an
especially bloody paragraph involving their dismemberment, catalytic
agents of that hungered-for 'something new' so perversely bequeathed by
a father's suicidal quest.

Steve Jobs had urged him to 'stay hungry, stay foolish'; the typewriting so confessional it might serve as evidence in his murder trial... especially if he'd foolishly stayed alive.

I'd come to divine yet another kind of sign—a sine, a desperate sound wave pattern made by those keys. Just a string of W's and Y's, oscillating waves of heaving angst monitoring his mad science—of an obverse life-denying Dr. Frankenstein's cry: "It's deprived, it's deprived!"

And there were other signs, the subtler sort for the eyes and the feet.

His hiked Joker-like now frozen eyebrows like the peaks of the sinusoid doubled U's oscillating from those keys' chorus of snaps, denoting other shocks that had become reflexes, unwitting signs of trauma since an early age. Once, while being unjustly punished for seeming to have been sloppy in dispatching his chores, a stinging slap across his as-yet-unblemished face exactly coincided with a moderate earthquake, toe-to-head Richtering in Joey's subterranean places delved by headshrinkers. Joey had always told himself that he'd felt something shrinking inside him, especially since that day's two branding's searing faults, their lines crossed, and crushed.

Joey's gut, used to uninvited blows from those rifle butts for eyes, spoke neuron-to-neuron with his brain's file marked 'air & mineral rights' belonging to the high ground he'd wished he'd stood.

His aunt, guilt-ridden, furious with her sister, unearthed the triggering primordial geology of the lad's tectonic slide—that same paterfamilias had arranged a surprise for the lad's 6th birthday.

A third-rate clown had been a no-show and his employer grew impatient for that rarity in adult experience: a new unfelt feeling.

Half out of envy for that child-like sensation, Daddy emerged from the attic wearing an antique operatic costumer from an old condemned house's auction.

As he slipped on the costume a reflexive smirk percolated as he realized what death felt like: 'one size fits all.'

The mask Joey had inherited felt supple, as if never worn, faintly redolent of his father's cologne, who'd related in the note to his son that it was the same feeling he'd hoped to satisfy in his young son, and his guests: that new, unfelt experience.

He'd then placed his double-barreled Remington between still-smirking lips, and French-kissed that entirely new never felt experience.

===
Addendum to Memorandum

I hereby resign from detective work. After twenty years of pursuing homicides and related incidents, I suppose I'm simply burnt out, as they say. I know one thing—I want to find what other experiences hold, new and never felt.

(Former) Det. A. Kingsley

----

*Note to file by Evidence Officer on Duty

Last known custodian of related evidence consisting of shoes, costume and mask now missing from evidence hold: Det. A. Kingsley

The Annual Luncheon

By Dean K. Miller

"Jesus H. Christ!"

"Greetings, Brother. Hot enough here for you?" Jesus said, dabbing his forehead with the sleeve of his simple robe.

"Fallen as I might be, I try to be reasonable. We are family, after all. Besides, this isn't the first time we've met in the desert." Satan tossed his head back, laughing.

"Yes, that's true. No worries, we won't run out of water, or wine, if you so desire." Jesus waved his hand over the table. A glass pitcher filled with ice water appeared, bracketed by two golden chalices, one marked with a "J," the other with an "L." "Father sends his best, that being that you give up on the sin-business, repent, and come back home."

"What, and ignore the current glut in the soul market? Have you been paying any attention to the electoral shenanigans in the United States? I couldn't have planned it any better myself. All them so-called Christians of yours are flipping the coin pretty fast." Lucifer poured water into his chalice. "If you don't mind, I'd like a nice red blend."

Jesus accommodated the request with a simple "sign-of-the-cross" motion of his hand over the goblet.

"I don't get it, you wouldn't even learn the simplest miracle-making, yet never hesitated to create wholesale disasters," Jesus said, filling his cup with water and taking a long draw. A light wind tousled his long hair. Across the table, Lucifer shivered from the same breeze.

"Simple things, simple minds," his brother replied. "Besides, Dad did enough destroying. I only watched and learned. Anyway, let's get down to business. As you know, I'm still against this 'repent and get in heaven' gig that Dad's been running. I mean come on, a lifetime of sin and then at the very end, all is forgiven? All these centuries and I've never understood that. But, given what's going on in the world, I think the slow times for me are over for decades to come."

"Our Father will never change that policy. Forgiveness is acceptance. Dad can't see it any other way. Ever since you 'rock-paper-scissor'-ed me out of denying humans free will, he had to find a way to let the redeemers in. He knew you'd never be able to manage the continuous influx of sinners into Hell, so he created the last-minute, get-out-of-jail-free redemption card. Besides, it gives the angels something to do. They can pick out the pretenders easily. Sort of like watching reruns of *To Tell the Truth*. A few simple questions expose the fraudulent ones." Jesus took a drink of water and continued. "And yes, Father is a bit worried about America. Look me in the eye and tell me you had nothing to do with it, the U.S. presidential candidates, I mean."

"Brother, on the word of our Father, I swear I'm clean. There were a few honest politicians interested in the Oval Office that had me worried, but they were railroaded out pretty fast. I couldn't be happier with the final two candidates. I thank the southern states for some of this. I mean, sure, I lost a golden fiddle down in Georgia, but overall, those folks keep sinning away. Their groundswell of support for both sides of the ticket made me proud. I can't lose either way, which is usually how it ends up. But this time, it's extra-special."

Jesus sighed. "Yes, it's plain to see the whole country is off its rocker, save a few brave pockets of genuine, god-loving people."

"Sometimes the scales of justice swing my way," Satan responded, then gulped down the wine from his chalice. "I know there's a 'but' coming. There always is. So let's have it."

Jesus leaned forward, elbows on the table.

"Okay, this is straight from the Father: Promise to stay out of the U.S. election. No influence in any way. Let the whole damn thing run its ill-fated course."

"And if I don't?" Lucifer asked.

"Look, Dad wants to turn that country around. God bless America and all that. I'm not sure it can happen, but he wants to give it the old Moses try."

"My, oh, my, has my brother started to lose his faith? In *our* own Father?" Lucifer snickered while motioning for a refill of his chalice. Jesus accommodated with a simple nod of his head. Jesus continued.

"Dad says if you get involved in any way, and trust me—he's watching closely—then the only thing you'll be watching on your porn-laden cable channel will be episodes of *Barney the Dinosaur*. And all your sinners will sing along every time a new episode begins and ends. Push him farther and it's reruns of *I Love Lucy*."

"Good God, Father really thinks he can turn them around, doesn't he? What do I get if he intercedes?"

"He'll reconsider your desire to blow the Yellowstone cauldron again. But you know he'll never cave. For Christ's sake, ironically enough, he let me die on the cross to keep a promise."

"You're right, but I would love to see that blow a second time," Lucifer said. "Very well, give Dad my word that I accept the terms of his offer. Anything else, brother?"

"Nope, that's it for this year. I look forward to seeing you again in 2017, especially since I get to choose the meeting place. I haven't decided just yet, the South Pole or the Vatican, but you'll find out soon enough." Jesus stood and extended his hand. Lucifer rose and grasped it.

"I look forward to our meeting as well. Give Dad a hug for me, and if you get a chance, check around to see if any of the angels aren't up to stuff. With the expected influx of new sinners, I could use a few high-level helpers around the place."

Jesus released the grip on his brother's hand.

"Over my dead body," he replied.

Both men laughed and vanished from the desert.

The Bell

By Tyler Denning

The Bell was made.

Born of steel and salt and sweat, it was forged in fire. It was made with one purpose: to announce the news of the church.

It was carried on the back of a cart, drawn by horses to the place where it would serve its duty. This small hamlet in the middle of the Rhineland had one church. It was the centerpiece of the village and it was getting a new bell. Young men surrounded the cart and with great effort carried the Bell into the church. There, it was attached to ropes and pulleys and hoisted into the air. The Bell felt the full weight of itself being raised high. Each pull was preceded by a call from the older gentleman. The Bell would come to learn that he was called the Priest. The Priest pointed and smiled as the Bell rose higher and higher. The Bell's swinging tongue swayed with each pull, occasionally striking the Bell, a tone slightly escaping the mouth.

The Bell was placed into a final pulley system and the young men descended from the top of the tower. The Priest walked to a single rope still attached and pulled hard. The top of the Bell tipped to one side and was allowed to swing back, hitting the tongue hard. The joyous cacophony sang across the village and cheers arose from those within the church and those without.

Soon, the sun came to sit upon the horizon, and rose again on the opposite side. When the sun rose to the highest point in the sky, someone would come and tug on the rope, and the Bell would ring. This occurred on many days. On some days, the people would gather at the church and the Bell would sing, and the people would hear the Priest speak of love and compassion.

The air grew cold, and the trees changed colors. Then they lost their leaves, and a light snow would cover the land. People would huddle in their houses, but this did not stop the Bell from bringing joy and hope to the land. It would sing every day, and ring for when a new person was born into the village. It would mournfully ping a sad note when they left this world for another. The Bell was especially sad to see the Priest leave, but a new one replaced him not too long after. The newer Priest was younger, and just as happy to speak to the village, even though he was a stranger. The Bell dinged for him just as happily as it did for the older Priest.

The snow lifted and the days grew longer. The trees would regain their green and life would flourish. As soon as it came, it would leave again as the land grew cold. This occurred countless times. Many priests came and left the church and it was the way of life.

Men came into the village one day, riding a strange device. They said that all young men able to hold a rifle must come to defend the Rhineland. Many of the village's sons and husbands left that day, and the Bell was sad to see them go, but happy to see them do their part. The seasons grew colder and warmer again, and the men did not return. Those same strangers came in and demanded that more of the village leave to fight. Again, more sons and husbands left, but this time some resisted and fought against their captors. The Bell could only sing sadly as they left, never to return.

Finally, the strangers came and pointed at the Bell. They said that it had metal, metal that could be used in the fight. The current Priest, defeated and crushed, agreed. The Bell was lowered by the strangers, their ministrations rougher then the men who put it up. It fought, and rang and clanged to no avail.

The Bell was placed onto the strange motorized vehicle and taken to a foundry. There, in the same fires that once gave it birth, it was melted. Agony raged through the Bell, heat scorching its once-proud surface.

The Bell was poured into a cast. The cast split the Bell up into multiple Shells. The Shells were then loaded with powder and explosive. The Shells knew only pain and misery and they knew only their purpose, to share that pain and misery with the world. Gone were the days of singing joyously, replaced only with a stinging feeling.

The Shells were loaded onto a train carriage. The Shells travelled to the West. Day and night, the Shells knew their time was coming to an end.

The Shells were unloaded off the carriage and reloaded into cannons. The cannons rang with calamitous intent, ceasing only to be loaded for the next volley. Each of the Shells was loaded into a cannon, separated for the first time in their existence.

The cannons thundered, and the Shells were propelled into the air. The Shells were high, higher than they had ever been before. They reached high into the sky, and for the first time in a long time, the Shells remembered. They remembered who they once were, a Bell, singing and ringing and dinging for the happy people of the village.

Gravity seized the Shells and they fell. Speeding toward the ground at an alarming pace. Going ever faster, a whistling sound trailing their descent. Faster and faster they fell. The Shells could see lines in the Earth. They saw people. The people looked back, and they feared.

The Shells struck, and spread their gloom and hurt across the land.

The Shells were no more.

The Big Cheat

By David E. Sharp

Honesty is not my policy.

I sit at my desk grinding my initials into its surface with a shiv I fashioned from a paperclip. Mrs. Maple, standing at the front of the class, drones in a voice like a harpy's song. Scrawled in chalky letters behind her are the words: Final Exam. On the far end of that test stand the sweet liberty of June, July and August.

Suddenly, I feel her gaze penetrating six layers of seated fifth graders and piercing my gut. "I do hope you're paying attention, Michael Flatbush. Any students caught cheating on the final exam will instantly fail the fifth grade. And won't you be happy to see me again after summer?" A wicked lipstick grin splits her face. The Maple. Like a shark in a floral print dress.

Walking home, Peanut hops around me like a caffeinated terrier. "Watcha gonna do, Mikey? The Maple's gonna fail you if she catches you cheating again."

"Whaddaya think I'm gonna do?" I kick a rock off the sidewalk into the street.

"I don't know," says Thud. "Maybe you should play it safe this time. The Maple's been gunning for you from Day One."

"And let her win?" I stop walking, grab Thud's shoulder and turn him to face me. "I ain't passed a test legitimately in five years of lower education plus half of kindergarten. I'm the best cheat this side of 2nd Ave., and I'll be *grounded* before I'll let The Maple make an honest scholar out of me!"

Thud removes my hand with two fingers like a bad fish. "Just sayin', Mikey. Next year's a new school. A new start. Middle school. That's a lot to risk just on principle."

"Just on *principle*?" I look away and bite my lip to keep my temper. I turn back to him and say with parceled patience. "*Principle* is everything, Big T. *Principle* is what separates us from wild animals. If you ain't got *principle*, whaddaya got?"

"But you're one of the smartest guys I know, Mikey," says Peanut. "You don't gotta cheat."

"What? You too, Peanut?" I give him a little shove on the shoulder. "What's *gotta* got to do with anything. I don't do anything 'cause I *gotta*. I do it to be the best. The best cheater there ever was. I want to go down with the greats. Capone. Nelson. Gargamel."

"Gargamel?" says Thud.

I shrug. "So I like old cartoons. The point is, he's a cheater. And when things got difficult, did he stop cheating? No. When the Smurfs held all the cards, did Gargamel go straight? No. When all the world seemed to be saying *Hey Gargamel. Give up. Get a day job in an office somewhere and stop chasing Smurfs*, did he give in?" I switch my gaze back and forth between them. "Well?"

"No," they say in imperfect unison.

Having properly shamed them I continue walking.

They fall in step behind me. "But what if you get caught?" says Peanut.

"I won't get caught."

"How can you be sure?" says Thud. "The Maple's got a sharp eye on you."

"I got a plan."

"What plan?"

"I say I got a plan, you don't believe me? Why I gotta explain it to you?"

"Are you gonna write down all the answers?" asks Peanut, jumping in front of me with unbridled enthusiasm.

I rub my temple and sigh. "Write down the answers, Peanut? Why don't I just stand on my desk with a bullhorn and tell the whole world I'm cheating? The Maple would frisk a cheat-sheet off me before the starting gun."

"What if you write it somewhere she wouldn't notice?" says Peanut, "Like the inside of a banana? You just tell her you brought a little snack. When the test starts, you're feelin' hungry. You peel the banana and, what's this? The answers? Where'd they come from? Then you eat the evidence!"

Thud and I just watch him until his mouth stops moving.

"What?" says Peanut, "It'd totally work!"

"No cheat-sheets," I say, "And definitely no bananas."

"Switch papers with someone?" asks Thud, "Maybe with Jenna Ludmeyer. She's smart. Always gets smiley face stickers from The Maple."

I fail to suppress a groan. "Are we savages, Big T? What do you think happens to Jenna Ludmeyer if I pin a failing test on her?"

Thud suddenly becomes very interested in his shoes. "Uh. She fails."

"That's right, Big T. She fails. And then she doesn't get to go to the university of her choice. That kind of cheating is just irresponsible. I can't abide irresponsibility."

"Besides," says Peanut, perpetually bouncing as though his bladder is full, "Mikey's sweet on Jenna Ludmeyer."

"Shut up, Peanut."

"Mikey and Jenna sitting in a tree. K-I-S-S-I-N-mphphph."

I wipe mulchy residue from my hand onto my jeans while Peanut spits and sputters. "No cheat-sheets. No swaps."

"Then how are you gonna get by The Maple?" asks Thud.

I stop again. I remove my backpack from my shoulder and unzip it. Peanut and Thud lean in with vulture expressions, peering inside.

"I don't get it, Mikey," says Thud, "All I see is schoolbooks."

"Schoolbooks, Big T. And some extras I picked up at the library. That's my ticket to the big cheat."

"How?" asks Peanut.

I smile. "All the answers on those tests are right here. Right here in these books. Most cheaters get caught 'cause they're lazy. They see cheating as a way of getting out of work. Not me. I'm gonna memorize all the answers ahead of time. When the test comes, I'll have 'em all right here." I tap my skull twice. "The Maple won't know what hit her."

"Mikey." Thud gives me a tilted face, "You know what that is, don't you?"

"What, Thud? What is it?."

Thud wipes some wetness from his eye. "Genius. Pure genius! Mikey, you may be the greatest cheater in the whole damn world."

"Time will tell, Big T. Time will tell."

The Ending

By Brandon Pyle

"I never peek at the end," she said. "I don't even flip through the pages I haven't read. I'm terrified I'll catch just one word and it will ruin everything."

"I'll do you one better," I answered. "I try not to read the chapter titles in the table of contents. They give too much away sometimes."

"Oooh, I never thought of that!"

"Do you think there really are people who peek at the end? People say they do, but maybe it's just one of those, 'Look how quirky I am' sort of things."

"Like playing the ukulele?"

"Right," I laughed, "or eating the pizza crust-first."

We walked to nowhere. A few blocks down, there was a street fair with stalls for crafts and food. We shared a bag of kettle corn and browsed things we had no intention of buying, like purses made out of candy wrappers. I normally avoided fairs like these, but today it was pleasant; I enjoyed watching her enjoy it.

We walked until evening and then went back to my apartment and ordered Thai. A DVD had arrived in the mail so we put it in.

"He looks guilty," I said halfway through the movie, "and he wasn't even in the room when everything went down."

"Shh... don't ruin the ending."

The movie ended (I had been right, the best friend had done it) and we talked about our lives and all of the Very Serious Things that occur to people at midnight. We kissed almost chastely when she left. It had been a perfect day.

I'm relieved now that we cannot peek at the end, because at that moment I would have. I was curious about what was to come, and if I had peeked at the end it would have ruined my perfect day.

The Fabulous And Multi-Talented Flaming Tommy Splinter

By Russell Dickens

The alarm radio went off fifteen minutes early, just as it did every morning. This time it blared the Sultans of Swing, which was acceptable, so Tommy Splinter sat up instead of hitting snooze three more times and listened to the guitar solo with crusty eyes, blinking them to pool the waves of sleep into his tear ducts, so that he could wipe them out. This was the only pop song that Tommy Splinter liked, so he allowed the drivel of commerciality to ooze from his alarm clock-radio's speakers. Tommy Splinter had a name to uphold, and pop songs did nothing for the turmoil within him, nor could he relate; his music tastes went another direction, further than anything related to soda pop.

Tommy Splinter looked at himself in his mirror, saw the reflection of his skeleton, wiped his eyes, then turned again, noticing the sockets in his skull were bloodshot, and thought, "Yeah. I'll comb my hair later."

The Splinter picked up a bottle of light peach airbrush paint, and began to shake it. Self-named to the public, nobody knew Tommy Splinter's real last name, but it wasn't Splinter. Friends speculated all kinds of possible names, like Kowalski, Smith, Poindexter, Jones, Rumpelstiltskin, Anderson, and the list went on. If anyone got his real last name correct, the Splinter never flinched, and he went to great effort to keep it hidden on the campus. The Splinter knew that a year from now he would be the manager of a Chevrolet dealership, one of the many his father owned, or was it a Chrysler dealership?

Heh.

Tommy Splinter would worry about that when it happened, for now he lived. As the days of his senior year dwindled, when his senior year ended, Tommy Splinter knew that the Splinter would die as he left school and entered the job force; this saddened him, dampening his mood, in these, the best days of his life.

Tommy Splinter looked in the mirror, noticing his flesh was beginning to fill in, but he was only up to muscle fibers and tendons, he still had a ways to go. The Splinter unscrewed the lid to the light peach airbrush paint that he had been shaking, attaching the jar to an airbrush and setting it aside.

"Coffee and a bird's nest (an egg cooked on toast) should do it," he fancied while scratching his nut sack, picking up a two-day-old pizza box from the floor that he had stashed earlier from the community refrigerator the night before. The Splinter, having procured 'za, now picked up every beer can, finding one half full, then taking a big slug to get rid of his morning cottonmouth.

"DAMN IT!?!", the Splinter exclaimed, spitting the leftover beer in his mouth out, "Beer cans are not ashtrays, assholes!!! Any other surprises I should know about?!? Assholes."

The damage had been done, it wasn't the worst-tasting thing he'd ever had before, just gritty. He surveyed the pizza hard before eating it, using it to get the taste of cigarette butts out of his mouth. It didn't overpower the taste, it just accented the pizza in a more desirable taste, as the taste from the ash beer can would remain for a while, so the Splinter would just enjoy this, hoping that the taste passed quickly.

The Splinter scratched his nut sack again, wishing that Christie was there, to scratch it for him. She could keep going. The Splinter stopped, looked in the mirror, and saw that his skin and hair had finished. Picking up the airbrush at an 8 % volume, the Splinter dotted out a pimple on his cheek, rubbed the paint into his skin, then turned the brush off, laying it down. He then got out his grease pencils and began contouring his upper and lower eyelids. Tommy Splinter didn't use woman's makeup, he made his own, but if a woman wanted to do a makeover on him, he always accepted, this was how he learned, even if at his own expense.

The Splinter picked up his acoustic guitar after finishing his makeup and eating the slice of pizza. The Splinter was never far from one of his guitars for very long while he was awake, sometimes even taking one to the bathroom with him, where he'd fill the air with his original guitar chords like Hawaiian Breeze air freshener. His friends said his music didn't help the smell, but it helped the Splinter, or else his funk would melt the flesh off his body. He didn't care about their nostrils; he didn't poo all the time, so these brief exchanges of solids and gases passed quickly, or at least the skin-and tissue-melting acidic part did.

With diet and eating properly, the Splinter could control his methane, but he didn't diet. The Splinter had learned about combining different foods for a larger, more potent radius of his gas flesh-eating capabilities. So he remained quiet, honing his music, while experimenting with the density of his passed gas, until he had perfected it. He abstained from meatballs, meatloaf, beans, Brussels sprouts, onion, garlic, and such, though he loved those things greatly. He planned his meals with great pleasure, for the day the Splinter would melt the flesh off the bodies of the crowd from one of his band's shows, and blame it on someone else...

"Their flesh would come back, the crowd's; mine does," the Splinter had surmised when he decided to go ahead with his plan.

Of course the Splinter never had his flesh melt down to his bones. That was caused by blurry eyes, transitioning from being asleep to waking up, a very dirty mirror, and gastrological disorder that caused him to fart a lot. Usually, he could hold it for hours, like a submarine underwater, before blowing his ballast. He always held it, for the sake of others, and now, he schemed for chemical warfare, just to see what happened. Best yet, because he was the star of his band, people believed him, and his plot to blame an innocent concertgoer meant his escape from detection and blame.

Actually, that was the best way to draw a small-venue crowd in, if they were tired, or quiet, or both; he'd get them cheering for something, a common enemy, then channel that initial jolt of crowd energy into his music. All it took was a REALLY good fart to stop the band, kill the sound, dim the lights, and everything else, as the aerial offense drifted to its intended target, to get the crowd into it, "NO MORE FARTS!!!" and then he would comply if the crowd showed some excitement. If not, the concert was explosive, to say the least.

But tonight's performance had been specially prepared with roasted onion, garlic, and capers in a white cream sauce over angel hair pasta, Brussels sprouts in a garlic butter sauce, with a large order of chicken gizzards and livers, and a large order of Popeye's onion rings. This would be his lunch as his plan fermented until fruition, snacking thereafter on bean burritos. The Splinter was going nuclear, and everyone knew about it. His fans looked forward to this blowout, bought the tickets to his concert, another sellout, with no refunds."...

...and then Tommy Splinter played with matches.
RIP

Tommy Splinter died of self-induced combustion while playing with a book of matches before the show. All that was left after the Splinter's flameout were several large pieces of burnt charcoal. It wasn't considered a successful combustion, because there is nothing left over in true combustion, so in a way, the Splinter just smoldered to death. He was twenty-two years old.

No one ever knew his real last name, or where to send his leftover charcoal. His car-dealing father figured Tommy had become a merchant sailor, and threw his son to the wind; he never searched, never knew that his son was essentially burnt toast.

There will be a memorial service next Wednesday at Wayside Waifs in the city, which will feature the burning of his leftover charcoal and a free hot dog roast at the same time. The burning of the charcoal means a lot to his friends, just to see the Splinter burn again, especially those not there the first time he combusted, and at the same time, to feed a few homeless people.

Tommy Splinter blamed his death on the third guy from the left in the fourth row of the concert at the Out House, and because of that, everyone bought the third guy from the left in the fourth row another beer. In a separate incident, the third guy from the left in the fourth row died when he fell and drowned in an outhouse reservoir while using the bathroom repeatedly.

Sources said the third guy from the left in the fourth row was full of urine at the autopsy; no shit...

The Father's Son

By Sarah Kohls Roberts

Joe King climbed into his Mercedes and sighed. Today was his day to visit his father at the nursing home. Joe went faithfully twice a week, and even attempted to be cheerful, even though it was his least favorite task. Not that he would let anyone else know; not his children, who questioned why he visited a mean old man who usually treated his son with derision, and certainly not his father. No, that was between him and God and good Father Matthew in the confessional. Joe's wife knew, of course. She was well acquainted with the sad resignation that accompanied Joe on his visits and the knowledge that Joe's father would never show Joe the love and approval he had hoped for his entire life. Still Joe went, dutifully, because he tried to be the son his mother had raised him to be, and because he felt it was the right thing to do.

As Joe pulled into a parking space, freezing rain began to fall. Joe pulled the collar of his overcoat close around his neck. Lately, his father was more and more confused. He refused to do his normal laps around the ward with his walker. Joe knew the end was probably near. Despite the difficult relationship, his heart felt as leaden as the sky.

Squaring his shoulders, Joe rapped on the door and walked into his father's room. "Good morning, Father."

Joseph King's wispy white hair floated like thin clouds around his head. He scowled. "It's about time you got up, boy. I've been waiting all day. You took so long the food's cold."

"I'm sorry. Would you like me to warm up your toast?" Joe said, pulling a chair next to his father's wheelchair.

"No need for that. The food's inedible. I'd like to see you eat this slop. But no, you get to eat at all those fancy restaurants and waste the money from my life's work."

Joe rubbed his temples. "The food is fine. Why don't you have some toast? You should eat something, and you know you hate to waste food."

Joseph's face became fearful. He looked around surreptitiously. "I can't waste it. Father doesn't like that." He leaned toward Joe and beckoned with a crooked finger. "He beats me, you know. My father. With his belt. He says I'm wicked and won't amount to anything. But I'll show him. I'm going to be as successful as Rockefeller! He'll see. And I'll never drink liquor like he does." Joseph paused and took a huge bite of toast, working it in his mouth with a vengeance. He continued in a whisper, "Do you know, if I smile, he says I must have done something wrong. Even if it's because I made him a present for his birthday." He took another bite of toast. "I made him a card, and whittled him a little house, because he builds houses, you know." Joseph's face lit up with the memory, then went out as suddenly as a candle extinguished by a gust of wind. "He said it was garbage. I worked so hard on that house! I just wanted to make him happy." His voice rose. "He threw the house into the fire, and beat me so hard I couldn't sit for three days. So I don't smile anymore." Joseph convulsed into sobs.

Joe sat in shock. He had never heard this story. He knew that his grandfather was a violent and abusive alcoholic. He knew that his grandfather's drinking had led him to an early grave and inspired his own father's rigid work ethic. But Joe had never known why his father had such a serious temperament. He had had many theories, but never had he imagined that it was due to heartbreak.

As his father sobbed, Joe patted his back gently and found himself feeling true sympathy toward him. So many pieces fit together. He had never understood his mother's gentleness with his father, even when his father did not act kindly. He had never realized why his father was so hard on him, why he had such high expectations, or why he punished Joe severely for getting into fistfights at school and never allowed Joe to treat or speak unkindly to anyone.

Finally Joseph's sobs turned to shuddery breaths. Joe retrieved some tissues from the bathroom. When he held them out to his father, he was surprised to see his father watching him with knowing eyes. Eyes that were suddenly Joseph King Sr.'s eyes, fully lucid and fully knowing who and where and when he was.

"Joey," Joseph croaked, using Joe's childhood nickname and looking him fully in the eyes, as he had not done in the long years since he slid into the fog of dementia. "Joey, I'm sorry. For all the times I yelled at you and put you down. You are a better son than I deserve, and you're a better man than I ever dreamed of being myself. I'm proud of you, son. And... I... I love you." Another sob escaped Joseph's lips as Joe knelt and hugged his father, as he hadn't since he was very small.

A short while later, Joe returned to his father's room with more toast and found the eyes of his father once again dulled by dementia. "I'm tired," Joseph said in a peevish voice. "I don't want toast. I want to take a nap."

Joe helped his father into bed. He squeezed the shoulder of the man who had taught him to throw a wicked curve ball, showed him how to treat a girl like a queen, and instructed him on the business of selling accordions. As he turned off the light, he said, "Have a good nap, Dad. I love you."

At his father's funeral two months later, Joe King looked around the church at those gathered to pay their respects. He began, "My father was a good man. I wish I had realized that years ago."

The Funk

By Vicky Gutierrez

Some days you just wake up in a funk. On this particular morning the funk swirls thick in the air, it seeps sour through the sheets, falls heavy from the ceiling, and gripes audibly from the rain outside. I look at the near-empty bottle of Beefeaters gin on the carpet and my gag reflex ignites simultaneously with the thought of finishing it off.

Always on foggy-headed middays like this the guilt invites itself into your mind. It barges in without knocking, opens your fridge, cracks one of your beers, and props its loafers up on your coffee table. And always, by way of greeting, it asks, "So what did you do this time?" boring into your soul with beady, squinting eyes. Often the answer is nothing to speak of, but the question comes so accusatorily, so pre-laden with the assumption of your guilt, that you burrow into your bed as deep as you can and hide your foul face from the world for a day or so, until gradually, friends call or text or comment on your Facebook page and you are absolved by their acknowledgement.

Today though, I don't have to scan my memory for long before the source of my funky shame throws my heart into my stomach in a sickening lurch. This time there is no ambiguity about the source of my guilt. The scene from last night replays itself in my head: the big dude with the gap in his teeth gloating when I missed the easiest mark on the pool table, his flabby chin shaking as he threw his head back in laughter at my "girlie shot," then "bonk" and his eyes grew wide, first in shock and then in menace when I hit him square on his fat, blocky head with the chalked end of my pool cue.

"Fucking bitch," he snarled through the gap in his gritted teeth. At the time, eight gin and tonics, two tequila shots and an IPA in, he suddenly resembled a large, angry ferret and I hit him again, having never much liked ferrets. This time though, I did it right, and I swear the sound the stick made on his head was hollow like a tinny thud.

"There's your fucking girlie shot." I slurred and he went jumping around the room flailing his arms and yelling, "Dude better get your bitch in check" to no-one in particular, even though I had come with no dude but had walked alone, my house being only stumbling distance from that particular hole. He was muttering that he "don't hit no girls" over and over in a sort of frenzied mantra and smacking the closed fist of one hand into the palm of the other when I slipped out the door, taking the pool cue with me.

It is leaning now against my dresser like a tangible souvenir from the top of the Beanstalk. Now I have the mental picture of his reddish eyes growing wide at the moment the cue stick hits his close-cropped dome playing on a loop, sometimes in fast motion like the old Charlie Chaplin films, sometimes slowed to a near stop, so I can see the chalk billowing around his head like a dust storm at the moment of impact. I hope I never see his face again, but with this mental scene stuck on replay, I know I will. I pass my guilt the bottle of gin.

The Hurricane

By Gale Sandler

The excitement was building. Our regular programming was preempted by our favorite meteorologist, who was on the screen again with a threatening weather map showing a large green blob known as Hurricane Matthew. We heard all the dramatic threats about how Matthew was going to hit the east coast of Florida and would be so huge that it would expand and cover all of Central Florida too!

OMG, so much to do to get ready. First and most difficult was to pack up the model train pieces and parts of my husband's layout. Do you have any idea how many pieces and parts make up a model train set? So after making fifty-two trips back and forth between the lanai and the dining room, I was exhausted. Whew, at last it's done. But what a mess in the lanai. Might as well vacuum all the little clumps of fake foliage that were on the floor of the lanai. If only I didn't have those stupid little vinyl window squares, I wouldn't have had to do all that. Of course now it needed to be cleaned everywhere.

Finally sat down to relax a minute and figured I'd do it in front of my computer and check my email and Facebook page before I turned everything off. Wow, here was a letter from our home insurance company with a checklist of to dos to prepare. Gee, growing up in Missouri wasn't like this. Tornado sirens would go off and we'd run down to the basement and an hour later it was all over. Oh dear, this is Central Florida. There are no basements and we don't have any sirens.

Ok, back to the list. Let's see, get water, get cash, fill up your gas tank and get extra cat food. Tornadoes sure were a lot easier.

So I started with the top of the list. Went to the bank and got some cash out of the ATM, then I headed over to the gas station and played "Dodge-em" cars juxtapositioning myself to get near the pump while everyone worked hard to cut me off. When I got up to the pump, a sign said, "Sorry, no regular left, just premium." Swell! At least I got some.

Then I headed up the street to the Walmart and got all the items I needed. We all played that game of which aisle had the shortest line. The answer was, "None of them." So I picked an aisle, got in line and had the strangest feeling I was being watched. Sure enough, the woman in front of me was dressed in a colorful assortment of clothing and had a real live parrot sitting on her shoulder. Its beady little eyes were looking right at me. Can you believe anyone would bring a real parrot into Walmart during this busy time when everyone is getting ready for the hurricane? Or for that matter, why would you bring a parrot in at any time? That's Walmart for you. I could do a whole story on that place.

OK, now I'm home and going back to my checklist. I figured the best place to be was our walk-in closet in our master bedroom because it's the only place with no windows. The only problem is, it's only four feet square, unlike our nice house in Atlanta. Well, let's see, I'll move all the show racks from the floor. Now I have to vacuum the floor of the closet and get the weather radio, flashlights, bottles of water, important papers and so forth. Now meteorologist Tony Manolfi (our Dean Martin look-alike) said we better put a disaster kit together. So I took an old swim bag and added our pills, wallets, birth certificates, etc. Now I'm really tired. I've just got to lay down for a little nap.

I jumped up thinking the storm was coming through the window when I heard a loud rattling sound. I looked over and it was my crazy cat, who had climbed between the window and the blinds, rattling her little heart out at the display of wildly dancing ferns beneath the window, populated by lots of chameleons that had really grown this summer.

OK, I'm up and back to work. Let's see, I have to remove all of the loose stuff from the patio door and by the front door, which I had just set up with a cute fall display.

So here we go with more trips back and forth to bring in flower pots and décor from the patio, the plants I was babysitting for my snowbird friend in Michigan, the straw people, the pumpkin, the gourds and the orange "Welcome Neighbor" sign. More to add to our overcrowded dining room loaded with model train stuff. Oh boy!

Let's see. Time to unload the stuff from the car and put all the bottles of water into the refrigerator in the garage, which now smells like a rain forest with all the plants in it. Oh, look, there's a giant roach in the garage window. It must have come in when I moved the plants inside. Great, something else to worry about!

OK, back to the checklist. Oh yeah, fill up the bathtubs in case the water and power get cut off. So I plugged up the tub in our master bedroom bath, turned on the water and looked at my checklist. Guess I better get something together to eat in case of power failure. I know, I'll hard boil some eggs; we can always have a big salad. Why not bake some of those slice-and-bake cookies I found in the fridge when I went to get the eggs. We weren't going to be caught empty-handed or hungry. So I put the eggs in a pot on the stove and set the timer on the stove to wait for the cookies I had just laid out on the tray.

OMG, I forgot to turn the water off in the tub. So I raced back to the bathroom and screamed. Now I had a flood to clean up all over the bathroom floor. No need to worry about flooding from Hurricane Matthew. Then when I took the mop back to the laundry room, I realized I had left the pot on the stove and the cookies in the oven. The water had boiled down to nothing and the pot was smoking and the cookies had burnt by now. Now it's 2 am, I am exhausted and everything is done. I'm tired of watching the same warnings from Tony about the hurricane.

Now it's the next day and the rain has started. Well okay, I'm ready now. Even called to find out where the emergency shelters are in case the grove of trees behind our home decided to come crashing down on it. The big winds in Marion County were due next. Okay, I'm ready....NO WORRIES! All of a sudden I heard a huge "Blam" on the lanai. I rushed out there to see what hit the windows and it's my crazy cat again. She's thrown all 7-1/2 pounds of might and fury against one of the little square vinyl windows—trying desperately to get at a big chameleon outside on the window. Oh just great. Scared the you-know-what out of me. Nope, Matthew hadn't hit yet.

Back to Tony showing us what's going on. Apparently, Matthew landed in Brevard County and was headed our way. Well, bring it on!

I was so tired from the preparation that I went back to bed after breakfast and fell fast asleep. I popped upthree3 hours later, turned on the TV, and the worst was over. Matthew was on its way north and had hit Broward and Volusia Counties; there was lots of physical damage but no loss of life. Then they showed the funniest thing I've ever seen. A reporter was showing scenes of storm damage and he was interviewing a guy named Dave, who had on a wife-beater shirt, a ball cap on backwards, and shorts. A huge tree was sitting over his pickup truck. The reporter asked him how he got out of his truck. He told Dave to face the cameras.

There stood Dave with a dizzy grin 'cause now he's on TELEVISION. Dave said, "Well, I just popped out the top of my truck, which had a window, and pulled myself up." The reporter asked him why he went out when there were warnings not to drive anywhere.

This rocket scientist replies, "Well, I wanted to get me some cigarettes." "Aren't you worried about getting the insurance to cover the damage to the truck?"

"No," says, rocket scientist. "Actually it belongs to my girlfriend." The reporter then asked him, "Weren't you worried about the storm." "Naw," he said continuing to grin at the camera. "This is the most exciting thing I've ever been through!" Oh boy!

Well it wasn't the most exciting thing, I've ever been through. But I can tell you one thing, I'm never going to do all this again. Let the lanai windows blow away, let the wind take my flag and let me house blow away. I'm sorry for all the damage that so many folks suffered, but I don't think I'm ever going to do all this again.

Next time, I'm going to do NADA, NOTHING, ZERO and let everything blow away. I might live a little longer that way.

The Jester's Runes

By Jennifer R. Povey

The princess watched the jester through narrowed eyes. Wrapped in motley, his face tattooed with the jester's mark, there was no mistaking him.

The mark that barred him forever from the life of a free man. Why did she have to be fascinated with the most unreachable of men?

Not only was he not of her class and available only for carefully-managed trysts that, of necessity, involved birthbane, but he was a jester—available to no one.

Jesters did not marry. Jesters did not father children. Jesters could never be anything but jesters.

Which was, of course, why he was so fascinating. Who had he been? Peasant or noble, it did not matter now.

He was telling some kind of joke to fat old Lord Tylt of... of... dang it... that was right, Tylt of Lorwood. Tylt was easy enough to remember, it was like what knights did in the lyst. Tilting. Lorwood she had more problems with.

The jester's name, of course, was known only to the jester. Was he happy? she wondered.

Happier, no doubt, than the field thralls, also branded into permanent slavery. Or perhaps not, for she had heard their songs, the rhythms to which they worked.

No, she decided. No slave could be happy, and no princess either, for her own freedoms were barely less curtailed.

She was a princess, and she would wed the foreign prince in two years, go to his kingdom and become his consort-queen. She would wed Prince Marek and pretend to be happy.

That was what princesses did, that were not the eldest and heir to the throne. They married princes. Younger princes became soldiers or priests. Well, she could have become a priest, but no thanks.

So, no. She was not much more free than the jester and he, at least, could never be punished for anything he said.

He came over to her. "You look as lovely as a rose, Lyrita."

He was a jester. He did not need to use her title. She smiled her thanks.

"But I see your thorns."

She actually smiled brighter at that. A princess was best cultivating her thorns.

Then he leaned over and whispered, "Tonight. Go. Go to the hunting lodge."

She did not understand. Did he want a tryst? He had to know that was forbidden, that even the rules that allowed an unmarried princess to take a paramour did not allow her to tryst with a jester.

"Do it." There was darkness in his tone and unfathomable pain.

She resolved to ignore him and, in any case, the servants were now bringing out dessert. Many of them were free men and women, not thralls. That made her feel better about her thoughts.

Or did it?

Nobody was free, but perhaps the jester's melancholy had now interacted with her own budding discontent and wrapped itself around her and was dragging her down.

But she was not going to the hunting lodge. Instead, she headed for the solar after the meal, but there was not enough light left to work by. Quietly cursing the fact, she decided she might as well go to her chambers, to read by torchlight until she was tired enough to sleep.

Out the window, though, she saw the jester in his motley cloak. He was not heading, as he should have been, for his quarters in the garden tower. No, he was heading into the garden.

Was he planning on trying to burn the castle down? Had he decided she was the one who would escape?

No. A shiver ran through her as he stopped in the center of the garden and pulled out a knife he should not have had.

Suicide. Did he intend that escape?

Nay. He started to draw forbidden symbols in the air. At first it was quiet, then lurid green fire began to follow the blade.

She clapped a hand over her mouth. Screaming would avail nothing. Instead, she ran from the room. "Raise the alarm, but quietly," she told the servant checking the torches in the corridor. "The jester. He's drawing runes."

The servant did scream, but it was stifled, and she ran off. The princess pulled her cloak around herself and took the quickest route to the garden.

It wasn't quick enough. By the time she was there he had the gate open. He turned towards her. "You should have gone."

"This isn't funny." It was a lame thing to say yet, somehow, fitting. There he was in motley, the runefire reflecting on his tattooed face. He seemed the darkest and gravest of monsters. But she knew she was right.

It wasn't funny, and abruptly she pulled the knife she, also, was not supposed to have, and threw. It landed in his throat, but around her she heard laughter.

"Too late, little lady. The joke's on us."

"Then take me and leave everyone else alone." The joke might be on them, the jester lay dead at her feet, but the gate had to be closed or everyone in the castle would be dragged to the netherworld.

"Brave princess, lovely princess." She sensed them walking around her, assessing her. "His princess."

Her lips quirked. "Never. That wouldn't have been funny, either."

Her breath froze in her throat.

"No. It wouldn't. Brave princess. Be free." She felt the fire close around her. She did not scream, but when the servants came out into the garden, there was no sign of her.

Only the jester's fallen body, his face twisted into a mockery of a laugh.

The Proposal

By Kari Redmond

Joey supposed he would have won whether or not Sally Harrison showed up. He would claim, for the next several years, that he had no way of knowing of her presence as he maneuvered the electronic arm for what must have been the thousandth time. Until finally the metal claw held tight to the giant stuffed ring and sent it down the mouth of the machine.

He would say that when he finally retrieved the ring from the chute, amidst the clapping and cheering of the crowd which had grown three rows thick with children, as well as adults, he had every intention of giving it to Sally even had she not been among them. The fact that she was, made it 'all the more romantic,' Joey would say as he recounted the story on the playground in the weeks and months that followed; Sally standing proudly beside him.

Joey had been playing nearly every Sunday after church when his parents would take him for breakfast at the Denny's, which had the only crane game in town. Joey saved his quarters all week. One for taking out the trash, another for keeping his bed made all week, another for collecting his laundry every Thursday, and another for loading the dishwasher every night. The latter was a job usually meant for his sister, but since the discovery of the grabber game, Joey had begged her to let him do it for her instead. She relented, preferring to watch American Bandstand, which played right after dinner most nights.

On this particular Sunday, Joey had not four, but five quarters, having found a beautiful shiny quarter on his walk home from school the previous Tuesday. It rested between two rocks, bright against the grass that insisted on growing between them. Joey took the quarter in his hand, inspecting it for authenticity, before placing it carefully in his pocket. He vowed that this Sunday, the Sunday he would have not four, but five quarters, would be the day he got the ring.

Sally Harrison knew about the kid who played the grabber game every Sunday. She listened in awe as children talked on the playground, and when she learned that the prize he was after was the ring, she quietly blushed. She had played the game only once since its arrival at the Denny's and was particularly fond of the diamond ring.

Joey was not particularly fond of the ring toy. It was simply the logical choice because of the nature of a ring. The claw would hold onto the loop of the ring much easier than it might a simple teddy bear. And for this reason Joey had his sights on the ring.

On Sunday Sally made her way to Denny's. She entered the double doors and found herself in the crowd of people already gathered around The Claw in the lobby. She had to stand on her tippy toes to be sure it was Joey playing the game. She then squeezed her way between an older gentleman and his wife to join the children in the front row. She asked the girl next to her exactly which quarter he was on. The fourth, the girl answered. Sally drew in a sharp breath, which she held, she figured, until the fifth quarter had achieved success.

A hush fell over the crowd as Joey carefully removed the coin from his lint-filled pocket. He settled it into the palm of his hand so he could blow away the remnants of his pocket before slowly and deliberately placing the quarter in the game. This gave Sally enough time to say a quick prayer to give Joey the steadiness to move the arm and grab the ring. By her assessment, the ring was in a perfect place, having been held and dropped so many times that it finally rested diamond side down, loop side up.

Joey had a ritual he repeated before depositing each coin into the slot. He would visualize his next steps. It was something his older brother, now at college, had told him about once. And he had never forgotten it. So when the crowd grew still, Joey was grateful for the silence and the time to visualize his hand on the joystick and the giant mechanical arm moving over the ring and dropping perfectly around the loop of the plush toy. He then saw the claw pick it up, dangling the ring in its arms. He watched it move forward in his mind and drop the ring into the chute.

After the quarter was dropped, Joey was ready. He saw his tousled blonde hair reflected in the glass on the machine and watched a drop of sweat roll down his cheek. He was grateful no one else could see this. When the game activated, he moved the arm of the machine just like he visualized, so much so, that when things happened just as he'd foreseen, he had to blink his eyes twice to be sure the ring had in fact dropped down the chute and deposited itself for retrieving in the tiny mouth of the game.

It was simultaneous: his sudden realization that it was not a visualization and the cheers of the small crowd that had materialized in the lobby. Claps and whoops surrounded him. He held the ring up for the crowd to see, and at the instant he turned around to face them, he found Sally standing in the middle, a shy smile on her face. He ceremoniously knelt on one knee and presented her with the plush toy.

Sally pretended to slip the overstuffed ring on her left ring finger. She patted herself on the back for placing the quarter visible enough for Joey to spot on his walk home from school. She remembered the look on his face as he held it to the light of the sun as she peered at him from the bushes.

The Psychic

By Rene Villard-Reid

The sun glinted through the windshield of my blue Audi as I drove to the coastal town of Santa Maria. My mind was at odds with itself as usual. Sometimes I have a non-stop tag team match wrestling in my head between my adult self and my more innovative inner child. This morning was no different.

The adult voice said, "Whatever could you be thinking?"

"I don't want to think," a smaller, younger voice replied. "I just want to know what it feels like."

"Are you nuts? Why are you seeing a psychic? I tell you all you need to know. This lady won't know anything. It's just a scam."

"I'm going because I'm curious." The child paused. "Think about that for a minute. Why don't you loosen up a little? Stop being so controlling and just see what happens? You have no sense of spontaneity."

"Loosen up? Are you kidding? Somebody needs to keep their feet on the ground. I just don't see the point in doing something that could make us look and feel really stupid. I hate it when that happens. Aren't you feeling just a little silly?" The voice wheedled on. "What if this person is full of bull? After all, you have only the recommendation of a pretty weird guy who's renamed himself Pasha. I mean REALLY. What kind of a name is THAT and what does it mean?"

"Well, I think he's kind of okay. Besides, lots of people change their names. That's not the issue, anyway. I just want to meet a psychic and see what she's like. Maybe she'll even tell me something special about myself that could make sense of my life."

"Special smecial. You know what your problem is kid? You NEED to feel special so you matter. For Chrissakes! Just for once, get your head outta the clouds. You're starting to sound like the flake who suggested you come over here in the first place. Come ON. Don't you think he's just a little strange?"

"Maybe... I don't know! You know what? Nothing interesting or unusual ever happens to me. So, frankly, I don't care what you think and I'm doing this, anyway. Strange guy or not. So... LEAVE ME ALONE."

The voices faded away, leaving a blessed silence in my head. "Finally," I sighed. I dragged my attention back to the road in time to make the turnoff and merged onto the street matching the directions I'd been given. A large faded sign announced the mobile home court where my fate would be determined... or so I hoped. I pulled in front of a single-wide trailer that was as short as it was wide. I couldn't imagine two people, a mother and daughter, could coexist in such a limited space. Its diminutiveness was punctuated even more by the tall obese woman filling the doorway. Breathlessly, she waved me through the door without moving. So I was forced to squeeze past her as she peered goggled-eyed through her Coke-bottle lenses. With effort, I made it across the threshold and saw a young woman seated in a chair.

Before I was able to greet her, Magda said, "This is Sandy, my schizophrenic daughter." There was a moment of stunned silence as I recovered from this feckless introduction.

Lamely, I said, "Hi." It wasn't brilliant or ingenious but it was the best I had. There was another awkward pause as they eyed me with curiosity. It began to feel as if I were the oddity in the room and not them.

Finally, Magda pointed to a tiny breakfast nook and gestured for me to take a seat. From the look of things, it was going to be a tight fit. I opted for angling my butt on the corner. It would make for a quick getaway should I need one.

She reached above her and took down a bottle of whiskey from the cupboard. I struggled to keep my face impassive as she downed several shots from a small glass and said, "It helps me to relax." Okay, that was a gross understatement. I kept my thoughts buttoned up while thinking with Alice, "Curiouser and curiouser."

As I perched on the hard, narrow bench, she began to babble in a disjointed fashion about some really strange stuff. You know, STUFF, as in 'raw material'... that which is unformed and mostly unintelligible. I don't know what else to call the contents of what spewed from this Southern Comfort oracle.

Without warning, the delivery came to an abrupt halt. It took me a second to realize it was over and I was expected to say or do something. I opted for discretion and self-consciously reached into my purse for the token silver. I placed it on the table, muttered a weak, "Thanks," and made for the door.

As I drove away, a strange numbing sensation began to ebb from my body and mind. Odd. I hadn't noticed it until it began to dissipate a few blocks from the trailer court. I tried to write the whole thing off as alcoholic drivel, when an unbidden memory stole across my mind. It surfaced through the haze of the departing trance, leaving a cold chill tracing down my spine. Two sentences crept through my head, leaving silver tracks of light.

"You are not from here. You are from the sixth heaven." As I pondered these words and their possible meaning, I heard the adult voice sneer and say, "What? D'ya think you're an angel now? Or better yet, how 'bout an alien? I suppose that makes you SPECIAL?"

The kid and I whispered back in unison, "Maybe."

The Recruit

By Brian Reid

"So what are we gonna do with him, Sal?"

"People with the business. We put them in the ground."

"It's fucking January, Sal. How come you always want to ace people in January? The frostline is forty-fucking-inches deep." Marco turned in the passenger seat to look back at the kid.

"See, kid, if we don't bury you past the frostline, you get heaved up out of the ground come spring. Your mom, she ain't gonna want to see that. Sal, he don't mind, but to me it's a messy job; we bury you above the frostline, your body freezes up, your skin splits all over the place.

"But getting you down deep? It's hard work. You need a pickaxe, or a contractor's shovel, which is what Sal uses. You use a regular shovel, the ground will snap it clean through." He turned back in his seat. "You want to ace him, Sal? Fine, but it ain't me doing the digging. I'm staying in the car. I ain't sweating and freezing at the same time. You ask me, you got some kind of seasonal disorder."

"What are you talking about?"

"Name one time you ever aced someone in August."

"Everybody's gone on vacation in August."

"It was August, you'd give the kid a break. How many windows you break when you was a kid? Nobody ever aced you."

"That's 'cause I never broke no fucking windows in January."

"So now you're being funny."

"Sometimes you got to send a message."

"To who, Sal?"

They drove in silence. Houses appeared less often, a small farm appeared on their left. Corn stubble poked through a blanket of snow.

"Sal, maybe I got an idea."

"We're putting him in a hole."

"Maybe so, but hear me out. We know where the kid lives right?"

"Yeah."

"He's what, sixteen. You sixteen, kid?" Marco turned in his seat, watched the kid's head, wrapped in a coffee sack, bob up and down emphatically. "He's sixteen. Where's he gonna run? So we let him go, he tells his little friends to stay away from certain windows, and if it happens again, we know where to find him."

When Sal didn't reply, Marco pulled a sheaf of round window stickers from the glove compartment. He turned back to the kid. "See, me and Sal, we run a business. We visit stores; we sell them stickers." He waved the window stickers in front of the coffee bag. "Can't see them? Well they say *South Chicago Police Association*. You buy a sticker, your windows don't get broken and your store don't catch on fire. Now you," he stabbed a hard finger into the kid's throat, below the coffee sack. "You broke a protected window, you little shit." The kid collapsed, gasping for air.

"Punks like him running around fucking with our customers," Sal said. "You let him go, he tells his little punk friends we're a joke. They start breaking all our windows. We nip this thing in the bud, we only got to dig the one hole." They turned onto a gravel road slicing through fallow cornfields.

The wind cut at their faces as they bundled the kid out of the car and yanked the coffee bag from his head. The bag had imprinted its rough weave on the kid's splotched face, his eyes were red. Sal tossed the shovel from the truck. The shovel rang when it hit the frozen earth. He pulled on a thick pair of gloves. "No need to waste a bullet," he said, "I'll do him with the shovel." He picked up the shovel like a baseball bat.

"Seems a shame, Sal. Like I said, we could let him go, pick him back up after the ground thaws, if we got to. We wouldn't even have to bury him, we could take him out on the boat, dump him in the lake. The lake ain't frozen in August."

"I ain't afraid of doing a little digging."

"I got an idea, Sal."

"We're freezing our asses off, Marco."

"Just listen. We get caught shooting out windows, it's three to five years, right? The kid here," he pointed to the shivering child, "he gets caught, he gets off with a slap on the wrist."

"Or a shovel in the neck."

"So what if he breaks windows for us?"

"Why's he going to do that?"

"We pay him."

Sal dug the shovel into the ground. "Better to bury him."

"Hear me out, Sal. What say we give him two hundred a window?"

Sal turned a shovelful of earth over. "Still leaves us doing the fires. Setting fires is twenty to life."

"So what if the kid does fires, too?" Marco turned his head "Hey kid, you kay setting fires?"

The kid stood frozen for a moment, then nodded quickly.

Sal stopped and leaned against the shovel. "How much?" he asked.

"A thousand." Marco said. "What say we give him a thousand a fire, Sal?"

Sal lifted another shovelful of dirt. "I say I got this hole started. Be a shame to waste it."

Marco huffed disapproval, "What's a hole going to buy you, Sal?" He looked the kid in the eye, "What if the kid took one-fifty for the windows and seven-fifty for the fires? Whaddaya think, kid? Two, maybe three jobs a month?"

The kid's face slackened as greed crept slowly through the last hour's fear. He nodded.

"Hey Sal, the kid says he'll do it."

"What about my fucking hole, Marco?"

"The kid'll make it up to you, won't you kid? First window's free?" He waited for the kid to nod. "See, he's a smart kid, Sal. You'll see." Marco pushed the boy toward the car. "In the car before we freeze our nuts off."

Marco slammed the car door behind the kid. Sal lifted the shovel and rubbed the dirt lovingly from the smooth blade and gave it a dry kiss. "Marco's right," he said, "You're the best recruiter we ever had."

The 7 Bar 7

By Joshua B. Lehman

"What'll it be, Cecil?" Red Ben boomed from behind the bar at the 7-7. Red claimed he was half Shoshone, but he looked like a full-blooded Irishman. His pale skin was flush with drink and slick with a sheen of sweat, his round face bordered by flaming red mutton chops.

"A ditch," Cecil answered as he took a stool at the bar. The cabin boasted the bar, three small tables, one long table with bench seating, and a pot-bellied stove. The log structure was chinked in clay mortar and sod covered the roof. Two small windows admitted slivers of late afternoon sun, leaving the cabin dim.

"The stew's over the fire out back," Red informed Cecil as the beefy barkeep ladled tepid water from a bucket into a glass. The water was mostly clear, Cecil noted. Red added a healthy pour of whiskey. "Too hot to cook in here just yet. How'd the dudes do today?"

"No one got themselves killed," Cecil grunted.

Red chuckled. The 7-7 was a dude ranch where greenhorns with a taste for adventure could experience the Wild West. Cecil guided them on such adventures. Today he had led some New Yorkers, three men and a young woman, up the South Fork on a fishing expedition. Cecil had made sure each guest landed a trout, but it hadn't been easy.

"Today's second Friday," Red noted. "You think Eddie'll visit tonight?"

Cecil pinched the bridge of his nose to stave off a headache. "I reckon so. I warned the dudes. They can't wait to meet him."

"That'll wear off." Red poured himself a finger of whiskey and slugged it down.

Eddie Antwin was a real mountain man. A trapper, he spent most of his time in a string of shacks he'd constructed throughout the backcountry. Once a month he appeared at the 7-7 to sell pelts and wet his whistle, always on the second Friday. Whether from a lifetime of seclusion or sickness in his head, Eddie was crazy. His tales of wendigos, lost tribes of little people, and beings from the sky often upset the dudes.

Eddie believed his own tales vigorously, and a tale told with utter belief is hard to discount, especially when accompanied by some "proof." The trapper always had some token to bolster his ramblings, usually a strange burn from lights in the sky or similar interesting wound. A miniature spear hung on the wall, Eddie's last artifact. It was a perfect replica, Cecil had to admire the man's artistry.

The heavy door to the cabin screamed in protest as the intrepid adventurers entered. Cecil shook his head, noting the men wore spurs, which jingled softly as they strode into the gloomy cabin. Each wore an expensive cowboy hat, two in brown, one in black. The woman wore a long black skirt, a white blouse, a red handkerchief about her neck, and a black, floppy-brimmed hat. A large white plume adorned her headwear.

"I love these dirt floors," the eldest gentleman exclaimed. "They're so authentic!" He wore the black hat. About fifty, he was father of the other two men and father-in-law to the woman. He had a white handlebar mustache, but his soft, supple skin betrayed his attempts to look like a real cowboy.

The other three dudes smiled as they seated themselves at the long table.

"Join us, Cecil," the woman invited.

"Don't mind if I do, Mary," Cecil played the genial cowboy, removing his own weathered hat and sitting across from her.

"Did Cecil tell you of our success today, Red?" The elder son crowed triumphantly.

"That he did, Robert!" Red's voice filled the cabin. "Moose is cleaning your catch now. We'll get 'em fried up to go with tonight's stew." Red ambled to the stove to light it. "It's time to fire up ole Polly here, once the sun sets, it gets cold out quick. And Moose'll be in any time now."

On cue the door squealed again as it swung open, revealing a gangly teen with shoulders as broad as a draft horse. He smiled shyly and ducked his head at the dudes. He carried a cast iron pot in one hand and a brown paper parcel under his arm.

"Moose! Yer ears must be burning," Red laughed. "Polly is just about ready."

Moose shuffled to the corner and placed the pot on the stove, letting the wire handle fall backward. He placed the paper package on the bar. "Here's the catch of the day," he announced awkwardly.

Red unrolled the paper to expose the tender orange fish. "You folks are in for a treat!" He grabbed a skillet from the wall, placed it on the stove, and dropped in a dollop of butter from a wooden crock. As the butter melted, he chopped an onion. Using the edge of his knife, he transferred the onion to the buttered pan. He added the fillets and their delicious aroma soon filled the cabin.

Come nightfall, the dudes were full of stew, fish, and drink. Ranch hands filtered in throughout the evening to entertain them with their stories, but what they really wanted was the company of the infamous Eddie Antwin. The loud braying of a mule announced his arrival.

"Ah, there's Melba!" Red grinned. "She's Eddie's mule. Now don't let Eddie's nonsense scare you. There's very little truth to it." The barkeep winked.

The door creaked loudly as it opened. The oil lamps in the cabin illuminated a grizzled, stringy man; he looked like a tough strip of leather that had sprouted an unruly gray beard. A filthy hat sat on his head, above oddly glazed eyes. He was silent.

"You okay, Eddie?" Cecil prodded. "Did the lights in the sky come for you again?"

The dudes laughed nervously.

"The little ones..." Eddie rasped softly.

"Close the door and tell us about it," Red chided. "You're letting in the chill."

Eddie fell, his face smashing into the earth floor. Three small spears, brothers to the one on the wall, jutted from his back.

The Woodcock

By Dave Scheller

I was driving home late one night on a Vermont backcountry road. Old Hyundai chugging along through the dark, Statler Brothers tape whirring around in the tape deck. I stopped for a bird in the road. It was a small one, strange for the woods, looked like it would be more at home by the ocean. Once my lights stopped dazzling it, it composed itself and seemed to fly off in ten directions at once.

What was this bird? A plover that got knocked too far inland by a hurricane? At home, I dug out the book of birds, looked for anything weird. And there it was, the woodcock. Little brown puffball with a long pointed beak like the prow of a ship. I drank more gin and went to bed.

Next morning, I was getting the little restaurant I worked at ready for a new day of food. Topping off ketchup bottles, making the first batch of coffee that the staff would inevitably drink all of. Sean walked by with a tray of salt shakers.

"Sean," I said, "last night I saw a woodcock."

And for a moment Sean looked like he had finally found his purpose in life. Then without a pause or thought he turned to me and said, "Dave, I'll tell you what. If you stop telling people you saw a woodcock, I'll stop telling people how you got splinters in your mouth."

Oh, Sean.

The Sartorial Spectre

By Adam Gottfried

The mall obdurately refused to yield customers. Jemeera Gomez Carlson, Jem to her friends, was so far beyond bored that she thought she might cry. She had adjusted all the display models, dressed and redressed the two full-size mannequins in the shop three times, a process that usually took the better part of half an hour. She had balanced the till (without the credit receipts) four times.

Sure it was mid-January, the retail equivalent of a yearly Great Depression, and sure she had homework to do (she wasn't THAT bored), but Jem had hoped for SOMETHING to do. Maybe stare at that cute jewelry store sales girl Jem had seen last week. Jem had never really been into guys, but then she'd never really been into girls. Not till she saw her. Most jewelry store sales reps were attractive, it was like a prerequisite for the job, but this one... this one was beautiful. Jem had spent the majority of her shift trying to avoid staring across the corridor at Whitehall Jewelers. The woman was a couple years older than Jem, and likely attended the local state college. Blonde hair, blue eyes and gorgeous in a natural sort of way. Jem could tell she wore very little makeup. Jem imagined she was gorgeous without her makeup, perhaps more so... for so many women used make up as their armor against the world. Certainly that was Jem's reasoning. She was lucky to have been born with her mother's smooth, flawless skin, but she spent 45 minutes each morning keeping it that way. Jem's naturally cafe-au-lait skin and flashing black eyes had caught the eye of several boys in her school, but she wasn't interested.

Jem blinked. She glanced around her father's shop. The Whitehall sales rep who had taken her fancy was not working today and her mind had wandered. Something in the shop had... changed. It was so subtle it might have been her imagination, but she was just superstitious enough to take a look around the shop. There had been shoplifters before, but mostly they targeted the higher-end fashion shops, Hot Topic and Spencer's Gifts, not the local tuxedo rental. She reached under the counter and grabbed an ancient pipe-fitter's wrench her father had inherited from her great-grandfather who had been, in his day, a pipe fitter.

She nosed around the shop, holding the wrench at her waist, not wanting any potential customers walking by (there were none) to see it. The shop was simple: the antechamber, which contained several display tables, half-mannequins dressed for a prom, and two free-standing mannequins (one masculine, one feminine) near the entrance decked out in the latest finery fresh from the Ohio clothier where her father did his business.

Racks of jackets and vests lined the walls, dressing rooms in the back, and the register, which had been upgraded to take Discover and American Express maybe two years previously. Jem had worked in this shop for five years, first unofficially, and now as a full-time paid employee. Her father had made a big deal out of making her an official "KEYHOLDER," which was his word for shift manager, but it was just another responsibility for her that she could care less about. She planned to leave as soon as she graduated and go to college. She wasn't 100% sure where yet, but she had been accepted at several fairly decent schools so...

There it was again. She walked back to the counter, opened a cupboard and turned down the XM radio station playing classical music, and there it was. Nothing physically had changed in her shop, it was auditory. Music played, soft and slow... she stepped toward the shop's large entrance and listened to the mall's canned Muzak, but that wasn't it. The music was something old-timey, something that reminded her a bit of Post-Modern Jukebox... but not. She glanced across the corridor.

Most times in the mall, even with zero customers, she could still see half a dozen people: the sales rep(s) across the hall, the bored kid at the Cinnabon kitty-corner from her, two or three kiosk workers staring blankly at their phones, and Jake the 30-something janitor who flirted with all the underage employees. He was harmless enough, she supposed, but she didn't like talking to him when she was in the shop by herself. Thus, the pipe-fitter's wrench.

But right at this moment, there was no one. Not a soul in either direction. The hair stood up on the back of her neck and a chill crept across her skin. She turned from the entry and froze, unable to move.

The mannequins were dancing. The freestanding mannequins, the male in a classic three-piece, and the female in the latest design for feminine tuxedos (her father was nothing if not progressive) were doing a fast sort of waltz in the center of the store. The half-mannequins, which were mostly headless, swayed in time, and the featureless heads lining the ceiling featuring the "largest selection of black-tie millinery in the city" were humming along with their freakish, mouth-less faces.

Jem screamed and closed her eyes... the music stopped. She opened them again... and everything was still. She dashed to the counter and dropped the wrench on it, and reached to scoop up the phone... but a white hand fell onto it. The male mannequin stood before her, hand on the receiver, offering the silk boutonniere that had adorned his chest. She reached out and took it, very slowly. He bowed, a smile stretching across his plastic face, and resumed his position on the floor... and all was as it had been.

Jem took a deep breath and exhaled. She could see a Whitehall sales rep across the corridor. The bored kid at Cinnabon was back. The music had stopped. She reached down, pulled out her backpack and removed her homework. Sitting behind the counter, she began her calculus, and did not look up again until closing time.

The Usual

By Kylie Cokeley

"You have to get out of bed," he says to the tuft of brown hair sticking out from the mound of blankets. His hand slams down on the alarm for the fourth time that morning. "I know you're tired, but we can't be late again."

The mountain of blankets, consisting of a comforter, two fleece spreads, and a knitted throw, begins to erupt. What was previously used to help Kaycee's anxiety is now drowning her. *Why can't I breathe?* She attempts to tear her way out of her cocoon. Once free, she moves her heavy, slender body across the room to the bathroom, wearing just her frilly panties. Her plain underwear is more comfortable to sleep in, but she is a devoted believer that wearing something beautiful might convince her that she is, too.

Kaycee brushes her teeth and washes her face. She stares at herself in the mirror, her face still dripping wet. She lets the hot water run over her hands for a second longer. She dries her face and catches a glimpse of her body in the mirror. Despite being desperately thin, she tugs at the small pouch that sits on her lower belly. She squeezes it harder and watches it melt off her body and ooze through her fingers. He sees her dissecting her body in front of the mirror and kisses her forehead. He knows that nothing he can say will make her believe just how beautiful she is. She tries to hide the shame she feels for having been caught.

After she's dressed, Kaycee makes her way to the kitchen. He is already there packing a lunch for them both. A pang of guilt fills her heart, because she knows that most of it will end up hidden in the trash under her desk. She pulls a small orange Prozac bottle from the cupboard and dumps a pill into her small hand. The bottle lingers as she contemplates downing the rest of the bottle.

"Would you like a muffin for breakfast?" She snaps back to reality.

"No thank you. I'll get something from the vending machine at work," Kaycee lies. He knows that she is not being truthful, but doesn't push.

Once they arrive to work, she goes down one hall, and he goes down another. Kaycee's cubicle looks as though a neat tornado had hit, the perfect disaster of cluttered organization. The small desk is covered in perfect stacks of paper, three staplers, two coffee mugs, and four half-empty water bottles. She grabs one of her mugs and makes her way to the kitchen to fix herself a cup of tea before beginning work. She is really craving coffee this morning, but will not allow herself to drink the extra calories from her creamer.

From down the hall, Kaycee sees a coworker walking towards her. Her mind begins to race. Her fingernails trace her palm, digging harder the closer they get. Kaycee mind turns in an endless loop: Should she say "good morning" and smile, or just smile and nod? She knows that she should do something, but what if something goes wrong? What if she makes a fool of herself? *Say good morning. Say good morning. Good morning. Good morning! Shit.* Kaycee smiles slightly as the two pass each other and immediately diverts her eyes downwards, her palm burning. She opens her mouth to say something. Nothing but a little gasp escapes. In her attempt to avoid looking like a fool, she makes a jackass out of herself.

Why didn't I say good morning? I should've said good morning. I should've said good morning, she thinks at rapid speed. Her face burns with embarrassment and anger. As the day ticks by, she replays the moment in her head like a horror movie until it's time to get off work.

She makes her way to the exit, and sees him walking towards her. She worries that he will be upset that she took an extra five minutes to contain her mess back into their neat stacks.

"Sorry, I didn't realize what time it was. I'm sorry," she apologizes. He tells her that he can't handle her anymore and that he is moving out. She feels the tears swell in her eyes even though the conversation never happened.

"It's fine." He smiles and takes her hand.

Her first real smile of the day spreads across her face. Despite her anger with herself from earlier, she feels almost playful now.

"How was your day?" he asks on the drive home.

She pulls out the candy she hides in the glove compartment. She doesn't want to allow herself the sweets, but her stomach growls loudly, and her sweet tooth starts to ache. She tilts her head back and empties the box into her mouth. She struggles to reply. "The usual." They both laugh. If there was a chubby-bunnies competition, she would be the Muhammad Ali. The rest of the car ride home is in happy silence.

Kaycee looks around at their small apartment and is thankful for all the freedom she and her man have. She doesn't allow herself to take the credit, despite working her ass off for all they have. A tinge of guilt washes over her. If she has so much to be happy about, why does life feel so goddamn awful? She doesn't linger on the thought too long. She makes her way through their bedroom to the small bathroom. She turns on the water in the bathtub and waits for it to heat up before adding a heaping spoonful of bubble bath. As she strips the clothing off her fragile body, a comforting sigh of relief escapes her. She is glad that she can relax for even just a few minutes. Kaycee sinks down into the tub until just her head is poking out and lets the scalding water burn her. For a moment, as the bubbles pop against her skin, her mind is finally silent.

Thief in the Night

By T.J. Perkins

The night was warm and the air was still as Jena stealthily picked her way along in the dark. It was slow going through the dense forest, but she had to catch up with that owl.

"Ohh ,how stupid could I have been!" She silently chastised herself at her negligence for losing the key. *"Master will be furious when he finds out."* Well—*IF* he finds out. Jena wasn't about to give up yet. After all, the owl did fly through the magik dust from her latest concoction gone awry and this time the explosion paid off. She could still faintly make out the sparkling trail glistening along the bare treetops.

She bumbled along, pulling her long blonde hair and robes free as they snagged on branches, and then spied firelight flickering ahead. Odd. It wasn't there a moment ago. The sparkling trail stopped just over it.

A cheery fire burned brightly in the clearing and welcomed Jena's curiosity until a tall, slender woman with cascading dark hair streaked with white emerged from the dark.

"I was wondering when you were going to get here." She spoke without looking at the young apprentice; energy sizzled and crackled as she moved.

The sight of the sorceress made Jena's stomach ache, but she gathered her inner light and faced the powerful woman. "I've come for my key. Your owl stole it."

The owl flitted from tree to tree, watching them.

"*My* owl? Whatever do you mean?" She casually tossed a handful of herbs into the fire and flashed a sly smile as thick smoke rose and tiny sparks climbed their tendrils.

"The key," Jena pointed at the bird. "In its beak." And crossed her arms. "I would like it back, please."

With a simple flick of her wrists power emitted off the sorceress' hands. She turned to Jena and smiled wickedly. "Only if you can beat me in a game."

"That's not within the guidelines of The Witches Grimoire. My master will..."

"Ohhhh, your master is nothing more than a cheap street performer." She tsked and waved the comment away. "*I*, on the other hand, wield far more power than he ever could. Be *my* apprentice and you will learn to control the very fabric of the cosmos!"

"You cannot just *steal* an apprentice, you know. You have to battle for..."

"I've had more than my share of battles with your master!" Her eyes flashed an orange/red hue as she clenched her fists. "He will regret trying to put me in a watery grave."

Jena gasped with fear and sudden recognition. Isabella! Master had spoken of her only once and it wasn't out of a fond memory. Isabella was scheming and conniving and would use any trick she could to get back at him. How *did* she escape that lake imprisonment?

"Stay with him and continue to fail at your spells—like the Time Alerting spell. He won't tell you what you're doing wrong. You can just magikally spin your wheels... forever."

"Have you been stalking me?" Jena couldn't help but be defensive. After all, this sorceress was treading onto personal space.

"Heavens no, child, there's no need for that. Your aura tells it all." She smiled slyly and took a few steps closer. The owl glided by and dropped the key into her hand. "You want this, yes?"

"O... of course." Jena's stomach did flip-flops as the sorceress drew closer and she couldn't help but take a few steps back.

"Then let's play." Isabella hissed the words with so much evil delight that it made Jena's skin crawl. With the snap of her fingers a fireball appeared in the palm of her hand and she threw it at the young apprentice.

Jena called on the element of water and raised a layer of moisture from the earth, extinguishing the fireball instantly.

Roots then sprang from the earth and started to wrap themselves around Jena's legs. The young apprentice conjured a pocket of air that pried them away.

Shaking with rage, Isabella opened a rift in the air next to her. "You cannot beat me!" and added a powerful vortex. Bits of trees and leaves were sucked in—then it caught hold of Jena. "If you will not be my apprentice then no one will have you!" Jena clawed madly at the trees to stop the pull and silently asked the elements for assistance—no response. "Will you submit?"

"No!" Jena shouted over the building wind. She turned her head to see Isabella holding the key outward like a prize. She had to get it back or time would be at the sorceress' mercy. Wait a minute—that's it! Jena began muttering her Time Altering spell and this time she was hoping to botch it up—again.

The time warp appeared before the vortex and bent it—a perfect alteration of space-time. All she needed to do now was make it bigger. This would require the use of her hands, but to let go would compromise her safety. She paused. Oh, what the hell!

Keeping her concentration, Jena released her hold and swept her hands in a spiral, stretching the warp, and then used the force of the wind to shoot forward and snatch the key from the sorceress.

"Noooo!" Isabella reached out to grab hold of Jena, staggered, and compromised her position. The suction of the vortex latched on and she was instantly swept in. With an earsplitting crack the rift closed, the wind ceased and Jena came crashing to the ground, as the forest grew quiet.

Jena kept her eye on the owl as she sealed the spell, sighed with satisfaction and smoothed down her tangled hair.

"Well, let's see how she survives that," she said to the owl. "She'll be in limbo forever, never emerging fully into either world." The owl took flight and followed her into the woods as she made her way back to Master's cottage. "*Humph!* Street performer, indeed."

Thursday Death Rode Through Town

By Stephen Vallee

At about mid-morning, Delia Majors was getting ready to repair an electric socket in her garden gazebo. It had rained the night before, but she gave the wet conditions in her backyard little thought as she lugged out the aluminum step ladder and set it in place. Looking for firm footing, she positioned the ladder directly beneath the hanging socket. Apparently the amount of water on the concrete floor did not generate any concern. She made sure that the ladder was stable and climbed up to remove the old socket and install a new one. Death rode by.

At about the same time, Delia's neighbor brought her daughter out to the garden to get a little sun before the temperature got too hot and the sun's burning rays might hurt the baby girl. The little girl immediately started to toddle, crawl and try to run around in her new-found freedom. There was so much here to see, touch and taste. How very wonderful of her mommy to bring her outside to see and experience this great big world. Yet she was not the only one seeing. Over by the fence, coiled and staring at her with its forked tongue flicking was a large diamondback rattlesnake. Death rode by.

In McGivney's Machine shop, Dwayne Ammons was doing his damnedest to keep up with the production crew. Some of the guys on piecework were pushing and bitching to get the line moving ever so much faster. He had taken off the safety guard covering the saw blade in order to pull the cut stock out more quickly. He was preparing to remove another piece of cut stock by reaching over the blade to grab the end of the metal. Death rode by.

Further down the street, in a dirty, grimy apartment, a disheveled and haggard Emily sat and stared blankly at the needle. She knew that she had way too much heroin in the cylinder; she knew that this was an overdose. "So what," she thought, "who would give a damn if I were here or not?" Sitting quietly, she looked long and hard at the needle filled with her release from this place, this pain-filled and wretched existence. She started to tie a tourniquet around her upper arm. Death rode by.

Earlier that morning, death had ridden by the power plant just to the East of the town and stopped. Ronald Parker had been dozing in his comfortable chair at the control panel. Death reached out and touched his aortic aneurism. Ronald bled into his chest and quietly died, never regaining consciousness.

Because Ronald died quietly, there was no alarm. Others in the control booth had no clue that he was not watching the gauges on the control panel. No one saw the indictor needles climb into the red zones to indicate a severe malfunction. Not a one of the dead man's colleagues were witness to the imminent meltdown of the transformers until it was too late.

Three of the huge transformers blew out and cast the town into an almost medieval darkness. All electric power to the town immediately ceased. The explosion at the power plant gave rise to earthly vibrations throughout the area.

The electricity going off at that moment allowed Delia to change the socket safely. She felt not even a tickle as she performed her task. Death had no need to stop.

The slight tremors in the earth startled the rattlesnake and it recoiled, its attention taken from the toddler for the moment. It slithered away from the edge of the garden and into a hole for its own definition of safety. Death had no need to stop.

Dwayne's saw stopped dead in the middle of a cut and snapped the saw blade. He cursed and swore as he pulled the inert blade from the piece of steel stock he had been cutting. Now the piecework people would surely be mad at him for slowing down the line. But he did still have all his bodily parts and then he noticed that the entire machine shop was eerily quiet. Coming back to an immediate reality, he reattached the protective guard plate to the saw before a foreman came by to catch him for his lack of safety protocol and report him to the plant manager. Death had no need to stop.

Emily saw the light flicker and go out. She stopped what she was doing to look out the window to see if she could determine what had happened. Standing, she nudged the table and the syringe rolled off and broke upon hitting the floor. She realized that she could not afford more heroin; she fell to her knees and pitifully cried. Death had no need to stop.

Thursday, Death rode through the town and did not stop. People complained and griped about not having electricity to power their gadgets, toys and machines. Inconvenience and irritation were the order of the day until the repair crews at the power plant were able to get the new transformers in place and online to facilitate the surge of electrical power back to the town.

At the power plant, a shocked managerial drudge found Ronald's body and a later autopsy revealed Death's handiwork. For Death, there had been no need to stop while riding through the town; he had stopped once and, in doing so, rendered other stops in the town unnecessary, at least for this day.

Tiger Pee

By Jesse Weiner

Today is going to suck. I should be excited to go on a field trip, smiling and talking with my classmates. Instead, my Cocoa Puffs slosh around in my stomach. I turn toward the open window and take a deep breath.

Emilio's voice rises above the chatter. He's bragging about his new kicks, a pair of bright red Jordans. I know I shouldn't look, but I can't help it. My gaze slides from the sunflowers growing by the roadside to the seat a few rows ahead of me. Emilio's dark head leans across the aisle to whisper to one of his friends. They turn and point at me, laughing and elbowing each other.

I cross my arms and sink low in my seat.

"Hey." My best friend Lu bumps my side. "You owe me a Coke."

"No I don't."

She rolls her eyes. "I knew you couldn't make it the whole way there without looking at him."

I point to the sign arching over the roadway, the words 'Cheyenne Mountain Zoo' painted in big white letters. "But we *are* here." I push up my glasses and wiggle my mouth, stretching the too-tight bands crisscrossing my braces. "Besides, he's my mortal enemy. I can't let my guard down."

She flicks her long black hair over her shoulder and gives me a withering look. "How many times do I have to tell you? Boys only..."

"Shh!" I slap my hand over her mouth.

Lu glares at me.

I point at the girl across the way. She faces forward, smacking her gum and twirling her hair, but I know she's eavesdropping. "C'mon, Lu," I whisper. "Marcy's right there."

Emilio's ex. Well, one of them, anyway. But she's the most recent, and most likely to run to her friends and repeat Lu's crazy theory. The last thing I need is to have Marcy's little posse tormenting me, too.

Lu's nostrils flare, but in a few seconds she nods.

I release her, quickly changing the subject to smooth things over. "Where you wanna go first?"

She shrugs and pulls a tube of lip gloss from her pocket. "I promised Bree I'd chill with them today." She applies a shimmery, pale pink layer and looks to the back of the bus, where all the popular girls are seated.

My face heats and I turn away quick. "Whatever." I lift a shoulder and pretend the betrayal doesn't sting. "I wanted to draw, anyway."

I thought Lu had given up trying to hang with them. We spent the entire summer together, catching minnows in the creek and riding our bikes and playing practical jokes on her brothers. *What's her deal?* She said she didn't like those girls, anyway. I press a thumbnail into the seat back in front of me and wish Lu understood. She keeps telling me to ignore him, but there's only so much a girl can take. Emilio's been bullying me for the past *month*. Whether it's my frizzy hair or knobby knees, the book I'm reading or the clothes I'm wearing, he always finds a way to humiliate me. If anyone has the right to be mad, it's me.

The bus stops and everyone jumps up and files outside. I tuck my thumbs under the straps of my backpack and plot my escape. Without Lu by my side, I know Emilio won't wait to strike. It's social suicide to stick next to Miss Woods or one of the chaperones for safety. I tried that once, at the beginning of the year, and the other kids are still calling me a teacher's pet. The only option is to duck and run. Even though I'm the tallest one in the class, I've gotten pretty good at not being seen. So long as I get back in time to make it back on the bus, no one will notice I'm gone.

I'm outta there the second Miss Woods turns her head. The zoo hasn't officially opened yet, so I sneak past the guy at the ticket counter and crawl under the front gate, its silver arms sticking out like a sideways jack. A bright orange sign cheerfully points to the newest exhibit, Jong the tiger.

Sweat collects under my backpack as I hurry to the cage. I slip under the railing to sit cross-legged behind a bush. In a patch of dappled shade just a few feet away from the cage, I take out my notebook and wait.

The tall grass inside the exhibit sways in the wind. I squint, searching for the tiger. *There.* She's pacing at the opposite end of the enclosure, restless. I lay my pencil down, deciding Jong's too beautiful to attempt to draw.

Suddenly, Emilio's whiny voice pierces the quiet. The tiger lays her ears flat. I peek around the bush to see him arm in arm with Lu.

"Hey!" He shouts, picking up a pebble and throwing it at the tiger.

Her fur bristles and she growls.

Lu shrieks and ducks behind Emilio, laughing.

"I bet I can get her to come over here," Emilio brags. He picks up another stone.

I fist my hands and search for the courage to tell them off. *Do something*, my mind screams. Lu pauses to punch out a text, and that's when it hits me. They'll only get in trouble if I have proof. I pull out my phone and hit record.

The tiger stalks closer. Emilio hits her right between the eyes.

I open my mouth to yell at them, but Jong is quicker. She flicks up her tail, lifts her leg, and sprays them both.

Lu screams while Emilio gags and spits. I smile, slow and sweet.

Till It Happens To You

By Zoe Dabbs

It had not taken very long to sleep with her. She said little, just drank the drinks he bought her and put her hand on his knee. When it came time, she said she was on the pill, but nine months later, Jason was born.

A few years later, Jason was old enough to talk. He was old enough to go to school. His mother made him breakfast every morning and put his lunch bag in his hand before he tottered off to school underneath a backpack that was much too large.

While Jack dressed and shaved, she washed her son's dishes, then turned on her daytime soaps just in time for Jack to make himself some toast.

Jack came home every night approximately half an hour after her son did, and always toward the end of dinner.

This particular night, Jack smelled of cigars, the cheap ones passed out by a new father at work.

His wife wrinkled her nose and shook her head. He paused before turning and going into the bathroom to wash up. When he'd been to the bathroom, he came back to the table to sit down.

Hand on his chair, his wife turned to her child and in the sickly voice used on dogs and by mothers unaware of their child's age said:

"He's been a naughty boy. Naughty boys don't get dinner do they?"

Jack grasped the chair. He looked at his wife and her son. Jason had gone back to eating and she had begun fussing over his cowlick.

Jack released the chair and walked to the cupboard, and when he opened it, he found a Wonder Bread heel. That night he had an open-faced sandwich with no filling.

The next morning was Saturday. Saturdays were when Jack went fishing, brought a few trout back, and his wife cooked them for dinner.

He was there just long enough to catch the fish, nothing more, before he was on his way back to the house.

When he arrived, his wife was flipping through a magazine, cradling her son in her lap.

"Did you catch anything?"

"A big one."

She walked over to him and took the fish. "Fish night," she said.

That night, and every Saturday, Jack ate dinner with them.

He knew that she loved fish. That much he knew. When they were through eating, Jack cleaned up while his wife watched TV with her son.

As they had for years, the weeks came and went. Saturday was fish day for the family.

One Saturday, he woke up to find Jason sitting in his truck bed.

"Can I come with you?"

"No Jason, this is the time I take for myself." He had to think of some excuse.

"Plleease. Please? Mommy said I could yesterday. She said one day I could do it so you didn't have to anymore. See? I'm helping!"

Jack stared at the boy and knew that his resistance was pointless. He could only hope the little boy was useless, or would one day tire of it.

"Fine. Get in."

They drove in silence, and when they got there, Jack thrust the rod into Jason's hand without a word.

"How do I...?"

"You either know how to fish or you don't. It's like breathing."

The little boy looked down at the rod and then the river. Frowning, he turned, and walked down to the bank, taking strides too big for his body and reached the water just before Jack.

Jack threw his line in and did not look at Jason. Jack could not stay still, and fidgeted so much he scared off the fish. Again and again he re-sank his boots into the muck, trying to find the best stance. And just as he sank his boot into the mud again, he saw Jason's line sail into the water beside his own.

Jack slipped and fell smack in the muck, which was already soaking through his jeans. The boy let out a giggle.

"Can't you do that somewhere else? You're making too much noise! You're scaring the fish away!"

The boy jerked his head at the words and quickly ran down the bank, away from the man, accidentally catching his line on an overhanging branch.

Jack watched the boy struggle with his line for a while before trying to settle in. It seemed like hours before his breathing settled.

By the time Jack looked up, his breath no longer ragged, Jason was nowhere in sight. Jack thought about looking for him, but didn't.

Jack stayed there, and cast his line again. He did it over and over. The cast wasn't smooth. He jerked it, and slid in the muck every time he did.

The next time he looked up, Jason was striding toward him with a grin that could break a heart. The little boy began to run.

"Look! Look! Look what I caught!"

The boy was dragging an enormous fish. Jack's eyes opened like soup being poured into saucers.

"Look! Look!" The boy stood grinning up at the man with the slack face.

The boy continued to grin as he ran to the car, as he clutched the fish to his chest the whole ride home and even as he jumped onto the cracked cement of their driveway.

Jack watched the boy as he walked to the front door of his house.

His mother had been waiting for him and opened the door up before the little boy had wiped his feet on the mat. Jack was too far away to hear the exclamation, but the woman's face lit up as the little boy held his prize over his head for her to take.

He watched as she took the fish and kissed her son on the forehead, grabbing him into the crook of her arm.

Jack sighed and turned to make sure the truck was locked. When he turned back around, the little boy and his mother had gone, and the door was closed.

Time of Death

By Jeb Brack

Watchmaker Simon Klein examined the tall man's pocket watch with interest. It was a handsome, peculiar piece, as big as Simon's entire hand. Solid gold. Intricate scrollwork etched on the cover. The face and works were fascinating, frightening in their baroque detail.

"I could trust it to no one else," said the tall man. He was thin, balding, nattily dressed in a suit that seemed a tad out of fashion. He had a gap between his front teeth, and eyes that glittered when he smiled.

"How come?" Simon asked him. "Abraham Goldberg's up the street, he does good work."

The tall customer chuckled. "No, only you can help me. Take another look and you'll see what I mean."

Simon didn't want to look at the watch anymore, but he did anyway. It was the most detailed and complex he had ever seen. It had the usual hands to indicate hours, minutes, and seconds, but it also had dozens of other connected dials, faces, and hands. One showed the date, another the year. Others told locations by pointing to... Good God, did this thing actually have a dial with a world map?

"Mister," he told the tall man, "Fifty years now I've fixed watches. Most watches, the customer waits for it less than an hour. But," he held the pocket watch back over the counter. "This watch I can't fix in less than three weeks."

"Do you have that much work keeping you busy?"

Simon shook his head. Hardly anybody came by the shop anymore. "It would take me that long just to figure out how it works."

The tall man did not take the watch. "Simon, I know you can do it," he said. "The thing is simply running a little slow. Open it up and you'll recognize the workings."

His smile was persuasive, even to such a stubborn man as Simon Klein.

Delicately, Simon removed the cover of the watch and peered into the workings. They were complicated beyond anything Simon had ever seen. The tiniest cogs. Infinitesimal wheels and gears. Hundreds, thousands of them. Awed by such intricacy, he opened his mouth to say no.

The tall man grinned now. Softly, but with conviction he said, "You know what to do, Simon."

And Simon did. He bent to work, removing mechanisms to reach the ones measuring the seconds and minutes. Such complexity! Here were the gears that controlled the world map he had noticed, and this mechanism ticked off... what?

Simon glanced at the watch face and shuddered. The unknown machinery counted off names. With the workings in the proper order, names would show themselves briefly in a small window on the face, before clicking out of sight. Furthermore, the watch would never display the same name twice.

He looked up at his customer, who still smiled, oblivious to Simon's dread. "Not as hard as you thought, is it?"

Simon Klein heard his voice quaver as he asked, "Who are you, Mister? What's this watch for?"

The man laughed, a sound like wind through a sunny cemetery. "Why, for telling time, Simon," he said. "Please do finish."

Automatically, Simon's hands pieced the works back together. "Mister, this watch is not just for telling time." The watch fit together with precision, only a few cogs left now.

"You're quite right, Simon."

"Then what does it do?" The shop seemed darker than normal. "Mister, are you... Satan?"

"Oh good heavens, no! This watch merely tells the time." He smiled again, but Simon was not reassured. "The time of death, Simon."

Simon's able hands faltered a little; he nearly dropped the man's watch. "You mean that this watch tells when people die?"

"Yes, that's right."

"But why do you have a watch like that?"

"So I can be on time, of course."

"For...?"

"Their deaths. So I can collect them. Then I escort them on their journey... wherever."

Simon's hands trembled hard now as he replaced the cover. "Then why did you say that only I could help you?"

"Set the watch to the proper time, Simon."

Reassembled, the watch was handsome and frightening as before, but now Simon understood the words and symbols on the face. He wound the knob at its top until the time was correct, the date today's. The location was the address of the shop, but Simon had eyes only for his own name, which clicked into view on the dial.

"You understand why I brought my watch to you? It's your time now, Simon," said the tall man, and rose from the stool where he had waited. He no longer smiled. "We'll step outside, and you will be struck and killed by a runaway bus. Don't worry..."

"Easy for you to say."

The tall man ignored the interruption. "Don't worry, you won't feel a thing. I promise." He held out his hand for the watch, then pocketed it and motioned toward the door. Simon stepped out, the tall man following.

Nothing happened.

The tall man frowned and reached into his pocket for the watch. "I could have sworn..."

He was interrupted, more forcefully this time, by the cross-town bus that jumped the curb, missed Simon Klein by inches, and flattened the tall man against the storefront. A storm of rubble clattered from the ruined shop. Dazed passengers and passersby formed a crowd on the sidewalk. The cops were not long in coming.

Simon stood rooted in place, his heart beating madly. At his feet glittered the tall man's pocket watch, dropped in the split second before impact. Simon picked it up. The dials, which still displayed his name, were not moving.

Simon stared at the watch a moment longer. Then he pressed the knob at the top of the watch. With a small click, the dials began to move. Simon's name passed from view. A thought occurred to Simon and he consulted his own watch. The tall man's watch was a minute slow. He set it once again to the proper time. The name dial remained empty.

Simon stopped the watch.

The Beautiful Child

By James H. Metaphor

Hair black as coal, skin white as snow, lips red as blood, that's what her mother wished for, upon discovering she was pregnant with Snow White. When she was born everyone agreed she was the most beautiful child they'd ever known. As she grew, her beauty became even more evident, people finding it ever harder to refuse her. Whatever she wanted, whatever she asked for, people around her were desperate to comply.

By the time she reached fifteen, she could have anything she wanted—or anyone—with but a look; she loved it. She moved through life with a cloud of people in her wake, just wanting to be near her, and she used them, like most popular teenagers use people who want their attention—carrying her things, buying her whatever she desired, attending to any need she had. Regardless of how badly she treated them or how awful her personality was, everyone thought she was wonderful.

She might have lived her whole life happily sponging off her fellow townsfolk and bathing in their praise, but for the fact that she learned a prince would be visiting her town. Upon hearing this, her mind was filled with covetous thoughts of being a princess and having vast riches to spend on whatever she wanted. She was so used to getting whatever she craved that she believed she deserved those things and that the prince would give them to her.

It was easy to arrange a grand ball to be thrown for the prince, for as soon as she suggested it, her followers rushed to fulfil her wish. The town hall was decorated and filled with food, drinks and music, ready for the prince, and a messenger ran to invite him to the ball, thrilling him with the idea.

That night, everyone who was able to attend filled the town hall, eager to dance with Snow White. Man, woman or child, all wanted to be beside her, simply to gaze upon her, but she pushed them away, darting through the crowds as she searched for the prince. Finally, he arrived and she rushed to the doors as whispers reached her of his entrance. She gazed upon him, frowning for he was not as handsome as she had expected, but she cared not, only wanting his crown and knowing that she could use her beauty to convince him to marry her and let her bed whomever she chose, without complaint. She had spent years maintaining relationships with multiple partners, and none of them minded having to share her.

Snow saw his face light up the instant he lay eyes on her and knew she had him. She acted coy, letting him dart forward to greet her, and feigned reluctance when he asked to dance. He persisted and she let him wrap his arms around her, discovering the smell of sweat upon him and his bad breath. She felt actual reluctance at that point, but he held her tight and the music was loud, so she had no choice but to let him drag her through the crowds, staring in adoration at her. That was enough to please her, in spite of the disappointment of a prince who was clutching her.

As the dance ended and she clawed free of his grasp, the prince dropped to one knee and snatched up her hand, lighting her face up with relief. She knew her struggle had been worth the effort, as the prince declared that he was madly in love with her. She was used to proposals, having received them regularly from various admirers of every possible appearance, but this was the first that she deigned to take seriously and a genuine smile filled her face as she accepted. The crowds around her seemed both happy and sad as they clapped, pleased for Snow, but afraid that they might not see her again if she was whisked away. All Snow could think of was the crown she would wear.

As the ball finished, the prince took Snow into his carriage, wanting her to accompany him back to the palace immediately. She filled the days of travel with vain talk about herself, as always. The prince clung to her every word, too smitten to care what she said, so long as he had her all to himself to listen to.

They reached the palace at last, and the prince led her inside, breaking her commentary to explain that he must introduce her to the queen, for only she had the power to allow them to marry, but he promised that she would be just as enthralled by Snow as he was, for who could fail to love one such as she.

Upon entering the queen's chambers, Snow paused to ask the prince why it was so dark, and he replied simply that the queen was blind, but the people did not know, so that she would remain strong in their minds. Snow didn't think, after so long with everyone loving her—until she was before the queen and facing questions she had never had to deal with before—that being blind would be a problem. It was only when the queen declared that this petulant, vain, brat was unfit to marry her son, that she realised the problem. The guards came at the queen's call, though the prince argued, but one look at Snow stopped them in their tracks. Snow realised that the queen was the only obstacle left, so ordered the queen's death. As the guards rushed to obey her, the queen lunged forward, scratching at Snow's face with her nails. By the time the guards struck her down, she had undone Snow's beauty without knowing what she had done. The prince took one look and cried out in horror, no longer mesmerized. He ordered her locked away for his mother's death and the guards obeyed, ignoring her demands and pleas as they threw her into the dungeon to rot, as a fitting punishment for her greed.

Very Specific Tastes

By Bert Edens

Mitch had just closed his eyes when the moaning started from the adjacent tent. He bolted upright, face flushed.

"Again? Damn it, don't they ever sleep?"

"Lay back down, honey," Jenny whispered. "They're entitled to a good time."

"Oh yeah, we have to whisper while they make enough racket to give the wildlife heart attacks." Rolling onto his knees, Mitch peeked through the mesh of their doorway. The top of the offending tent wobbled back and forth, only further irritating him.

"It's almost three in the morning," he growled, looking at his watch. "This is the third time tonight. They need a new hobby." Mitch plopped back down on his backside, barely missing Jenny's foot. "This is ridiculous."

After yawning and stretching, Jenny propped herself up on an elbow. "You're just jealous because you can't make me scream like she does." A wink was meant to soften the jab, but it only served to heighten Mitch's aggravation.

"Oh yeah, thanks a lot, bitch." He picked up a pillow and clutched it tightly, staring at her. The feigned threat only made Jenny giggle, not helping Mitch's mood at all.

"I should go over and tell them to shut the hell up," Mitch said, still flexing the pillow in his hands. "They have no consideration at all for others."

Jenny figured that as long as he was pissed off, she might as well get all the mileage she could out of it. "Yeah, well make sure you take a notebook, in case he gives lessons. Can't hurt, that's for sure."

"What's that supposed to mean, huh?" He threw the pillow at her, but it bounced harmlessly off her shoulder. "Don't I make you happy?"

She sniggered. "You make you happy, that's for sure. You pound away until you're done, then roll over and go to sleep. I'm left to finish up with my faithful Magic Wand." Jenny looked away. "Not that you would notice or care."

Mitch stared at her, palms up, genuine surprise covering his face. "Fourteen months together, and now you tell me? Why didn't you say something before?"

"I have very…" Jenny paused, searching for the right words. "I have very specific tastes. Ones you have never bothered to ask about." A glare darkened. "You just think a cock, and not even a big one I might add, is all a woman needs. You're so concerned about busting a nut, that's all."

"Oh, don't you even think I'm going to get my mouth down there. That's fucking nasty," Mitch said while flapping his hands at her. "Not a chance."

"But it's okay if I suck you off when you want it, isn't it? I promise you, he's over there licking her into oblivion." When Mitch didn't say anything else, Jenny turned her back to him. "Never mind. Just lay back down."

As Mitch began to get settled, a loud squeal emanated from their neighbors' tent, followed by an enthusiastic, "Oh fuck! Yes!" Unable to handle being embarrassed further, Mitch reached under his pillow, grabbed the hatchet he kept to protect them from animals, and tore out the entrance of their tent, stomping toward their neighbors.

"Mitch, wait!" Jenny called after him, but he either didn't hear her or ignored her. Soon after he plowed his way into the adjacent tent, Jenny heard a combination of screams, hard thumps, and sounds that reminded her of the comedian Gallagher smashing watermelons on stage. After a couple of minutes, silence.

Jenny heard Mitch's shuffled footsteps and heavy breathing before she saw him. He ducked into the tent and had barely stood up again before Jenny was kneeling before him, stripping his shorts off. She began taking care of him, and he responded quickly.

Soon Jenny guided him down to the sleeping bags, where she straddled him and continued taking control of the situation. Mitch closed his eyes, enjoying having her do the work for a change.

Lifting the hatchet from where Mitch had dropped it, Jenny wiped the blood from it across her breasts. Then she raised it high above her head, smiled, and helped Mitch finally understand her very specific tastes.

Well You Know, Maybe It Was

By Melissa Gale

"Well you know, maybe it was," she says, shifting uncomfortably in the wire café chair.

Sitting outside in the back patio area of a well-known coffee joint for their first "date" felt safer before, when she first set up the meeting. Publicly reluctant, despite the visible loudness of her red hair, Carlie wasn't used to dating someone so openly opinionated. All of Joseph's reviews were positive (with the exception of that one) so she thought she'd give him a try, and hey, isn't that what this is supposed to do? Help her grow and push through some social and personal barriers?

"Yeah?" Joseph asks. "Well, I doubt that." He leans back and takes a sip of his coffee, smirking at the nearby table of trendy 20-somethings.

Strong and black. Carlie thinks. *Just like him.* She takes a moment to inspect him while his thoughts are elsewhere. *Is he black? Is that even politically correct anymore?* Skin tone aside, his height and athletic build added to her belief that he'd be quite popular in his trade. And those eyes—stunningly green like Rhianna's. *What was her nationality again?*

"Hey, you're not drinking your latte." Joseph points at her cup. An oversized, artistically painted behemoth that seemed to be the staple of every trendy coffee shop in Seattle. "Correct me if I'm wrong, but your profile said that a grande latte with 2 raw sugars was your favorite."

Aware he has caught her staring, Carlie quickly looks down at her cup. "You're not wrong. It did and it is." She spins her coffee cup with her fingertips, not able to look up at him. "I've just never done this before, and I'm not really sure what I'm supposed to say or do with you."

"Look." Joseph says quietly, gently placing his hand over hers. "We don't have to do anything you don't want to. The whole point of this is to allow you the safety to try new things, socially, sexually, or otherwise, with someone who's experienced and able to help navigate you through it. Think of me as your 'guide,' okay? And no pressure from me." He squeezes her hand, finding her eyes. "I'm yours however, and whenever, you want me." Removing his hand to take another sip of coffee he says, "If spinning coffee in that garish monstrosity while I drink mine is what you want to do, that's just fine with me."

Carlie looks up at Joseph and sees his eyes sparkle as a playful smile slips across his face. It takes him only one step to move beside her. Holding out his hands, he gives her his most trustworthy look and waits. Her eyebrows knit together as she tentatively reaches out and places her hands in his. She feels a sharp tug as she's swept up into his embrace. Joseph holds her tightly with one arm, and with the other brushes her hair back and softly kisses her neck. The warmth from his mouth quickly spreads goosebumps across her shoulders. "And unquestionably a waste of my special talents." Joseph breathes into the back of her ear. "Just tell me what you want me to do."

"I, um, you..." Carlie stammers, unable to catch her breath. She realizes her fingers are digging into his biceps and forces herself to loosen her grip.

Joseph smiles at her and skillfully places her back in her seat, slipping his arm from around her waist and gently kissing her on the forehead. Carlie looks around the café and seizes her coffee. Her cheeks burn and her eyes dart from one table to the next. "I, um..." she stammers.

Joseph laughs then. A full-throated laugh. If people weren't looking at her before, they sure are now. "C'mon," he says as his laugh settles into his chest, shaking it now and then. "I promise I'm not scary. 'Always a gentleman.' Right? That's the promise we make when we sign on with the agency. I was recruited because of my... talents... but part of the gig is to gently guide and encourage you to try new things. And besides," Joseph caresses the handle of his coffee cup. "I like my job and I'm not about to do anything to mess it up."

What If...

By Aimie S. Randall

She woke to October 5, the day of What If. "IF" is a destructive word. It is not so much a word, but a place, a place buried deep in a heart full of lost and broken promises. A life could be lost in that place.

What If started with his smile, pure glee after a sheepish proposal that came with the tiny diamond teenagers can afford. It's the diamond that sparkles with the dim light of a star long dead, dreams that could never survive the truths of adulthood.

But his smile... it was so pure, it was the way she imagined her own son would someday grin across the table over pancakes hot off the griddle. There could never be another boy whose smile would sparkle with joy. Only this boy, the boy lost in What If.

For her What If was danger, but for him it was life. It passed in front of him the first time he saw her and suddenly he wished for more. He wished he was taller. He wished he was thinner. He wished he was... more. He lived for more. He chased her, but he didn't understand the game. She was the flag-bearer for a life he could not have. She ran across the court with promises of happiness, children, golden retrievers and picket fences. Her flag was the storied American Dream, and though he chased her, he really only wanted the promise. Carrying the flag was never his intent.

She was his biggest lie, a lie to his family and his friends and most of all to himself. He had no use for her, only the promises she bore. When he first saw her walking, his heart pounded. She wore heels with a skirt that showed her legs. Her legs looked older, like a cheerleader, so he had expected to see the face of one of his sister's friends. She was new and beautiful. Her lips smiled kindly, but her eyes were haughty, clinging to innocence so skittish that he could almost watch it flee. He wanted to know her now, while she was yet a child. And he wanted to understand her later, when she would be a woman. She scared him, but he was drawn to her, so he ran after her.

He asked to carry her books and she laughed. The laughing made him angry, but the sound of it made him breathless. She said that she didn't think he could handle it and he wished he were stronger. He wished he were more. She was elusive. Suddenly this boy was on his first hunt.

He hunted, she ran. She found stronger, taller, thinner boys and she loved them. The last of the innocence left her and she was a cheerleader, showing strong, haughty legs that matched her eyes. She changed and he learned. He watched her grow and he grew into her.

Finally, broken by a Taller Boy, she came to him. The innocence was back... it had pushed the haughtiness from her eyes and he recognized that girl he had met, the girl who had become prey. The Taller Boy was gone and for the first time, he stopped wishing. This wasn't What If anymore for him. It was finally What Is, and he knew who she was. He reminded her of the girl he met, the one just learning to be a woman. He reminded her of the chase, the distances they had gone and lives they had lived. He was part of her history and she discovered that her heart wasn't broken over the Taller Boy. Her heart was broken because she couldn't be alive without this boy by her side, this boy who wished.

His hunt was victorious, so he came to her with a ring. It was a tiny ring tucked into the back of a Matchbox car, their dream car. He promised to make her dreams come true. She couldn't say no to the smile. She couldn't say no to their dreams.

But dreams can't be shared. It may seem so, but a dream comes from the place in the heart that lies next to What If. Dreams are the soul's fingerprints, a dusty reminder that the soul exists alone. And while they look the same at first glance, no two really are. They hoped for the same car and the same picket fence, but up close it still looked different. She wanted him. She wanted a son who smiled like he did. She wanted to leave and return to this home they built on a love they found when they were still children.

He wanted normal. He wanted to belong. He thought she was his missing piece, but it was really the feeling of having the most beautiful girl in the room. When he wasn't in the room anymore, it felt different. It was something he wouldn't admit, not even to himself, so he chose to be lonely.

The Taller Boy didn't break her, but he broke him. He was broken every time he saw the two of them together and in the distractions of daylight he could say that it was because he feared losing her. But alone, in the night, the part of him that wished for more screamed the truth at him. He was broken by the Taller Boy because he bore an unbearable truth.

She knew he was distant. She knew that she loved him more. After years of running, she didn't understand, but she was lost in him and he had gotten lost somewhere else.

So she walked away before she could be exiled. She turned her back on the son they would never have and the picket fence with no home.

To her, he became the What If, an unwelcome visitor in the wee hours. A danger to What Is. To him, she was the What If, a reminder of a life simple in its construction, but only as big as he could build it. What Is.

The Weight of Glass

By M. K. Martin

"Is that him?"

Ned's voice is in my ear, whispering into my soul. He's always with me like a shoulder devil. I adjust the clear nuplex straps of my off-the-shoulder robe. This season the clothes are bright hues and large prints. Below the balcony where I stand, a sea of partygoers washes back and forth each a single color is like lonely petals of crumbled roses. Across the ceiling, ropes of sparkling lights pretend to be stars, but no one's looking up.

Soon there will be the toast. "To the bride and groom." And then the speeches, the dancing, the flock of children with their fat little faces squished into an expression somewhere between seriousness and bewilderment. They don't want to be here anymore than I do.

But I have a job to do. I have a purpose in life.

An artificial person passes, collecting drinks. This AP is a female model with proportions belched from the darkest part of the primitive male brain, the part that loves fire and blood and sex, the part that no one here is allowed to meddle with. Here we are civilized people. We are the pillars of society, paragons of civic virtue.

And yet.

I hold out my glass, perfectly balanced on my fingers. My pinky hovers. Today the polish is the blue-green of the sea with an iridescent topcoat. I watch my hand as if it belongs to someone else. It moves so gracefully, languid. A refined hand, free of scars, blemishes. Pale as cherry blossom moonlight.

The AP slides her (its?) tray under my outstretched glass. The pressure is calculated precisely - just enough for me to know it's there, not enough to jar the glass. All I have to do is let go.

I look into the eyes of the Mark before me. I try to anyway. He's engaged with the cleavage spilling from the front of my blue-green top. Unlike the pretty petal people below, my robe is tight in front. The skirt is short and loose, freeing my legs. My robe has gold braid and buttons, giving it a military appearance. It goes with the black ankle boots. Dressy, but they don't violate our first rule about clothes - never wear clothes that prevent you from escaping.

In my ear, Ned asks again, "Is that the Mark?"

I turn my head and see the AP out of the corner of my eye. Her face is frozen in a bland smile, lips slightly parted, submissive. She registers that I'm looking at her and blinks twice, resetting as she meets my gaze.

"How else can I be of service?"

I can't even resent the sexy-baby voice. The AP no more wants to have that voice than I want to be here, holding the Mark's life in my hand in the form of an unreleased cocktail glass. The muddled liquor distorts the goji berries staked through the glass like beaded blood.

"You ever see an AP like this? So life-like nowadays," the Mark says.

Aren't we all?

The weight of a life, so small I can hold it on two fingertips. And yet the glass seems infinitely heavy. It chimes against the other glasses on the AP's tray as I release it.

"That's my girl," Ned's voice carries his smile to my ears, the implant making it sound as if he's standing right behind me. Ned has been looking over my shoulder since my first day at the Finishing School.

"I'm an adult." I'm annoyed with Ned's patronizing paternal tone and I speak aloud.

"Don't I know it?" The Mark smiles. If his gaze were getting customer loyalty points at My Tits, he'd be platinum class. "Why don't we-"

The AP reaches out and stiff-arms him in the chest. She moves so fast it creates a wind around me. For a second, I think that creak is thunder, but it's the Mark's sternum.

The AP's next blow snaps his head back. I know his neck is broken before he does. He doesn't feel any pain. He's dead before he hits the floor.

Behind him a woman screams, waves her hands uselessly at her face. Her nails are so long and manicured she dare not touch herself.

I mimic her panic. It's hard for me to have the right emotions, but I'm good at follow-the-leader. Ned taught me the art of blending in.

Several of the guests join our cacophony. Some rush forward, eager to get a look. Others flee, driven by that instinct to avoid violent actors.

I don't wait to see what happens to the AP.

I thread the crowd, tracking the faces, the lessening levels of panic as I make my way out of the ripple caused by one dropped cocktail glass.

By the time I exit the Grand Pah Nangha Hotel I look like the calm, bored socialite that I am supposed to be. I lift a hand, wrist back as I hail a cab. Of course there's no driver. No one wants to go back to the bad old days when you might have to talk to a laborer en route from here to there.

Still, as I step into the cab, I wonder how easy it might be for someone like Ned to find a hacker to break open the cab's code and turn it against its passenger.

I wonder if the AP apologized to the Mark. They're programed to simulate remorse when they make a mistake or are confused.

I imagine her symmetrical face, large eyes with just enough fold to still be attractive, her pliantly parted lips as she breathes, "Oh, I'm terribly sorry. Whatever can I do to make amends?"

I wonder if she knows she's about to be erased. Some of them are programmed for self-preservation.

I wonder if Ned understands we killed not one, but two tonight.

See That You Remember

By Jesse Bradley

The man with chainsaws for arms waits for a date outside a pizza place. The town is used to the man since he grew up there. Any stares come from children, or people who aren't from around here.

How did it happen, the man's date asks, points at his arms. He pecks at the pizza, waiting for a better question.

The Blood of Kings

By Jason Brick

Grandfather didn't join the revolt against the Immortal Emperor because he thought he could outrun the tyrant's wrath.

He figured if he ran enough farther and enough faster than all the other rebels, he might just die of old age before He Who Shall Not Be Mocked got around to him.

It worked, too. Grandfather died in his sleep, wealthy and comfortable, king of an island nation out in the Blood Sea. But he got stupid, fell in love, and fathered three kids. Two of them died outright when Old Boneshaver's eye fell upon our island. The third had already gotten stupid his ownself.

So here I am, mucking out scorpion shit in the sewers beneath the Caves of Torment. Nothing but the cleanest possible tortures for those who displease His Magnum Excellency. Like I've been doing since my fourteenth birthday, and they tell me I will be doing until at the very least the day of my natural death.

But I have a plan of my own, one that doesn't mean running. I stole the idea from the mind of a rebel alchemist, using a spell Gran taught me back in the bright years on the island.

A careful enough person can distill a potent toxin out of scorpion shit. A patient enough person can wait for the distillation to dry into a powder. A lucky enough person can carry it on His Royal Skullfucker's annual visit to taunt and tease his prisoners.

And a quick enough person could use it to put an end to this "Immortal" horsecrap with an opening hand and a strong outward breath.

I don't know if it will work, but I know I have to try.

You see, I got stupid, too, and my daughters can't spend their lives shoveling scorpion shit for the wrinkled giggles of a thousand-year-old stain on the undershorts of the world.

They need to live free.

After all, they have the blood of a king in their veins.

Abaddon

By Andrew Hiller

Radle grabbed my shoulder. The shadows jerked. I turned, rubbing against the rough wall. Glints of quartz and pyrite shimmered. The fool's treasure threatened to cut me. Still, my bony companion pulled at me, forcing me to bend down, to study the ground. My eyes widened. Our lantern revealed pictographs etched on the floor. An arrow, a sun circle split in half, and a man standing above all.

"Abaddon," Radle whispered, recognizing one of the symbols.

I nodded.

My fingers traced the notches chipped into the rock. The surfaces were old, smooth, eroded. Radle shifted position to get an even better look. His movement rippled in soft chamber echoes.

"Could be a false trail," I warned. Radle shook his head and whispered "Abaddon" again.

Abaddon. Sword breaker. City splitter. The blade no man or army could stand against. Could it truly be near? The greatest of all the legendary swords? I took a deep breath and blew dust from the floor, willing more carvings to emerge from beneath the dust.

Could we be lucky enough? Now, when the need was greatest, when the armies of Sythros rampaged across the land, when their foul beasts clawed and bit. I shook my head and tried to still my thoughts.

"I get to wield it first," Radle announced, making a fierce gesture, a stab with an imaginary blade. I caught his grin. It pulled at my own lips. Ten years of hunting through libraries, listening to old stories told by toothless beggars, and debasing ourselves had led to this cave. A cave that held long-forgotten writing. A scrawl of cursive and pictograms that belonged to a nobler time.

"Abaddon," I said, aiming the lantern into the darkness. Radle trotted down the passage. Pebbles skittered in his wake, scrambling mice on a ceiling.

I moved slower. I counted the runes, the pictographs, and even the barely visible scratches of a misaimed chisel.

We pursued the greatest weapon in history by squirming down channels, slithering down holes, and leaping across breaks in the rock. As we got deeper into the cave, the floor became more and more sculpted. Eight hours in, a distance no sane man would travel alone without a pick and the smell of riches to spur him, the walls became smooth. Our fingers traced filigrees of gold hammered into the wall. Faces drawn in relief. Faces familiar to every boy of our nation.

Abaddon.

Then, our fingers found wood. The lantern guttered. Radle searched for extra oil. My knife probed the wood and I pried. It took two of us. So mighty were the builders who sealed Abaddon in.

There it rested. Not in a skeleton's hand or wrapped in snakes, or some foul curse, but lying plain on a frayed blanket. Even faded, the material looked like something of wealth. Seven colors wove in and out. Silver stitching drew pictographs of broken men, shattered swords, felled demons and one hero atop all of them.

I knew no doubt.

I nodded at Radle to take it. To wield it first.

He backed away. His courage stolen.

"What if I'm not worthy? What if it strikes me down?"

Shadows crisscrossed his face. My own fingers trembled. My breath shivered like candle flame.

"Me then?" I asked. Radle nodded.

How strange for a scholar to be the first person in three hundred years to bear Abaddon. Me, a man whose toughest duel was against mosquitos and rice. Whose callouses came from pushing a pen, not swinging a sword. To say that I was not worthy would be to say that the sun rose in the morning.

I waited, but it only made Radle retreat. When he stood at the edge of our light's halo, he stopped.

"Feather and spit!" I swore and reached down.

I closed my eyes, prepared for a poison dart to claim me, lightning to hail down, or the sword itself to rouse and cut me. My knees pressed at the wood of the box as I bent lower. Then, my hand closed around the hilt. It felt worn... smooth. Any leather around the grip had worn away or been stripped, but it felt good in my hand.

Warm.

Could I be a better man than I supposed?

When I pulled it upright Radle fell to his knees.

Then, my heart broke. Abaddon, the invincible sword, had flecks of red against its edge. I put it down on the wooden edge of its cradle and drew the lantern closer.

Of course, I thought, and sighed.

In the days of Abaddon, this sword would have been the mightiest of all. It would easily chop swords in half and none could stand against it. It was an iron sword in a bronze era. That made it seem magical, but it was only a smith-forged blade... though, in fairness, probably the first of its kind.

I shook my head at Radle.

He advanced, but I put my hand out to stop him.

"False trail," I lied. How could I kill hope?

A rusted Abaddon in an age of steel swords and pikes would fare as poorly as bronze had against its greatness. To reveal Abaddon was to destroy all hope and kill our nation.

Gently, I put the sword back and covered it with the blanket, then set the wood over it and found a rock to jam the pieces closed again.

"Come," I said, pointing towards the exit. "We must still hunt."

Radle looked back, but he followed.

Life from Life

By Shreyasi Majumdar

It was tiny. Miniscule. Barely visible to the naked eye. None save itself knew of its existence. Few cared to ponder. And yet, amidst their ignorance and the cares of the world outside, somehow, by some strange magic, it had come into existence—a tiny sentient being pulsing with life, small and beautiful. It did not know where it came from. It did not know who its mother and father were. Indeed, it did not know what a mother and father were. Was it male or female? What about siblings? Did it have any brothers or sisters that might tie it to them by some strange invisible bond of affection? It had no knowledge of family and the bonds that ensue. It just knew that it WAS, as it lay there, asleep under the vast cover above. It did have some memory of reaching its current resting place. Not really thoughts, but images, blurred and shaky—visions in the deep recesses of its mind. It remembered a funny sensation, half of itself was floating... or being carried. Strange buzzing and flapping sounds, tremulous movements up and down, oscillations from one side to another, and finally the sensation of freefalling. That was its strongest—no—its only memory of life before now.

When it awoke again, it was here. The place was moist, strangely to its liking. It was filled with a sense of nurture and nourishment as it lay between its two guardian angels on either side. They were growing with it and they had said that their only job was to make sure it ate well and was healthy and became strong enough to be independent. The three of them spent many hours together in the isolation of their home under the 'mother sheet,' as they called it. It became stronger as the days rolled on and the urge to break out of itself became greater. Not yet, its two friends said. Wait till you are more robust, more resilient. You will need it when you meet the outside world head on, they advised. So it waited. And waited some more. One day it turned to them and asked anxiously, "Can I break free of this cage now? I need something badly, something warm and bright, but I don't know what it is."

Strangely, no sound came to it in reply. Its friends lay beside it, silent and unmoving—almost like their duty was over—the time had come for it to move on. It took this to be a sign of assent and began its journey. Part of it dug deeper into the mother sheet while the other part strained against its outer shell to find a breach, an opening that it could stretch out from. Somehow it knew what it had to do. All the knowledge of its life and the lives before it were within its tiny form. Somehow it knew of the warmth it needed. Somehow it knew that it would grow and creep and anchor itself in every available bit of mother sheet that it found along the way. Somehow it knew what its brood would look like and it knew that it would continue to have children for seven or eight years at least. It suddenly felt happy. A strange vibrant vigor filled its being. It pushed harder as memories of humans and its past offspring welled up inside it.

Humans. It knew what they were and how much they loved its kind. It remembered a time when its offspring were so precious, humans traded them as currency. They were worth their weight in the most precious of human possessions – gold. The mother sheet was beginning to thin out over its head. Just a little bit further, it thought, aching to see the outside world, wondering how much things had changed since its last lifetime here. Had humans changed with the world too? No, it could not be. Not much time had elapsed since its last existence. Did the trade in its offspring still flourish? Did they still bargain over its babies' prices? Was its essence as much in demand as it had been when it was here last? How funny, it thought. Humans desired its progeny so much and how little it needed humans for its survival. Yes, survival was key. Survival was foremost in its mind. Survival was what life was all about.

It pushed harder as the jumble of frenzied thoughts ran through its mind. A gazillion emotions and memories raged through its being. One last thrust and a crack appeared in the mother sheet. With ecstasy oozing from every pore, the little peppercorn plant pushed its head out of the soil, felt the first breeze on its skin, opened its arms wide and reached out towards the sun.

Write of Passage

By Jenny Cokeley

I could only reach the ranch by following an endless maze of dirt roads that cut through the high desert. Getting there was a four-hour drive from home and I had lost radio reception two hours back. I found Poison's Greatest Hits crammed in my glovebox and Bret Michaels rode shotgun the rest of the way. By the time we belted out *Every Rose Has its Thorn* for the fourth time, the caravan of eager writers I followed idled in front of the locked gate that separated the ranch from the rest of the desert.

The pungent smell of sagebrush seeped through the car vents, punched me in the face, and knocked me back to 1988 for a split second. I was no longer the woman with her shit together following a caravan through Central Oregon. I was a sixteen-year-old girl in the middle of the Mojave Desert. After the sheriff knocked on our door and locked us out of the house, we left California and drove to Oregon. A trip that should have taken two days at the most had taken six. Six days of sleeping at rest stops and empty campgrounds in December. *Every Rose Has its Thorn* played every half hour on the radio while my parents screamed at each other. I had thought about California over the past twenty-something years. I had even talked about it a few times, but it was like giving a book report. My body never told the story.

Five miles from the gate, ten writers who were each paying $600 to be creative for the weekend piled out of their cars and stood in front of the ranch house. Even if they called it a ranch, it was really just the desert. And this was really just a small house without air conditioning in the middle of August.

Our writing instructor, Helena, invited us inside and told us how excited she was we were there. She promised we would be creative. How she could guarantee that was beyond me. No distractions whatsoever, she told us. She had no idea I was my own distraction. I could pay $600 not to write, I did it for free all the time.

She gathered us in a circle, told us to introduce ourselves, and tell why we came. My explanation was short and sweet. "I'm just here to make myself write."

Leslie was next. She said she was a banker whose life was full of order and exactitude, perfection and fine details. I was a perfectionist, too, but in a different way. In the way one's afraid to make a mistake because of a shitty childhood, not because numbers had to balance or the economy would tank. She used outlines, deadlines and discipline. I was a write-in-the moment kind of gal, which explained why I just stared at a blank screen with the cursor taunting me and reminding me of why I wasn't a writer. One day, that cursor's going to be my bitch. The other eight writers introduced themselves. Blah, blah, blah, boring, boring, boring, give me a break, show-off.

Helena had asked us to bring a piece of literature that spoke to us to share with the group. I couldn't remember the last time I had actually read an entire book. My house was littered with half-read books. I could have lied to the group and spoken of a classic, but I had forgotten everything I learned in my high school English class. To this day, I only heard rumors about how *The Catcher in the Rye* ended. There was one poem that stuck with me, not that I could remember the words. For goodness sake, who could remember sixteen words?

When it was my turn, I read *The Red Wheelbarrow* by William Carlos Williams. I had always loved its simplicity and the image it evoked, the contrast in colors. I mean, really, how many poems actually have the word chicken in them? It took me 15.4 seconds to read the poem and say why I liked it before turning to the person to my left.

"That's it," I said. Crickets. I believed they were waiting for something more meaningful, how the poem impacted my life in some profound way. Something more than how I liked the way the color red looked against white, so much so I painted my living room to match the poem's color scheme. They were waiting for writer stuff.

Helena sent us on our way to be inspired. No pressure there. I decided to search outside for it, getting more pissed off the longer I looked. I paid good money to wander around the desert like an asshat.

I came across a beaten-down, sunbleached barn hunched to one side like a craggy old man. The once-stalwart wood structure was nothing more than a splintered, bowed skeleton. It had outlived its purpose, cast aside and forgotten, just like the men who had nailed each pristine board in place when it really was a ranch.

The side door hung from its rusty hinges and lured me in. The midday sun peeked through the splintered roof and scattered fragments of light and shadow across the floor. "What do you have to tell me, old man? I'm waiting. Tell me a story." The old man was silent. "Listen, asshole, I don't have all day." Evidently, I did, and the old man knew it.

It was dusk by the time he whispered the poem. I hadn't written - one since I was a teenager going through my woe-is me phase, an old friend who still visits from time to time and outstays her welcome. She's the kind of friend who tracks dirt in the house, puts her feet up on the furniture, and drinks the last beer without telling you.

And just like that, inspiration vanished. At least it made an appearance. Not $600 worth. $20, tops.

Thank You, Backers!

You may or may not know that *FLASH* happened because of the support of 81 generous backers who helped make it a reality. Those backers were (in chronological order):

Julie A. Fast, Zoe Dabbs, Ronda Simmons, Walt Socha, Adam Gottfried, Jeff Campbell, Sharon Rose, Jim Rosenbaum, Don Wright, Diana Hauer, Bronni, Melissa Campbell, Daniel, Brandon Hewitt, Michael Wild, Mary Sparks, Teresa Hook, Adrienne Dorris, Denzil Hook, Laura Mahal, Emily Voigt, Gale Sandler, Kathlene Postma, Herbert Voigt, Cinda, Michelle Knight, Joe Beiker, Lise Kauffman, John Houihan, David, Barry Sparks, Lawrence Paz, Chris Jordan, Kristin Owens, David Sharp, William Donohue, Rene Reid, Carol Thompson, Belle Schmidt, Jake Gonnella, Megan Gilbert, Kylie Cokeley, Mark Emery, Fear the Boot, Joseph Taylor, Denise Schuck, Jennifer V Gray, Runester, Daryll Lynne Evans, Lorna Simons, Debbie Sands, Ryan, Bert Edens, Kailea Saplan, Allen Stenger, Bri Castellini, Joe Sharp, Lindsay Lunda, Lynann Dunker, Nessa Kerr, Angela Stanfield, Eddie Padron, Gregg E Townsley, Mike Mavilia, Kim Dietz, Roberta Mavilia, Antonio Montalban, Meike Buesseler, James Bass, Sarah Roberts, Yannet Interian, Michelle Cain, Kenneth Hall, Andrew Wilbur, Abhilash Mudalair, Charles Warrington, Jeanette Roberts, Aimie, Owen Palmiotti, Melissa Breeding Voet, Josie Ruth

Made in the USA
Middletown, DE
27 September 2019